To my friend
Billy Griffin,
Roger W. Crook

OUR HERITAGE AND OUR HOPE

A History of
Pullen Memorial Baptist Church
(1884-1984)

by
Roger H. Crook

Published by
The History Committee
Pullen Memorial Baptist Church
Raleigh, N.C.

PUBLISHER'S PREFACE

This book was published by the History Committee of Pullen Memorial Baptist Church in commemoration of the church's one hundredth anniversary. The publication of the book was made possible in part by the generous gifts of Bea Anderson and Nancy B. Nahikian.

Library of Congress Catalog Card Number: 84-62984

ISBN-0-9614485-0-4

Copyright, 1985, by the Board of Trustees,
Pullen Memorial Baptist Church

Sparks Press, Raleigh

TABLE OF CONTENTS

FOR ALL THE SAINTS . . .

O may thy soldiers, faithful, true, and bold
Fight as the saints who nobly fought of old,
And win with them the victor's crown of gold.

Alleluia!

FOREWORD

Pullen Memorial Baptist Church has been so busy making history that it has neglected keeping a complete record of what it has done. That may be too ingratiating a statement, for as a matter of fact most churches do not maintain good records. The problem of getting the facts of Pullen's early history, however, has been unusually difficult. The second building which the church occupied was destroyed by fire in 1921 and all records kept in the church at that time were burned. The records for the next ten years, however, have also been lost. Minutes of the meetings of the Board of Deacons between 1931 and the present are fairly complete. Minutes of church conferences for all periods are extremely spotty.

Pullen has always been a church that has made the news. The *Biblical Recorder* and the Raleigh *News and Observer*, therefore, have been invaluable sources of information about what has happened at Pullen. Without those two periodicals little information about the earliest years of the church would have been preserved. Material from these periodicals is documented within the text of the book, with *BR* referring to the *Biblical Recorder* and *N&O* referring to the *News and Observer*.

Prentice Baker, who was baptized into Pullen Memorial Church on May 5, 1907, wrote a brief history of the church from its beginning through 1930. That history was never published but was circulated in mimeographed form. It preserved a great deal of information and relayed impressions that could not have been found in any other source.

A special word of appreciation is due several persons. Alicia Hutcheson, a student at Meredith College, designed the dust jacket. Nona Short, of the faculty of Meredith College, made the copy photograph of the Fayetteville Street Church building which appears on the dust jacket and on page 29 of the text, and the photograph of the present building of Pullen Memorial Baptist Church which appears on page 136. Hilda Highfill did the painstaking work of preparing the statistical table found in the Appendix. Inez Ray has been helpful in providing materials from the church archives and in finding many of the photographs. Mary Ruth Crook and William C. Harris have made helpful suggestions about the manuscript. Carolyn McGill, faculty secretary at Meredith College, has typed the manuscript.

5

EPILOGUE

This narration of the history of Pullen Memorial Baptist Church begins with an epilogue, a word "spoken upon" what has gone before.

The heritage of Pullen Memorial Baptist Church is a long and honorable Baptist tradition. From their beginnings as the radical wing of the Reformation, Baptists have stressed the grace of God in his dealings with people, the freedom of each person to respond to God's grace in his own way, and the responsibility of God's people to reach out into the world with the good news of God's love.

Thomas Helwys, the leader of a little band of people who formed the first Baptist church on English soil, was the first person in England to call for absolute religious liberty. In *A Short Declaration of the Mistery of Iniquity*, published in 1612, he wrote:

> Our lord the king is but an earthly king, and he hath no authority as a king but in earthly causes, and if the king's people be obedient and true subjects, obeying all human laws made by the king, our lord the king can require no more; for men's religion to God is betwixt God and themselves; the king shall not answer for it, neither may the king be judge between God and man. Let them be heretics, Turks, Jews, or whatsoever, it appertains not to the earthly power to punish them in the least measure.

On the flyleaf of the copy which he sent to King James I he wrote:

> Hear, O King, and despise not the counsel of the poor, and let their complaints come before thee. The king is a mortal man and not God: therefore hath no power over the immortal souls of his subjects, to make laws and ordinances for them, and to set spiritual Lords over them. If the king have authority to make spiritual Lords and laws, then he is an immortal God, and not a mortal man. O King, be not seduced by deceivers to sin against God whom thou oughtest to obey, nor against thy poor subjects who ought and will obey thee in all things with body, life and goods, or else let their lives be taken from the earth. God save the King. Spittlefield, near London. Tho. Helwys.

Not many years later (1644) Roger Williams, who is credited with being the founder of the Baptist movement in the United States, and who is memoralized in one of the stained glass windows in the Pullen sanctuary, wrote in *The Bloudy Tenent of Persecution*: "Hence I affirm it lamentably to be against the Testimony of Christ Jesus, for the civil state to impose upon the souls of the people, a religion, a worship, a ministry, oaths (in religious and civil affairs), tithes, times,

7

days, marryings and buryings in holy ground." Instead, he said, the state should give "free and absolute permission of conscience to all men in what is merely spiritual . . . and provide for the liberty of the magistrate's conscience also." As a minister of the gospel—not in good standing with the Massachusetts Bay authorities—he preached to the Naraganset Indians, having learned their language and having reduced it to writing. It was he alone who championed the cause of the Indians against the power of the King of England.

Near the end of the eighteenth century William Carey, who is memoralized in another Pullen window, began a movement that was ultimately to involve Christians of all persuasions in a mission to the world. His controversial little book calling for the sending of missionaries to the non-Christian world was entitled *An Enquiry into the Obligation of Christians to Use Means for the Conversion of the Heathen.* In making his case for the support of missions he said:

> Many can do nothing but pray, and prayer is perhaps the only thing in which Christians of all denominations can cordially, and unreservedly unite; but in this we may all be one, and in this the strictest unanimity ought to prevail. Were the whole body thus animated by one soul, with what pleasure would Christians attend on all the duties of religion, and with what delight would their ministers attend on all the business of their calling.

> We must not be contented however with praying, without *exerting ourselves in the use of means* for the obtaining of those things we pray for. Were *the children of light,* but *as wise in their generation as the children of this world,* they would search every nerve to gain so glorious a prize, nor ever imagine that it was to be obtained in any other way.

After a lengthy illustration drawn from the world of commerce, he concluded, "Let then every one in his station consider himself as bound to act with all his might, and in every possible way for God."

Absolute freedom in one's response to the grace of God and a sense of responsibility for the world are hallmarks of the Baptist heritage. The story of Pullen Memorial Baptist Church is the story of a congregation that is both independent of and cooperative with other Christians, that is both a worshipping community and a ministering fellowship, that is prepared for its future by an appreciation of its past.

Chapter 1
Pullen and His Times

"John T. Pullen dies Suddenly," the Raleigh *News and Observer* announced in a front page article on May 2, 1912. The brief news report stated that Pullen had died "this morning at 2:05 o'clock at the residence of Mr. John W. Harden on Hillsboro street." Five days later, on Wednesday evening, May 7, 1913, the members of the Fayetteville Street Baptist Church honored their founder by voting unanimously to re-name their congregation "Pullen Memorial Baptist Church." For twenty-nine years Pullen had so closely identified himself with the work of Fayetteville Street Church that someone said of him, "he served God for a living and ran a bank to pay expenses."

John Turner Pullen was born on December 1, 1852, the son of Nancy A. and James D. Pullen. He had two sisters. The older one, Anna, married Dr. L. W. Crawford, of New Bern. The younger, Lizzie Lee, married Charles Binton Belvin. Belvin eventually became president of the National Bank of Raleigh.

While John Pullen was a small child, in the early 1860's, his parents managed the Planters Hotel, located on the corner of Wilmington and Martin streets in Raleigh. After that, until about 1876, they operated a boarding house in their home situated on the corner of McDowell and Hargett streets. In 1865 William Holden, the newly-appointed Provisional Governor of North Carolina, appointed James Pullen a court clerk in Wake County. He probably did not hold that position long, for Holden was defeated in the election of November, 1865.

In 1876 James and Nancy Pullen, along with their son John, their two daughters, and their son-in-law Charles Belvin, took up residence in the home of Richard Stanhope Pullen, brother of James. The house was located at 213 East Edenton Street, property which in the early 1890's was acquired by the Baptists of North Carolina for the location of the Baptist Female University. Opened in 1899, that institution ultimately became Meredith College. For a short time during the period in which the James Pullen family lived with Stanhope Pullen, John Pullen's mother was a housekeeper for Mrs. Octavius Coke. Apparently she was a live-in employee, for the Raleigh City Directory of 1880-1881 gave her address as that of the Cokes. The rest of the family, however were listed as living at the residence of Stanhope Pullen.

No records of John Pullen's formal education remain. He could have received good schooling in Raleigh, however, for public schools had been in operation since 1842, and a number of private schools were also open at the time. The fact that he went into banking suggests that he must have been well-taught.

John Pullen grew up in an era of change. He was only nine years old when the Civil War broke out. He could not have been immune to the intense feelings of the time, even if he did not understand the political and economic and social currents. He must have heard people discussing *Uncle Tom's Cabin,* which was first published in the year that he was born. He surely sang "Dixie," which was composed in 1859. He may have been frightened by news of John Brown's raid on Harper's Ferry, also in 1859. He must have felt the electricity in the air when Lincoln was elected President, when South Carolina seceded from the Union, and when North Carolina eventually took the same course and joined the Confederacy.

Raleigh's wartime activities created an atmosphere that affected everyone. Three major recruiting and training centers were located in or near Raleigh. A major military hospital was located in the city. Careful preparations were made for the defense of the city, though fortunately they were never called into service. After Raleigh's surrender near the end of the war, it became a Union camp, with some 60,000 soldiers based in and around the city. General Sherman spent some time in the city, using the Governor's recently-vacated home as his headquarters. He was there when the news of Lincoln's assasination came, and it was he who kept control of the angry Union soldiers and kept them from resorting to new violence.

Pullen was a teenager in the Reconstruction era. He might have been in the crowd that greeted President Andrew Johnson, a Raleigh native, on the occasion of his visit to the city in 1867. He surely was aware of the presence of Federal forces which remained in the city until 1876. He saw the black population of Raleigh double in size and reach the point that it even equaled the number of whites in Raleigh. He heard about the rise of such black self-help groups as the Union League, and he also heard about the growing strength of the Ku Klux Klan.

If Pullen had any early interest in religion he was aware of division in the churches. During the early 19th century the question of the morality of slavery had been debated in the churches. Toward the middle of the century, however, opposition to slavery had almost disappeared from the south. Several major denominations split along regional lines. The Methodists divided in 1845, and so did the Baptists. A number of Presbyterian synods withdrew from the national organization in the 1850's and early 1860's. When war broke out the southern churches rallied to the support of the Confederate cause. This was true not only of those newly-formed denominations, but also of the Episcopal Church, which had not divided, and of the Lutheran churches, which had never united. After the war, feelings were so strong that there was no immediate movement toward a reunion of the denominations which had divided. As a teenager, therefore, John Pullen would have known only the southern variety of Christianity.

Pullen's entire business career was in the field of banking. His first job was with the State National Bank, an agency which had been organized in 1868. He remained with that institution until 1887, and was, therefore, with it at the time of the beginning of the church that ultimately was to bear his name. The bank with which he was longest associated, and which popularly came to be called "Mr. Pullen's Bank," was the Raleigh Savings Bank and Trust Company. It was chartered in 1885 and opened in 1887. Pullen was the cashier at the time of its opening, and in 1889 was elected president. Joseph C. Brown, president of the Citizens' National Bank when Pullen died, said that "it was under his guiding hand" that the bank became one of the leading institutions of the state. The term which was frequently used to describe Pullen's operation of the bank was "conservative." Brown said:

> In the management of the bank, Mr. Pullen was almost ultra conservative, but he recognized that the people, and many of them of limited means, were trusting their money to the care of his bank because they felt that its management would be first of all safe; and nothing could ever cause him to vediate (sic) from that rule which he early marked out for himself—to seek safety for depositors first and profits for stockholders afterwards. (N&O, 5/7/1913)

Few details about John Pullen's early religious life are available. Both his father, who died in November, 1887, and his mother, who died in August, 1888, were buried with funeral services conducted by the pastor of Edenton Street Methodist Church. His mother's name appears in the church records beginning in 1882, but his father's name does not appear in them at all. His uncle Stanhope was a member of Edenton Street, having been converted in 1878, following a revival there in which Mrs. Mary Moon was the preacher. Edenton Street records report that Stanhope was baptized in May, 1879, and then received into the church. Hope Summerell Chamberlain, in her *History of Wake County*, reports that

> When Edenton Street Methodist Church was being built, he came and supervised the construction day by day, and saw all go right, but no one dared to ask, "How much are we to depend on you for, in paying for the new church?" After everybody had given all they could, and then stretched it a little further, Mr. Pullen placed a check in the collection plate which made him the largest contributor to the building fund. (pp. 235-236)

Records of the First Baptist Church do not reveal when John Pullen first became a member of that congregation. His involvement in the life of First Baptist, however, was not at first significant. In its monthly conference on Friday, August 5, 1881, the deacons were given a list of "those absent for three meetings" and instructed to remove from the list the names of people who had valid reasons for not attending. The rest were to be dealt with by the church. John T. Pullen was one of twenty-two men cited to appear before the conference on September 2 to account for their absence. None of the men appeared. The deacons were instructed to continue to work with the absent brethren. On November 6, 1881, the church cited Pullen "to answer to the church for unchristianlike conduct toward the church in that he declined to conform to a rule of the church."

What Pullen's "unchristianlike conduct" was is not specified in the records. At that time, the church was trying to "correct" its rolls, however, and similar action was taken against a large number of persons. In a few instances "drunkenness" was named as the offense for which a person was to be disciplined, and in one case "adultery" was cited. In Pullen's case, as in most others, nothing is stated beyond not conforming to "a rule of the church." His offense, therefore, may well have been nothing other than absence from the church meetings.

There may have been more, however. In an article published in *The State* in 1934, Josiah Bailey described Pullen:

> He was as a young man living the worldly, self-indulgent life rather than the really bad life. He was a good fellow—the best field-shot in Raleigh, if not in the state, and one of the best at pool. The bar-room and the pool-room in his day were usually one—and the bar-room was his loafing place. He drank but was not a drunkard. He kept late hours, and coming home late, would find his mother on her knees praying for him. She loved him with a mother's love and would not give him up. (1/6/34, p. 2)

According to Bailey, Dr. T. E. Skinner, pastor of the church, went to Pullen in the pool hall to inform him of the church's action. Admittedly Bailey's report, written more than fifty years after the event, may be embellished a bit. Human nature being what it is, Pullen himself may have romanticized the story as he told it to his friends. Nevertheless, Bailey's report, the only one that we have, is true to the situation, if not accurate in every detail. Bailey wrote:

> He (Skinner) found him in a saloon playing pool, apprised him of the accusations, and urged him to attend the church conference that night. John, quick of temper and impatient of the minister's intrusion, retorted with an oath: "I am not going to be there—they can do as they please; I don't care."
>
> "Young man," replied the minister, "you do not know what this means. I cannot compel you to come. But all this day you will have on your mind what you have said, and tonight when the church bell rings, with every stroke you hear, remember what you have said—and you will come."
>
> John did remember. All day long he bitterly reproached himself. His pride urged him not to attend the conference. "I ought to be turned out of the church and I shall be—why should I go?" Upon the first stroke of the bell he was resolved not to move. But as the sound came again and again, he found himself on the way, and with the last stroke he entered the church door.
>
> When the accusations were presented he came forward, and with profound humility, confessed his wrongdoings, and declared that no one realized as keenly as he that he ought to be turned out. But, he added, he believed he could do better; that for years he knew his mother had been praying for (him) while he was indulging himself; that he hoped he might have a chance and it was for her he hoped not to be turned out of the church.
>
> The church readily responded. His name remained on the roll—he was given the chance.

The minutes of the First Baptist Church conference on Friday, December 2, 1881, report:

> Bro John T. Pullen was present to answer to the charges preferred at the last conference meeting. He stated that he felt that he had done wrong in failing to comply with the rule of the church, but that he would try to do better in the future and hoped that the brethren would pray for him.

John Pullen himself, in an unsigned tract written many years later for the benefit of mothers of wayward sons, wrote:

> Many a time I have buried my head in the pillow, and covered it up, to escape hearing the cries of that Godly woman as she poured out her complaint before Him. I did not know then what it all meant; but I know now, my precious mother, and I thank thee for every tear, and every sigh, and every groan thou didst make for me, thine only boy.

This experience was a turning point for John Pullen. Bailey reports that on the next day he told his friends of his intention to live a Christian life. For him that meant the abandonment of a carefree attitude and of that way of life which Bailey characterized as "worldly" and "self-indulgent." So determined was he to be a different kind of

13

man that he even gave away his shotgun and buried his shells! Immediately he became actively involved in the work of the First Baptist Church. Within months he was elected an usher, and shortly after that he was chairman of foreign missions for the church. Soon he was elected church clerk, a position he continued to hold until 1884, when he took up the mission work at the end of Fayetteville Street.

When the Federal forces left Raleigh in 1876 John Pullen was twenty-three years old and was working for the State National Bank. For most people in the city the times were difficult but not depressing. Indeed, for the business world the future was hopeful. Thomas Briggs had opened his hardware store in 1865. The Royster brothers were operating a store selling candy which they themselves made. In 1867 Alfred Williams began publishing school materials and supplies. In 1871 Needham B. Broughton and Cornelius Bryant Edwards started a publishing firm. The Tucker brothers had a thriving mercantile establishment in Raleigh. Dozens of other businesses, some of which still survive, were prospering. Although no major industry existed in the city, several small-scale manufacturers were thriving, particularly those engaged in producing farm implements.

The fact that it was the state capital remained the major factor in the economic life of Raleigh. Not only government officials, but also visitors to the capital, were a boon to the merchants. While no figures on the number of visitors are available, the thriving hotel business testifies to its significance. The Yarborough House, situated on Fayetteville Street, was the largest and most famous of the hotels. In addition, however, there were numerous smaller inns, taverns, and rooming houses.

John Pullen's Raleigh was a city in transition. The population had increased to just over nine thousand. The streets were unpaved and poorly lighted, but improvements were being planned. The city aldermen were trying to find ways of providing an adequate water supply for the growing population. Fire protection, limited by the insufficient water supply, was provided only by volunteer fire departments. Doctors and nurses were few in number and hospital facilities were almost non-existent. There were thirteen churches, eight white and five black. The fourteenth church, the one now called "Pullen Memorial Baptist Church," would come into being in 1884.

Chapter 2
A Mission Church
In A City Coming of Age
(1884-1900)

The nation was hardly tranquil in 1884, the year of the establishment of Raleigh's third Baptist church. Grover Cleveland had just been elected president of the United States, winning by one of the thinnest margins in the history of the nation. The contest with James Blaine had been bitter and filled with mud-slinging. It had been complicated by the activities of two minority parties. The one was the National Equal Rights Party, which ran Belva Lockwood for the presidency. The other was the Prohibitionist Party, which ran John St. John. While neither of these parties polled many votes, they were an important factor in the election because Cleveland's margin of victory was so close.

If things were bad in politics, however, they were booming in business and industry. The last quarter of the nineteenth century saw an unparalleled exploitation of the natural resources of the nation. New machinery was created for the mass production of goods: drills and saws and rock drills and typewriters and elevators and so on *ad infinitum*. Factories were built in which masses of people working with machines increased productivity ten-fold, and even a hundred-fold. New cities came into being and older ones grew phenomenally. A rapidly expanding network of railroads crossed the country. It was the age of invention, the age of Thomas Alva Edison, of Alexander Graham Bell, of George Eastman, of George Westinghouse. It was the era of burgeoning fortunes, with untold wealth being amassed by Andrew Carnegie, J. P. Morgan, Leland Stanford, Henry Clay Frick, John D. Rockefeller, Philip Armour, Gustavus Swift, Cadwallader C. Washburn, and Charles A. Pillsbury.

The rapid and unplanned growth of cities created new problems: transportation, communication, sanitation, fire protection, police protection, and the like all had to be dealt with by the city. The working conditions in most of the new plants were bad and wages were low. That fact gave rise to the labor movement, under the leadership of men like Charles Lichman, Uriah Stephens, and Samuel Gompers. The period was marked by strife, and often by violence, as the relationship between management and labor increasingly became an adversarial one. Labor used the method of the strike, and management used the method of the lockout. Both sides engaged in threats, subterfuge, and violence—and the nation was torn.

Although agriculture remained basic in the economy of the South, manufacturing began to play an increasingly significant part. Many new cotton mills were built, and the mill-town became a familiar landmark, especially in the upper South. Tobacco processing came to be a major industry, as did the processing of iron ore, the production of turpentine, and the production of lumber. Employment in those industries was available only to whites, a fact which contributed to the social problems of the South. In the textile and tobacco plants both men and women were employed—and young children as well. Working conditions were oppressive, the hours were long, and the pay was poor. Furthermore, the paternalistic pattern which developed in the southern mill villages was to continue well beyond the middle of the twentieth century.

Politically the South was solidly in the Democratic fold. The Republican party was popularly associated with the Reconstruction era, and Republicanism was, therefore, anathema. The real political battles were fought out within the Democratic party, and the real electoral process took place in its primaries. Within the party the divisions were significant and candidates for leadership were abundant. For local elections, therefore, there was often real choice between candidates and positions. For national elections, however, there was no question about which party would get the southern vote.

The rapid growth of a newly organized church in Raleigh was one expression of the evangelical fervor that swept the nation in the latter part of the nineteenth century. One significant manifestation of that zeal was the work of itinerant evangelistic preachers who traveled all over the nation, spending weeks at a time in one city, then moving on to another. Those evangelists were rarely identified by their denominational affiliation. Their meetings were not planned by the local churches, and were in fact quite independent of them. Yet most of the local churches supported the meetings and received new members as a result of them. The best known revivalist was Dwight L. Moody (1837-1899). Moody was a Congregational layman who worked for the YMCA in Chicago, and in fact began his evangelistic work through that agency. His first successful revival was held, not in this country, but in London in 1872. There he preached to thousands at once, and hundreds of conversions resulted from that meeting. Not a small part of his success was due to the help of his song leader, Ira D. Sankey. After the London success, Moody and Sankey conducted campaigns throughout the rest of Great Britain. When they returned to the United States they had developed a system for preparing a city for their arrival, for the time that they would spend in that city, and for follow-up on the converts after they left. Employing that method they moved back and forth across the nation for more than twenty years, preaching to thousands at a time. Their methods were emulated by more than a score of other men who earned national reputations and by untold numbers of still others whose activities were restricted to a more local area.

Another significant aspect of the religious life of the nation was the growth of separate black denominations. Even before the Civil War, in both North and South, there had been some separate black churches. After the Civil War, blacks in the South moved in large numbers into separate local churches and into separate black denominations. There were many independent black Baptist congregations in those years, but the first successful attempt to form a national organization of those churches occurred in 1895, with the formation of the National Baptist Convention.

The years before the turn of the century were a period of great and growing interest in foreign missions. All major Protestant denominations enlarged their overseas missionary force, particularly in Africa, China, and Japan. The Student Volunteer Movement for Foreign Missions came into being in 1888, capitalizing on the great enthusiasm of college students for the cause of missions. The Student Volunteer motto soon became famous: "the evangelization of the world in this generation."

This era also saw the time of the growth of the Sunday school movement. Originating in England late in the eighteenth century, it spread rapidly in this country in the nineteenth century. The organizational meeting of the International Sunday School Association was held in 1875. At that meeting the concept of a uniform system of Bible study was debated, and soon afterward the Uniform Lesson Plan was adopted.

Yet another feature of the religious scene was the temperance movement. That movement was pre-Civil War in its origin, but was interrupted by the war. The Prohibition Party was organized in 1869 for the purpose of pushing the cause of temperance at the national level. In the last two decades of the nineteenth century it was quite active, and among other things fielded a presidential candidate in every election year. The Woman's Christian Temperance League was organized in 1874, under the leadership of Frances Willard, with the avowed purpose of pressing for teetotalism for the entire nation. The Anti-Saloon League was organized in 1895, drawing support from all evangelical churches, to press for a constitutional amendment to end the sale of intoxicating beverages.

One other major factor on the religious scene during the last two decades of the nineteenth century was a theological ferment. The rapid expansion of knowledge in the realm of science, and the increasing pervasiveness of the scientific world view, was raising many questions of religious significance. Particularly important were Darwin's two major works, *The Origin of the Species* and *The Descent of Man*, and his theories were to cause great controversy within the nation in general and the church in particular. Many religious leaders were open to the theological re-formulation necessitated by scientific developments. Logically, therefore, they were also open to the new approach to the study of the Bible which made use of the techniques of literary criticism and were involved in the formulation of the concepts of liberal theology. Most theological schools began to utilize the new approach in their teaching and in their practice.

Many other religious leaders rejected out-of-pocket any scientific theory that raised questions about the traditional interpretation of the Bible and of religion. The literary-critical approach to the study of the Bible was anathema to them. A clash between this group and the liberals was inevitable. The division was severe in most of the major denominations, and a number of them had the bitter experience of heresy trials. The Southern Presbyterians ousted James Woodrow from the faculty of Columbia Seminary in 1886, and in 1893 the Northern Presbyterians suspended C. A. Briggs, president of Union Theological Seminary in New York, from its ministry. The Southern Methodists dismissed Alexander Winchell from the faculty of Vanderbilt University in 1878. In 1879 C. H. Toy was forced to resign from the faculty of the Southern Baptist Theological Seminary, and in 1898 W. H. Whitsett was forced to resign from the presidency of that same institution.

In that same period of reaction against the new learning certain new fundamentalistic movements came into being. The Jehovah's Witnesses were organized in 1874, the Christian and the Missionary

18

Alliance in 1877, the Churches of God in 1881, and the Church of the Nazarene in 1895. The Salvation Army, a theologically conservative evangelical and social activist group, was established in London in 1878 and reached the United States in 1880.

A development of major importance to the Southern Baptist Convention was the formation of the Woman's Missionary Union. The status of women in the Baptist churches was in a stage of ferment. In some local churches the women were organizing for the support of missions. In 1877, for the first time, a woman was recognized as a messenger from a local church to the Convention. For a number of years many women had been meeting for the support of missions while their husbands were serving as messengers to the Convention. From time to time they sought recognition as a Convention agency, but always failed to receive it. In 1884, however, at a meeting held in the Westminster Presbyterian Church in Baltimore, the women decided to make their organization a permanent one which would meet while the sessions of the Southern Baptist Convention were being held. In 1888 the organization was officially recognized by the Southern Baptist Convention.

Like the rest of the South, Raleigh experienced great changes in the last two decades of the nineteenth century. The streets were being paved, with work progressing on Fayetteville Street at the rate of about one block a year. Street lighting was being improved, and the system of horse-drawn street cars was being expanded. The first telephone exchange was opened in 1882. A more adequate water supply was provided, and fire protection became more of a reality. Rex Hospital was opened in May, 1894, and St. Agnes Hospital was opened two years later to serve the black population.

Efforts were being made to bring to Raleigh a share of the industrial and business growth of the region. A Chamber of Commerce was established in 1888, and it engaged in the kind of "industry hunting" which is familiar to us today. Its chief success was in bringing cotton manufacturing to town: Raleigh Cotton Mill was opened in 1890, on what is now Downtown Boulevard; Caraleigh Cotton Mill was opened in 1892, and Pilot Mill was opened in 1893. Other small industries were also brought in, and the banking business was expanded. In 1887 Stanhope Pullen donated to the city sixty acres of land to be used for a public park, in the event that it was not needed for a new major industry. Fortunately for the city, the industry did not materialize, even though a new street car line made it much more accessible to the city.

Education was a major concern in the city of Raleigh. In 1885, less than a year after the establishment of Fayetteville Street Baptist Church, Edward P. Moses came to Raleigh to serve as superintendent of the school system. His work was to be one of the major contributions to the expanding public school system. The need for a better school system throughout the state was documented by the finding of the 1900 census that North Carolina had the highest illiteracy rate in the nation!

Provision for higher education was in the air as well. In 1883, just months before Pullen began his mission at the end of Fayetteville Street, people on the other end were talking about the establishment of an agricultural and technical college in Raleigh. Walter Hines Page and L. L. Polk and others formed in that year the "Watauga Club," which pushed for the establishment of a school. Two years later the General Assembly voted to establish such an institution "in a city that would donate land and contribute to construction costs." Raleigh won out, holding out a number of enticements including a gift of eight and a half acres of land from Stanhope Pullen. Classes in the new institute were begun in October, 1889.

In 1889 also the Baptists of North Carolina decided to establish a "Baptist Female Seminary,." Raleigh outbid other cities for that institution, and the "Baptist Female University," later renamed "Meredith College," was opened in 1899. It was housed in a new building on the corner of Blount and Edenton streets on land that had been owned by Stanhope Pullen. The financial agent for the Baptists who raised funds for the school was O. L. Stringfield, who was to be one of the early pastors of Pullen Memorial Church.

Raleigh was a "Baptist town" in the 1880's and 1890's. According to James Vickers: "In 1887, out of a total church membership of 3,590, the Baptists led with 2,005." First Baptist Church was the oldest and largest Baptist church in the city. Known first as "The Raleigh Baptist Church," it had been established in 1812, and from its beginning it had both white and black members. A group of some two hundred blacks had separated from this church in 1868 and formed an independent congregation now known as "The First Baptist Church, Wilmington and Morgan Street."

A second white Baptist church had developed from a mission established by First Baptist in 1874. It was located on Swain Street, and for a time was called "Swain Street Baptist Church." Beginning with ten charter members, it grew rapidly. In 1881 the congregation moved into a new building on the corner of Hargett and Person streets and changed its name to "Tabernacle Baptist Church." The new building had a seating capacity of 600, and for several years following the move, from 50 to 75 persons annually were added to the church rolls.

At the time of the organization of the new mission on Fayetteville Street, the Reverend T. E. Skinner was the pastor of First Baptist Church. In addition to being an able administrator, Skinner was a popular preacher. Most of his sermons were evangelistic ones, and he was much in demand for preaching in other places. In 1884, however, the membership of First Baptist apparently had stabilized. The church's letter to the Raleigh Association in August, 1884, reported four baptisms for the year, four received by letter, one restored, three excluded, and seven died. The total membership that year was 536, of whom 190 were males and 346 females. It is interesting to note that although the female members outnumbered the males by almost two to one, First Baptist, like other churches of the era, was male-dominated. Only males were allowed to hold office and to participate in the decision-making process in the church conferences.

The minutes of the First Baptist Church for the early 1880's reflect a great concern for enforcing attendance at the church conferences. The roll was checked, and persons not attending were contacted and called upon to give reasons for their absence. The deacons decided whether their explanations were satisfactory. If their reasons were not valid, the absentees were cited to appear before the church for explanation. The records frequently report that fellowship was withdrawn from persons for non-attendance. Upon occasion, members were dismissed for other reasons as well, such as drunkenness or joining a church of another denomination. Sometimes persons who had been excluded were restored to fellowship when they asked for such action and promised to be more faithful members. Frequent efforts were made to "correct" the church roll by getting absentee members to ask for their letters, or to report to the church at least once a year and to make contributions for the support of the church.

The initiative for the establishment of a mission at the south end of Fayetteville Street came from John Pullen. Pullen had fulfilled his promise made to the church on December 2, 1881, that "he would try to do better in the future." He became such a respected member that on September 29, 1882, he was elected an usher in the church. On May 5, 1883, he was elected Chairman of the Committee on Foreign Missions. Two months later he began keeping the minutes for the church conferences, and on January 4, 1884, was elected clerk by acclamation.

The first mention of the mission on Fayetteville Street appears in the minutes of the First Baptist Church for May 2, 1884:

Bro. Jonathan Womble Jr. sent forward the following resolution which was adopted. The Church having heard of the efforts of Bro. John T. Pullen to collect funds and purchase a lot and erect thereon a building for a mission station, hereby approve and endorse his actions and recommend that Brethren W. N. Jones and Eugene Harold be appointed with Bro. Pullen as chairman, to cooperate with him in securing the lot and raise funds for the same and for the erection of the building.

The committee reported "progress" on May 30, 1884. On Sunday, June 8, the pastor called the church into conference to "consider the propriety of taking up a collection for the Mission House." The church decided that it was a proper thing to do, and after the service a collection was taken amounting to "something over $27.00."

On August 1, 1884, according to the minutes, "Bro Pullen reported progress on Mission House. Bro Harris Vaugh at his own request was appointed a committee of one to raise $50 to pay for the Mission House lot." In that same conference

> The following resolution offered by Bro. J. T. Pullen was carried. Resolved, that this church extend to any of the members of the Second Church a most cordial invitation to participate and take an active part in any of the services that may be held at the Mission House located on South Fayetteville Street.

On October 31, 1884, in church conference

> Bro John T. Pullen stated that it was very probable that a Third Baptist Church would be organized soon, and that he wished to get the approbation of this Church in the movement, whereupon the Church heartily approved of the movement. A collection amounting to nearly $40.00 was taken up to aid in procuring a deed for the ground on which the Mission House is located.

On December 17, 1884, the *Biblical Recorder* reported that

> The third Baptist Church in **Raleigh** is an established fact. A number of the most active and useful **members** of the First and Second churches have taken letters and will be **organized** into a church at an early day. The church is located on the old Palace grounds near the buildings of the Centennial Graded School.

The minutes of the First Baptist Church for December 28, 1884, indicate that

> On Sunday evening, Dec. 28, 1884 the Fayetteville Street Baptist Church was organized. This Church is located on Fayetteville Street in the Southern Portion of the city. Rev. T. E. Skinner, C. T. Bailey and Alvin Betts constituted the presbytery. Thomas W. Blake and J. T. Pullen were made deacons. Trust in God and do its duty is inscribed upon the banner of this little church.

In the church records these minutes are followed by a report of a meeting on December 5, a little more than three weeks earlier, in which letters of "dismission" were granted to "J. T. Pullen, Peter Francis and his wife Mrs. Peter Francis and Annie Francis to join the 3rd Baptist Church of this city."

From time to time in 1885 other persons from First Baptist united with Fayetteville Street Church. On July 3, 1885, a letter was granted for C. T. Bailey, who had been a member of the organizing presbytery, to join the new congregation. Bailey was at the time owner and editor of the *Biblical Recorder*, which he had purchased in 1875 and which he continued to publish until 1895. He had studied at William and Mary and at Richmond College, had served for a short time in the Confederate army, and after the war had come to North Carolina as a teacher and a minister. He served at various times as trustee of Wake Forest College and of Shaw University. He was president of the Baptist State Convention of North Carolina in 1885-86, and was, therefore, a member of Fayetteville Street while he held that office.

On September 4, 1885, First Baptist granted a letter for Sallie Bailey, daughter of C. T. Bailey, to join Fayetteville Street. She was seventeen years of age at the time, and had attended school at the Peace Institute in Raleigh and at the Richmond Female Institute in Richmond, Virginia. Her move to a mission church was entirely in keeping with what proved to be a life-long interest in missions. In January, 1886, only three months after she joined Fayetteville Street and a few days before her eighteenth birthday, she accepted the position of corresponding secretary and treasurer of the Woman's Central Committee of Missions of North Carolina, the organization which was to become the Woman's Missionary Union of North Carolina. She served as treasurer of the Woman's Missionary Union from 1900 until 1916, and president from 1916 until 1936. She was vice-president of the Southern Baptist Woman's Missionary Union from 1916 until 1938. She did not remain permanently in The Fayetteville Street Church. At the age of nineteen she married Wesley Norwood Jones, a leading member at First Baptist Church. She probably returned to First Baptist at that time.

The site of the new church was a spot known as "the Fayetteville Street Crossing." It was located in an area of the city occupied by working-class people. While the other churches of Raleigh would not have admitted that they were "class" congregations, few people from that area were in any of them. Pullen intended this church to evangelize a group who were not being reached by anyone else. At the time of his death the editor of the *Biblical Recorder* wrote of him and of Fayetteville Street: "He was at the heart of it, and all the poor felt at home there in a degree that they would not feel in any other. . . . They could be neither pitied nor patronized there." At the time of the building of the church, the Centennial Graded School occupied the property of the old Governor's Palace, where Memorial Auditorium now stands. The "crossing" where the church was built was just behind that spot. The new building was a frame structure approximately forty-five feet by seventy feet, with two small rooms in the rear. Across the front was a sign, in large letters, "Prepare to Meet Thy God."

The character of the church as a mission in an underprivileged area is evidenced by a report that appeared in the *News and Observer* on December 28, 1884:

> At the Baptist mission chapel, lower Fayetteville Street, the first Christmas tree in that part of the city gave the children great delight. That kindly gentleman, Mr. John Pullen, was in charge. The room was tastefully decorated and was so full of people that there was no room for even one more. After giving everybody every thing they wanted, Mr. Pullen said he had two barrels of flour left, which he would distribute among the poor. This church is only a few months old.

Records of the early years of the church have been lost—if, indeed, they were ever kept. There were only five members at the time of its organization, and its ministry was viewed primarily in terms of evangelism. That emphasis characterized the church throughout this entire period. The "Personal and Other Items" column in the *Biblical Recorder* carried frequent references to the work of all three Baptist churches in Raleigh. The first note about the work of Fayetteville Street Church was an announcement on February 14, 1885, less than two months after the organization of the church, of a "series of meetings" held by Rev. F. M. Jordan. In December, 1885, there was another meeting, with Jordan again doing the preaching. According to the *Biblical Recorder*, "Bro. Jordan has done some of his best preaching. There have been so far nine professions—principally among the adults. The meeting still continues. Bro. Jordan left for home on Monday." (BR, 12/23/85) For weeks afterward that meeting continued, even without a preacher. On January 6, 1886, the *Biblical Recorder* reported: "The meeting at the Third church still goes on. There have been twenty professions of faith. The only services held are singing, reading the word, prayer and a short exhortation from some brother." Thereafter the *Recorder* made almost weekly reports, and on February 24 announced that the meeting "has resulted so far in over seventy conversions. Thirty have united with that church and several have joined the other churches." The last reference to this particular meeting is dated March 3, 1886.

C.A.G. Thomas became pastor of the church in January, 1887, and began almost immediately a series of meetings which lasted for more than a month. The *Recorder* reported twenty-two professions, with seven new members being baptized. In the fall of the year, after Thomas had left the church, there was another "protracted meeting." The *Recorder* reported on September 28 that it had "been going on at this church for three weeks, although the church was without a pastor at the time, conducted by the lay members, with occasional ministerial help."

S. H. Thompson became pastor on February 25, 1888, and almost immediately began a meeting. This one apparently started without a great deal of planning. On April 18, 1888, the *Recorder*, reporting on the activity in the Raleigh churches on the previous Sunday, said that "The Churches in Raleigh on Sunday were crowded with deeply interested congregations." Then, following brief statements about First Church and Tabernacle, the article added:

> The interest at the Fayetteville Street church, has been so great that pastor Thompson preached every night during the past week, and will continue to do so during the present week. Twelve have professed faith and about thirty others are penitently seeking salvation. The church is greatly revived and a great work is in progress.

That meeting lasted for another two weeks.

The January 8, 1890, issue of the *Recorder* reported that

> Rev. O. L. Stringfield of Wakefield, spent last week in a series of meetings with the Fayetteville Street church, Raleigh. The meetings were largely attended, and ten or more persons professed faith in the Redeemer. He baptized seven on Sunday night and received four others by letter.

Jonathan Wood became pastor of the church in July, 1891, and, following the pattern of previous pastors, almost immediately began a series of meetings. He was aided in that series by the Reverend J. F. Long, of London. That meeting must not have reached any significant number of people, since the *Recorder*'s only comment (10/7/91) is that it "continues with much interest." In April of 1892, however, Wood was assisted in a meeting by O. L. Stringfield. About that revival the *Recorder* commented: "Several persons have professed conversion. On last Sunday night they had a very precious meeting." (4/20/92) How long that meeting lasted is unknown, but a note in the May 4 issue of the *Recorder* stated that the meeting "continues with good interest."

In May, 1893, during one of those periods when the congregation had no pastor, Stringfield preached in another revival at Fayetteville Street Church. On May 31, the *Recorder* noted that "On Sunday morning last three persons were received into the Fayetteville Street Baptist church, Raleigh, by experience. Ten were baptized, and others are awaiting the ordinance." The next week five more were received "by experience." The next week four others in the same way, and twelve were baptized. In November, 1893, Stringfield accepted the pastorate of the church. Even though he was the best-known evangelist in the state, and even though he had led in revival services in Fayetteville Street Church, Stringfield had a visiting evangelist preach in a series of meetings in April, 1894. In the fall of the year, however, he conducted another meeting himself, with the help of John Pullen.

In January, 1895, the Baptists of Raleigh employed the Reverend A. D. Hunter as "city missionary." The Fayetteville Street Church was without a pastor, Stringfield having resigned in December, 1894, and Hunter played a significant part in the continuation of the revival spirit throughout the period. He preached in the church often in 1895 and 1896, and on a number of occasions conducted baptismal services. The *Recorder* reported on May 1, 1895:

> A great work for the Lord has been wrought in the Raleigh Fayetteville Street Church and our out-stations since the beginning of the year. There has been a gracious revival in South Raleigh, many conversions being made. Pastor and missionary Hunter, Brethren Pullen, Blake, and others have been active in this quiet but faithful work.

The next issue of the *Recorder* reported the fourth week of the revival, and on June 5 it announced:

> Fayetteville Street Baptist church closed its meeting last week, and on Sunday night last, Rev. A. D. Hunter baptized five. This is forty-one recently baptized into this church, three of whom were old men, one in seventieth year. Others have joined by letter. Bro. Hunter says he is glad to work with such helpers as Bro. John T. Pullen and those who labor with him. Many of those who attended this meeting also attended the meeting at Caraleigh Mills.

It would be a mistake, however, to assume that evangelism was limited to those periods when a revival meeting was in progress. Almost every Sunday people responded in some way to the preacher's invitation. Often persons came forward as "inquirers." Frequently people would come forward to move their membership to the church. But the most frequent responses were professions of faith, and hardly a week went by without someone being accepted as a candidate for baptism. The church conceived of its mission as essentially one of evangelism.

In addition to the evangelistic work that centered in the church, there was a variety of other activities. In August, 1888, open air evangelistic services were held on Sunday afternoons in the southeastern part of the city. One reference was made to "the brush arbor" where services were held, and another to "some manifestation of religious concern by the impenitent of the congregation." These statements are found in paragraphs on activities of the Raleigh churches, and follow immediately on reports on the Fayetteville Street Church.

Beginning in mid-1894 and continuing for many years, John Pullen and Fayetteville Street Church were involved in a mission at Caraleigh Mills. Caraleigh Cotton Mill had begun operation in 1892, and, following the pattern of such industrial development, a mill community had grown up around it. Just about the time that the Fayetteville Street Church completed payment for its own new building, "Brother Pullen . . . commenced the erection of a mission station at Caraleigh Mills." (BR, 5/10/94) As has already been noted, in January, 1895, the Reverend A. D. Hunter was employed by the Baptists of Raleigh as city missionary. A report on a general meeting dealing with the city mission work, held in early January, included the statement that "The Caraleigh work is going on well. The chapel is ready for occupancy." It also noted that Pullen was one of the speakers. (BR, 1/9/95) Three months later the *Recorder* reported:

> There have been seventeen professions at Caraleigh Mills, and the meeting is still in progress. The converts are mostly grown people. Last Sunday afternoon and night four men from twenty-two to sixty years of age claimed a hope. Rev. A. D. Hunter is being helped in the work by Bro. John T. Pullen and the members of Fayetteville Street Church, which is a live, active church. (4/10/95)

A further remarkable development was reported in the *Recorder* on May 19, 1897:

> The Fayetteville Street Baptist Church of this city has employed a teacher and established a night school at the mission at Caraleigh Mills for the benefit of any of the operatives who desire to attend. A good many are now in attendance upon the school.

The judgment of the editor of the *Biblical Recorder* that Fayetteville Street Church was "a live, active church" was quite correct. It had been organized on December 28, 1884, with five members. When it was accepted into the Raleigh Baptist Association, on October 19, 1886, it reported a membership of 69. Of that number, eight had joined by letter after the organization of the church, and fifty-six had been baptized into the church. Services were held both Sunday morning and Sunday night, as a rule, although at times there were night services only. Normally there was also a Wednesday evening prayer meeting. Two or more revivals were conducted each year, and they often lasted for several weeks. The congregation grew rapidly, and by early 1894 the membership of the church was 113. At the end of the century it had passed the 200 mark.

The Sunday school program was a vital part of the church during this period. John Pullen was superintendent from the beginning. Within a year after the establishment of the church more than 200 persons were members of the Sunday school. Again, there is no clue as to the content of the program, but it is highly likely that it was a Bible study, with a strong evangelistic flavor. The International Uniform Lesson system had just been formulated, and it is possible that that plan was being followed. On October 13, 1897, the *Biblical Recorder* reported:

> The Sunday school raised fifty dollars last Sunday for missions and the Orphanage. Two little girls for two weeks arose early each morning and worked hard picking peas and bringing water, and thus earned a dollar each and put it in the collection.

The rapid growth of the church, and of its Sunday school, soon made the original building seem inadequate. The *Biblical Recorder* announced on January 4, 1888, the decision of the church "to commence work on their new building next March and to complete it during the year." The plan to move apparently was a bit premature, however, for the total membership of the church at that time was still quite small. In addition, the pastor, S. H. Thompson, resigned about mid-year, and for the next eighteen months the church was without a minister. When a new one came, he remained for slightly less than a year, and his successor for only a year. Furthermore, the church was struggling financially; in 1888 the total offerings were only $532.26, and $400.00 of that was promised the pastor as his salary. There is no record that the church decided to delay the move, but there was no further reference to moving until 1890. On March 26, 1890, the *Recorder* reported that "The church has arranged to move higher up on Fayetteville Street." Again on June 4 the *Recorder* referred to the decision, saying that "The Fayetteville Street Baptist Church of Raleigh have arranged to build a new house of worship, and have secured a most eligible lot for the purpose." That lot was about two blocks north of the original location, on the corner of Fayetteville and South streets.

At long last, construction of the new building was begun in 1892, with most of the work being done by the members of the congregation. The church was without a pastor while the work was going on, and John Pullen did the preaching. What might have gone into the pastor's salary, therefore, was used to help pay for the building. At the end of 1893 the *Biblical Recorder* reported:

> The new house of worship of the Fayetteville Street Baptist church, Raleigh, approaches completion. The seats are now being placed in position, and the house will in the near future be ready for occupancy. The Lord has greatly blessed the efforts of this band of brethren. Nearly all of their membership has been gathered by conversions in their own meetings, and they have more than a hundred on their list of members. (Dec. 13, 1893)

A service of dedication of the new structure was held on Sunday, January 28, 1894. According to the *Biblical Recorder*:

> On Dec. 28th, 1884, the Fayetteville Street church, Raleigh, was organized. This result grew out of years of labor in prayer meetings, Sunday school work, visiting and helping the poor, &c. A site was purchased from the State during the administration of Gov. Jarvis and a mission house erected thereon at the lower terminus of Fayetteville Street. Brethren Jno. T. Pullen, Sylvester Betts, T. W. Blake and others were prominent in the labors of that section of the city. After the church was organized, God blessed the work and many have been added to the membership. The house was enlarged; but the Master has so constantly

Fayetteville Street Baptist Church
1894

blessed the labors of this flock, that the building became inadequate for its purpose. A more eligible site at the corner of Fayetteville and South streets was secured, and a larger, handsomer and more convenient edifice has just been erected. The old house will be sold to colored people. On Sunday 1st the new church edifice was dedicated to the service of God. By special request, Rev. C. A. Jenkens, the eloquent Goldsboro pastor, preached the dedicatory sermon. His subject was "God's Supreme Command of Love," and he treated it in a style that was at once broad, clear and convincing. His remarks with especial reference to the new house were very well taken. After the sermon, Dr. Carter, Bro. Simms, Bro. Stringfield, the pastor, and Bro. Pullen, who has labored so faithfully in this field, made short talks. They were all timely and forceful. Bro. N. B. Broughton made a "collection talk," and about $275 was raised to help pay the indebtedness of the church. The new church building is indeed an honor to the taste and judgment of its builders; is neat, well-arranged and roomy. It is situated in a location to do much toward bringing souls to Jesus, and the church has within it some of the best workers we know of. The attendance at the service was very large. Brethren Cobb, Carter, Betts, Simms, Stringfield and Hunter were on the pulpit. (BR, 1/31/94)

By May, 1894, the cost of the building had been paid completely, a sum amounting to $3,500. A small amount, however, was still owed on the lot. (BR, 5/10/94) Three years later an "infant class room" was added, at a cost of $600, and an "elegant church bell weighing about 1,000 pounds" was installed.

From the outset it was clear to everyone that the real leader of the Fayetteville Street church was John T. Pullen. Years later, Mrs. Bernice Stringfield McKay, daughter of O. L. Stringfield, recalled: "Mr. John T. Pullen had a church and a parsonage. What a wonder he was. He was a rich man living just this side of Meredith. He was a bachelor and loved church. He told Papa to come to his church as pastor, with a parsonage for us, at the end of Fayetteville Street. The church was Pullen Memorial." If Mrs. McKay's memory about the parsonage is correct, this is the only information we have that the church (or John Pullen) owned one. But she apparently had a clear perception of the relationship of Pullen to the church. The new church had no pastor until 1886, and Pullen did most of the preaching for the congregation until that time. He was superintendent of the Sunday school from the beginning until his death in 1913. He was church clerk from 1893 through 1897. In the years when the church had no pastor (1889, 1892, 1893, 1895, 1896), he did the preaching. Without raising any question about Pullen's devotion or the effectiveness of his work, one might wonder whether his forcefulness and his prominence might help account for the short tenure of most of the pastors in those early years.

John Turner Pullen
1852-1913

Throughout his life Pullen was an evangelist. One of his earliest kinds of evangelistic activity was the distribution of literature aimed at conversion. In 1888 he notified the *Recorder* that he would send "80 nice chromo cards with Scripture texts thereon, free to any address; provided said person will distribute them to the unconverted." (5/23/88) From time to time thereafter he had similar notices published in the *Recorder*. One Sunday in July, 1894, he preached in the First Baptist Church of Raleigh on the subject, "Personal work for Christ" (BR, 7/11/94). On September 21, 1898, the *Recorder* printed in full an address by that same title. Commenting on it, the editor said:

> We never printed better reading than that you will find in the address on Personal Work, by John T. Pullen. It is long, but you will treat yourself badly if you do not read every word carefully. We believe every paper in the land could print it wisely for the upbuilding of the cause of Christ. The address becomes a wonder when, in view of the Scripture quotations, the reader is told that not one word of it was written. Brother Pullen speaks off-hand. Miss Carrie McLean, who has so admirably performed similar service for us, took the address in shorthand, and Bro. Pullen was as surprised as he could be when he saw how his talk appeared in written words. What an incentive to self-education it is that Brother Pullen has become able to make such a speech, not by aid of school or college, but by devout study of the Bible. Neither Moody nor Spurgeon ever made a better speech than this one. Read it; keep it; live it.

For some ten years after the establishment of Fayetteville Street Church, Pullen's preaching was done chiefly at that church. Beginning in 1895, however, he was in some demand for preaching in revivals in other churches. Bear in mind the fact that that was an era of revivalism. In the editorial just quoted, the names of "Moody" and "Spurgeon" were assumed to be so well-known to the readers of the *Recorder* that the comparison would be immediately appreciated. The *Recorder* for August 21, 1895, reported that "Bro. John T. Pullen of Raleigh has been aiding Pastor Jonathan Wood in a good meeting at Bryson City." Wood knew Pullen well because he had been pastor of Fayetteville Street Church in 1891. In November of 1895 Pullen preached in a revival at Littleton. (BR, 11/13/95) In February, 1896, he preached in a series of services at Fayetteville Street. (BR, 2/2/96) In April of 1896 he and the Reverend A. L. Betts, a former pastor of Fayetteville Street, were in services in Reidsville. (BR, 4/15/96) In June of the same year he held services at East Durham Church in which, according to the pastor, there were twenty-six "professions of religion, and twenty were baptized Sunday night." (BR, 6/10/96) The June 16, 1897, issue of the *Recorder* carried a note from the Reverend W. A. Smith:

Our meeting at West Durham Baptist Church closed June 1st. It continued about three weeks. Bro. John T. Pullen, of Raleigh, was with us two weeks, and did some of the purest gospel preaching it has ever been my privilege to hear. He relates no ghost stories nor death-bed scenes, but preached *the* Gospel, believing it to be the power of God unto salvation to all them that believe. About thirty-five professed faith in Christ, and eighteen have already been received for baptism; others, I think, will join. Brother Pullen holds a warm place in the hearts of our West Durham people, and we hope he will come again. In our hearts, we thank God for sending him among us, and for His blessings upon us in the meeting just closed.

In March, 1898, Pullen preached in Baymore, New Jersey. (BR, 3/30/90)

One of the periods during which Pullen did most of the preaching at Fayetteville Street Church was the years 1895-96. For about five months in 1896 the *Biblical Recorder* carried brief notes on a number of his messages. From those notes, and from the verbatim report of his address on "Personal Work" (BR, 9/21/98), we can get an understanding of the kind of preaching he did. His sermons were basically expository, explaining and illustrating selected passages of scripture. They were full of biblical quotations, allusions, and examples drawn from all portions of the Bible. Clearly the man spent a great deal of time studying the Bible, because he ranged over both the Old Testament and the New for quotations and citations. The religion which he proclaimed was intensely personal, stressing one's individual relationship to God and one's duties to God. While he proclaimed salvation by grace, there can be no doubt that for him the evidence of that salvation was a rather rigid standard of personal mortality and a commitment to doing good deeds. The messages were always climaxed with an invitation to Christian commitment. Pullen always preached as if at least some of the congregation were sinners who needed conversion.

Long after the death of John Pullen, Charles Hinton Belvin III, his nephew, wrote that "John long had been occupied with good works especially with food baskets, groceries, clothing, fuel, medical attention to the lesser privileged whites and blacks." The context of that statement suggests that that was the case even before 1881. That should not be surprising, because many philanthropists are not religious persons. Some of the things Pullen did in the late 1890's, however, were unusual. While some of the local churches provided each year a Christmas dinner for the poor white widows of the city, for example, he did the same thing for an even more neglected group. The *Biblical Recorder* for January 5, 1898, reported that "The week of Christmas in Raleigh was made worthy of the meaning of the season by the great dinner given by John Pullen to the old colored women."

Another example was his ministry to the men in Central Prison. Several members of Fayetteville Street Church regularly went with him to teach Sunday school in the "Penitentiary." When the century-old building of Central Prison was razed in October, 1983, the demolition crew found in the cornerstone a box containing, among other items, the following letter from John T. Pullen, dated July 15, 1885:

> For several years I have been a teacher at the Penitentiary Sunday school. I can say from the depths of my heart, that I love to come and tell the prisoners of Jesus and his love. Some people think it a yoke to walk out here every Sabbath. If it be a yoke, I say My God give me more yokes.

The first pastor of Fayetteville Street Church was C.A.G. Thomas. The *Biblical Recorder* announced on October 6, 1886, that "Rev. C.A.G. Thomas has accepted a call to the pastorate of the 3rd Baptist Church of Raleigh, and will preach for the church every Sunday evening." Thomas had been pastor at Warrenton for several years and had also served two other churches at the same time. He preached at Kittrell every other Tuesday night and at Middleburg on the third Sunday mornings. Shortly after his marriage he had resigned at Warrenton and accepted a pastorate in Newport News, Virginia. After he had been there for less than a year, however, he resigned. The *Recorder* announced that "Rev. C.A.G. Thomas, the former pastor at Warrenton, and who had been doing a good work at Newport News, Virginia, has to leave the latter place on account of the health of his wife." (BR, 7/29/85) Thomas soon accepted calls to Mt. Moriah and Hepzibah churches in Wake County. (BR, 9/6/85) The work which he began at Fayetteville Street in October, 1886, was simply a responsibility added to an already busy schedule. At the end of 1886, however, he gave up his other churches, moved to Raleigh, and devoted all of his time to Fayetteville Street.

Thomas' coming to Fayetteville Street Church coincided with the church's affiliation with the Raleigh Baptist Association. At its annual meeting on October 19, 1886, the Association accepted Fayetteville Street Church into its fellowship. The total membership of the church at that time was sixty-nine, with fifty-six of that number having been received by baptism. Almost immediately after beginning his full-time work at Fayetteville Street, Thomas started a series of revival services which continued for nearly a month, and a number of people were baptized as a result of it. In a general statement about life in the Raleigh churches the editor of the *Recorder* said of Thomas, "He is one of the finest of our young preachers and is doing a good work in Raleigh." Thomas' pastorate was quite brief, however, for he left at the end of July, 1887, to become pastor of a church in Yanceyville.

The Reverend Alvin Betts was called almost immediately after Thomas' departure. Betts was already well-known to the members of Fayetteville Street Church. At the time of the establishment of the mission which became Fayetteville Street Church he was pastor at Bethlehem Church near Raleigh and attended the meetings of the Baptist ministers in Raleigh. (BR, 8/10/84) A note in the *Recorder* for October 8, 1884, shortly before Fayetteville Street Church was formed, stated that "A protracted meeting held by brethren Alvin Betts and John Pullen at the mission Chapel, resulted in the conversion of fourteen persons. This mission will soon result in the organization of the 3rd Baptist church in Raleigh." Along with C. T. Skinner, pastor of the First Baptist Church, and C. T. Bailey, editor of the *Biblical Recorder*, Betts was a member of the presbytery at which the church was organized. In 1885 he served several churches in Harnett County. In that same year he was also a frequent visiting preacher at Fayetteville street. In the summer of 1886 he "canvassed Wake County in the interest of the American Bible Union." (BR, 7/14/86)

Less is known about Betts' work as pastor at Fayetteville Street than is known about his involvement in its formation. The *Recorder* reported nothing about his work there in 1887; the only reference to him is the announcement of the death of "another of his sons in the prime of early manhood." (BR, 7/27/87) His tenure at Fayetteville Street was concluded at the end of the year.

In April, 1888, S. H. Thompson began his work as pastor at Fayetteville Street Church. Prior to that time he had owned and operated the High Point Classical Institute, a school which he had established in January, 1886. Almost immediately upon his arrival a revival was begun. According to the *Recorder* for April 18, 1888:

> The interest at the Fayetteville Street church, has been so great that pastor Thompson preached every night during the past week, and will continue to do so during the present week. Twelve have professed faith and about thirty others are pertinently seeking salvation. The church is greatly revived and a great work is in progress.

Thompson was much in demand as a revival preacher in other churches. The *Recorder* carried frequent notices about his being away from Fayetteville Street and frequent reports from other churches about his work with them. In November, 1888, after only eight months in Raleigh, he accepted a call to become pastor of a church in South Boston, Virginia, where he had just preached a revival.

For a year Fayetteville Street Church was without a pastor. Early in 1890, however, O. L. Stringfield accepted a call from the church. Stringfield was one of the best known and most highly respected ministers in the state. He was a native of Wilmington and a member of a family that before the Civil War had been quite wealthy. With his older brothers in the Confederate army, Stringfield, although not yet a teenager, had a man's responsibilities at home. His struggle with poverty during the days of the Reconstruction created in him a sympathy for the underprivileged which was to characterize his adult ministry. At the age of twenty-three he decided to become a minister and went to Wake Forest College. At the time of his graduation in 1882 he was serving a field of four churches. In September of that year he became principal of a new school at Wakefield, near Wendell. For eleven years he was the moving force behind that school which was widely known for the quality of education it gave students. During all of those years he served as pastor of a number of churches, and he was in constant demand as a revival preacher.

In January, 1890, Stringfield conducted a series of meetings at the Fayetteville Street Church. On February 9 the *Recorder* announced:

> Rev. O. L. Stringfield, one of the principals of the Wakefield Classical and Mathematical School, has agreed to preach for the Fayetteville Street church, Raleigh, on the fourth Sunday of every month at eleven a.m. and every Sunday evening at 7:30 p.m. This will in no way interfere with his duties as co-principal of his school at Wakefield.

Throughout that year he met his obligations both at the school and at Fayetteville Street. In addition, he preached in revivals all over the area. There is no record of when he terminated his relationship with Fayetteville Street, but it probably was at the end of the year. After ending his pastorate, however, he was a frequent preacher at the church, and some years later would again become its pastor.

Jonathan B. Wood assumed the pastorate of Fayetteville Street Church in July, 1891. As was the case with his predecessors, and as seems to have been usual in Baptist churches in the area, very shortly after his arrival he began a series of evangelistic metings. Rather than doing the preaching himself, however, he was assisted by a visiting minister, the Reverend J. F. Long, of London, England (BR 9/30/91), whom the *Recorder* characterized as "a consecrated man, a zealous worker, and a good preacher." (BR, 10/7/91) In April, 1892, there was another revival, with O. L. Stringfield doing the preaching. Wood was in poor health, and in May, 1892, he resigned and moved to Colorado.

A new day dawned for the church in January, 1894. For two years after Wood's departure the church had been without a pastor, and during most of that time John Pullen had done the preaching. It was during that period that the church renewed its efforts to move to a site higher up on Fayetteville Street. In January, 1894, the church had a new pastor and began its work in its new building.

The new pastor was not really new, but was a former pastor who had returned. O. L. Stringfield had served the church in 1890. In the years 1891-1983 he had continued his work at Wakefield, had preached in countless revivals throughout the state, and had been pastor to other churches. In April, 1892, he had been elected to the Board of Trustees of the Baptist Female Institute, which was still in the planning stage. In May of the same year the Trustees had engaged him for part-time work seeking support for the Institute, and soon afterwards they had made the position full-time. He was to devote most of his time and energies to that work until the school opened in 1899. He was an ideal choice, for no other man was better known in Baptist circles in North Carolina. At the time that he was beginning that work he accepted a call to return as pastor to Fayetteville Street. According to the *Biblical Recorder* for November 15, 1893:

> Rev. O. L. Stringfield, the worthy agent of the Baptist Female University, has accepted the pastorate of the Third Baptist church of this city, and will locate his family here. We welcome Bro. Stringfield to our city and congratulate the Third church on their admirable selection.

For a full year Stringfield served the church, and apparently served it well, for the *Recorder* frequently reported on the evangelistic work there. It also reported that the new building was completely paid for, although a bit remained to be paid on the lot. (BR, 5/10/94) The total membership of the church reached 147, a figure that represented an increase of thirty-four over what it was at the beginning of the year. Stringfield concluded his pastorate at the end of the year.

For nearly three years the church was without a pastor, and again John Pullen did most of the preaching. During 1895 he had a good deal of assistance from the Reverend A. D. Hunter, the "city missionary" employed by the Baptists of Raleigh. Hunter worked chiefly with the West End Mission and with the Caraleigh mission. In that work he was closely associated with John Pullen and was a frequent visitor to Fayetteville Street Church. The *Recorder* for June 5, 1895, noted:

> Fayetteville Street Baptist church closed its meeting last week, and on Sunday night last, Rev. A. D. Hunter baptized five. This is forty-one recently baptized into this church, three of whom were old men, one in seventieth year. Others have joined by letter. Bro. Hunter says he is glad to work with such helpers as Bro. John T. Pullen and those who labor with him. Many of those who attended this meeting also attended the meeting at Caraleigh Mills.

During 1896 and 1897 Pullen was responsible for the services, usually conducting them himself, but often having visiting preachers.

The next pastor was W. C. Barrett, who came to Raleigh from Sampson County. He was visiting preacher at Fayetteville Street on the last Sunday in November, 1897. The *Recorder* for December 15 carried the notice: "Rev. W. C. Barrett of Sampson Co., who is one of the best of our younger men, has resigned the pastorate of his churches in Sampson, and will give up his school the last of this year.

His purpose is to devote full time to the work of the ministry." On December 22 the *Recorder* announced that "Bro. Pullen having need of rest, arrangement has been made for Rev. W. C. Barrett of Sampson County to supply the pulpit of the Raleigh Fayetteville Street church." Soon the *Recorder* was calling him "pastor," although it never noted his having been called by the church. He was with the church through the end of 1899. The editor of the *Recorder* commented about his work at Fayetteville Street:

> Rev. W. C. Barrett also has resigned his pastorate, that of the Fayetteville Street Baptist church. He came to Raleigh a young man from a country field. He brought an earnest soul, a studious mind and a consecrated life. His labors have been richly blessed. He has grown steadily as pastor and preacher. He leaves his church prepared for a larger work and he himself is similarly prepared. No one who has watched him here can doubt that he has a future of abundant labors and great usefulness before him.

Barrett himself wrote for publication in the *Recorder*:

> I have had a very pleasant pastorate at Fayetteville Street Church, Raleigh, N.C. One of the most pleasant things connected with my work there has been my association with brother John T. Pullen. He is a theological seminary in himself, and I believe that my acquaintance and work with him will be worth more to me in the future than a year spent under any other influence. His consecration, faith, and beneficience can not be forgotten by any who is associated with him. He is faithful to his pastor and to his church, making his duty to them next to his duty to God.
>
> He and the church have stood by me and supported me in all my efforts to advance the cause. When my resignation was accepted, every cent of my salary had been paid. When I had preached my last sermon as pastor of the church Brother Pullen came to me and gave me a library of one hundred and fifty volumes of very valuable and useful books, together with book cases and room furniture which I had been using two years, amounting in all to more than $200.00, and gave me $50.00 in cash as a special purse.
>
> I will say something about the faithful workers, the church and the field at Fayetteville Street at some time in the future. (BR, 1/17/1900)

At the turn of the century, Fayetteville Street Church was playing a vital role in the religious life of Raleigh. In fifteen years it had grown from a mission church, with a charter membership of three men and two women, into a thriving congregation of more than two hundred persons. It had reached those people whom it had been intended to reach, the unchurched people of south Raleigh. Most of its members came into the church by profession of faith and baptism. It had taken its place as a vital church in a denomination noted for its evangelistic emphasis.

Chapter 3
A Traditional Church
In An Era of Progress
(1900-1920)

The Christian Oracle, an ecumenical religious journal, began publication in 1884, the same year in which Pullen Memorial Baptist Church was established. In 1900 its name was changed to *The Christian Century*. That name change symbolized the optimism that pervaded the United States at the time. The new century was greeted with a hope and a belief in the future that has been unmatched in American history. The Civil War was nearly a generation past, and the nation was doing a good job of covering up its scars and ignoring the unresolved problems which it had left. Only recently the nation had emerged the victor in a war with Spain. The people were confident that the United States was the greatest nation on earth and were anxious to share with the rest of the world the benefits of America's presence. Everyone shared the belief that God had blessed the nation, and that the future was bright because those blessings would continue so long as the nation maintained its fidelity to God.

In 1900 America was well on the way toward becoming an industrialized and an urbanized nation. Great new economic empires were being built by Frederick Weyerhaeuser, James Hill, Edward Harriman, Philip Armour, Gustavus Swift, Robert Morris, Cyrus McCormick, James Duke, J. P. Morgan, and many others. The masses of industrial workers, however, did not share in the wealth of those economic empires. They labored in the mills and the mines, working long hours for short pay, often working in hazardous conditions, and totally dependent upon jobs which they could lose at any time because of their personal failure or because of changes in the economy. A large middle class of business and professional people nourished the American dream, confident that there were no restrictions upon their initiative, no limitations except those of their own abilities. They saw education as the key to success. They were comfortable and secure in their belief that the blessings of God came upon those who deserved them.

A major social factor in the South was the presence of a black minority in a white-dominated society. The establishment of new patterns of relationship between blacks and whites was begun immediately after the emancipation of the slaves. Beginning about 1885, however, the southern states enacted laws requiring racial segregation in education, in transportation, in all kinds of public accommodations. In addition to the laws there developed a whole complex of social customs which rigidly regulated all contact between blacks and whites. The process was not complete until shortly before the outbreak of World War I. The first two decades of the twentieth century, therefore, were a period of the establishment of barriers and the fixing of restrictions within which our people were to operate for half a century.

In reaction to certain elements in the developing patterns of race relations, the National Association for the Advancement of Colored People was created in 1910. While the NAACP did not become strong in the South until well after World War I, it did begin to draw some support in cities such as Raleigh. In its early years, through its Legal Defense and Educational Fund it provided legal assistance for blacks accused of crimes.

Another agency which was active in the first two decades of the twentieth century was the Ku Klux Klan. Originated soon after the Civil War, the Klan began to lose members in the last two decades of the nineteenth century. Beginning in 1915, however, it experienced a revival, and after the end of World War I it grew rapidly in membership and in power.

In the same year that the Klan was born the Boy Scouts of America was organized. The Scout movement had originated in England in 1907 with the work of Sir Robert Baden-Powell, and in only a few years had become an international movement. An idealistic and self-help kind of organization with a stress on wholesome group activities and on personal development, it made a significant impact upon the lives of literally millions of American youth. In a real sense it capsuled the optimism and the idealism of the American dream.

In these first two decades of the twentieth century, religion was as up-beat as everything else in American life. The modern missionary movement, begun in the first half of the nineteenth century, had progressed at a steady pace. The Student Volunteer Movement, organized in 1888, was having its greatest impact in history under the leadership of John R. Mott. All major denominations were affected, and more than ten thousand men and women served as missionaries in the first twenty years of this century. The movement's motto was "the evangelization of the world in this generation."

Revivalism, too, continued apace. In the early twentieth century Sam Jones was called "The Moody of the South." B. Fay Mills was conducting carefully planned campaigns which involved the churches in each city he entered. Gypsy Smith, Cyclone Mack, Mordecai Ham, and scores of others moved back and forth across the nation preaching a gospel of salvation from the fires of hell. The best-known evangelist of the period was William Ashley ("Billy") Sunday, a former professional baseball player with a flair for showmanship.

The main theological current in America, however, particularly in the Northeast, was not revivalism but liberalism. The theological schools and the universities all made use of the new methods of biblical criticism, and all tried to come to terms with the new scholarship in the realms of science and technology. Their approach to faith was less authoritarian and less exclusive, and more dependent on reason and more humanistic. They dealt less with the personal application of the gospel and more with the social implications.

In the major denominations a vigorous reaction against liberalism developed. Reactionary efforts came to a focus in 1910-1915 in the publication of a series of twelve small volumes of essays on *The Fundamentals*. Those essays were widely distributed among both lay and clerical leaders. While they did not halt the trend toward liberalism, they did clarify the differences and tended to harden them. Because of the general educational and cultural isolation of the South from the rest of the country, the churches here were not as seriously affected by the division as were the churches of the Northeast. They were not completely unaffected by the controversy, however, because at least echos of the discussions were heard.

The Sunday school movement spread rapidly in the early twentieth century. The avowed purpose of Sunday schools was Bible study; the chief objective of that Bible study seems to have been the winning of converts.

Another feature of church life of the period was support for the temperance movement. The work of the W.C.T.U. and the Anti-Saloon League was supported by the efforts of many denominations.

Even Southern Baptists, who had a reputation for resistance to political action and to cooperative efforts with other denominations, joined in the campaign. Most evangelicals found it difficult to distinguish between light, moderate, and heavy drinking and believed that the best thing to do was to press for the complete avoidance of the use of alcohol. Their efforts culminated in the ratification of the Eighteenth Amendment to the Constitution, which went into effect in 1920.

The major denominations were deeply affected by the Social Gospel. This movement was an effort to bring the gospel to bear upon the new and urgent social problems that were brought on by the rapid industrialization and urbanization of the nation, and, therefore, upon a wide variety of economic issues. It was also concerned about the problems of minority groups, international relations, political power, the court system, and so on. Washington Gladden, who died in 1918, has often been called the "father" of the social gospel, and Walter Rauschenbusch, a Baptist minister who also died in 1918, has been called its "prophet." Rauschenbusch's book, *Christianity and the Social Crisis*, published in 1907, was one of the best read and most highly influential religious books of the era. There were varying degrees of openness to the social gospel, but all of the major denominations were affected by it.

In the early years of the twentieth century a concern for Christian unity was expressed in cooperative efforts in the cause of temperance, in the support of foreign missions, and in the Sunday school movement. In addition, in 1907, thirty-three evangelical denominations formed a cooperative agency called the Federal Council of the Churches of Christ in America. The Southern Baptist Convention, however, never affiliated with that Council.

Although Southern Baptists have insisted that they are a "denomination" and not a "church," in this period they took a number of steps to strengthen their denominational organization and thus took on the essential features of a church. One such step was the coordinating of the work of the State Conventions. Another was the encouragement of the use of denominational publications in the educational program of the churches. Still another was the establishment of a second theological seminary, Southwestern, which was opened in Texas in 1908. Yet another was the establishment of the Relief and Annuity Board to help provide retirement income for ministers.

The city of Raleigh was experiencing rapid growth at the turn of the century. In 1890 the population was 12,678; in 1909 it was 19,218. That growth was due largely to the fact that the city was the center of state government, and government was growing. The city limits were enlarged several times, although not all of the residents of the newly-annexed territories were convinced that incorporation into the city was an unmixed blessing. In 1910 a local realty company, over some local opposition, began a housing development known as Cameron Park. First Baptist Chruch acquired some property in that area to provide for the establishment of a church, and in the 1920's that property was to play a part in the decision of Pullen Memorial Church to relocate in West Raleigh.

Some problems associated with the growth of the city were already being recognized before 1900, and efforts were made to deal with them. Those efforts were intensified during the first two decades of the twentieth century. The paving of the city streets continued, and the provision of a more adequate system of electric lighting followed quickly. Telephone service was improved and expanded. Carolina Power and Light Company took over the streetcar system and expanded it. Still something of a novelty in the city in 1900, the automobile was common enough by 1920 to make at least one service station a profitable venture. Steps were taken to solve the water problems. Hospital services were increased and improved, with both Rex Hospital (in 1904) and St. Agnes Hospital (in 1909) entering new buildings.

Educational institutions were very much in the public mind. North Carolina State Agricultural and Mechanical College had begun operation in 1889, and was attracting more students every year. Meredith College was opened in 1899, and it drew support from all over the state. The public school system was prospering, particularly with the opening of the Raleigh High School in 1906, with Hugh Morson as principal.

The growth of state government required additional space for state agencies, and the second decade of the century was a period of the expansion of facilities. A number of imposing new government buildings were erected, and there was considerable construction on the campus of North Carolina State College. In addition, expanding business and banking concerns, particularly on Fayetteville Street, required new buildings. County government too was growing and had to erect new facilities.

The entrance of the United States into World War I, in April of 1917, brought an immediate change to Raleigh. Within two months over 2500 Raleigh men were in uniform, and within a year a third of those men were on duty in France. A number of Raleigh women served in the medical corps. Camp Polk was made a training ground for the tank corps. Thousands of soldiers from all over the country who were trained there spent some time in the city, and many of them enjoyed the hospitality of Raleigh residents. Then, in 1918, as suddenly as they came, the soldiers were gone. Two months after the end of the war Camp Polk was deactivated. For Raleigh, the last great hurrah of the war came on March 23, 1919, when a crowd of 50,000 people welcomed home Raleigh's native son, Colonel Albert L. Cox, and the 113th Field Artillery. Colonel Cox and his regiment had played a major role in the break in the Hindenburg Line which had turned the tide for the Allies and was the prelude to victory.

In spite of economic uncertainty, therefore, in spite of festering social problems, and in spite of the war, the first two decades of the twentieth century were an era of progress in the United States. Like the rest of the South, the state of North Carolina and the city of Raleigh were not in the mainstream of all the developments in the country. Yet they could not have been completely isolated from any of them. Life in Raleigh was, on the whole, upbeat. The city was growing and prospering, and Fayetteville Street Baptist Church was in step with the times.

When W. C. Barrett left Fayetteville Street Baptist Church in December, 1899, the church was in good condition. During the two years of his leadership it had increased in membership by a total of twenty-two persons. The Sunday school was thriving, with more than two hundred on roll. Although a decline in financial contributions had occurred because of uncertainty in the national economic situation, the future of the church was not in any serious danger.

For the first seven months of 1900 the church was without a pastor. As usual, John T. Pullen did most of the preaching during the interim. In June, 1900, Edwards and Broughton published his little book, *What Saith the Scripture?* The editor of the *Biblical Recorder* called that document "the product of his incessant study of the Scriptures." (7/11/1900) A large part of it is a beautiful arrangement of quotations from the Scripture to answer a wide variety of religious questions. Another section is a collection of Pullen's comments on Scripture, simple and direct and practical. The final portion is a reprint of two of his addresses, "Personal Work" and "Likeness of God's Word to Fire." The book sold for fifty cents and the profits from it went to the Students' Aid Fund of the Baptist Female University.

From time to time during the interim visiting preachers from throughout the state spoke at Fayetteville Street Church. Apparently some of them were delivering "trial sermons" to give the congregation an opportunity to hear persons who might be considered for pastor. One such person was A. A. Butler, of Franklinton. Noting that Butler had preached at Fayetteville Street in early June, the editor of the *Recorder* commented that he had "greatly pleased the congregation of our Fayetteville Street Baptist Church," and that "Franklinton had better look out!" (BR, 6/13/1900)

Butler was called by Fayetteville Street and became pastor on the first Sunday in August, 1900. He served the church through April, 1902. Shortly after his arrival the editor of the *Recorder* commented that he was "making a fine impression" upon the church. (8/29/1900) A few weeks later he commented that "Butler had taken the Fayetteville Street people by storm." (10/3/1900) During his tenure the membership of the church increased only slightly, however, and enrollment in the Sunday school remained about the same. With a membership of 232, the church sems to have stopped growing in size, at least for a time. The changing character of the area in which it was located may have been a major factor in this development. Butler certainly did those things that a pastor was expected to do. On the occasion of his first anniversary as pastor the *Recorder* said that "He had rendered very effective service, preaching ably and visiting constantly. His work is highly successful." (8/14/01) He apparently was well respected in the area, for in November, 1901, he preached the introductory sermon at the annual meeting of the Raleigh Baptist Association. One Sunday in February, 1902, he occupied the pulpit of First Baptist, while the pastor was away, and the report of that event noted that "This young preacher continues to make substantial progress." (2/12/02)

John Pullen continued his evangelistic and philanthropic work as usual. On January 9, 1901, the *Recorder* described at length one of the activities for which he was noted:

> One of the most unique and thoughtful remembrances of the poor that we have seen, is in the Old Folk's Dinner, given at the Fayetteville Street Baptist church in this city, by the Young Ladies' Society of the First Baptist church and Mr. John T. Pullen. On New Year's day of each year the young ladies of the First Baptist church prepare a bountiful spread for the aged poor. Invitations are issued and when necessary private carriages are used to bring the invited guest to the feast. The young ladies serve the meal, acting as waitresses. Tables are spread, comfortable seats provided and in every way the feast is a spread of which any up-to-date hostelry might be proud. In this work the young ladies are ably assisted by Bro. J. T. Pullen, who is the presiding genius of the Fayetteville Street church and the active friend of every worthy enterprise. Surely this is a good work and will bring its reward to those who gave it.

Another philanthropic interst was revealed in a letter signed by Pullen, along with W. N. Jones, N. B. Broughton, C. J. Hunter, and R. N. Simms, who constituted the "Central Committee of Education," and published in the *Recorder* for February 6, 1902. That letter appealed for support in the denomination's commitment to raise $50,000 to pay off the debts "on the Baptist Female University, the Chowan Baptist Female Institute, and our Baptist academies."

At the end of April, 1902, Butler left Fayetteville Street Church to become pastor of the Baptist church in Beaufort. Although his ministry at Fayetteville Street had continued the evangelistic tradition, that does not seem to have been his major emphasis. Twice, at least, the

45

editor of the *Biblical Recorder* had spoken of his pastoral work. On the first anniversary of his coming to the church the editor had spoken of his "visiting constantly." And in announcing Butler's resignation the editor had spoken of his doing "good and strong work here, in pulpit and in the homes of the people."

For approximately a year Fayetteville Street Church was without a pastor, and as usual, John Pullen either preached at the services or was responsible for inviting a visiting preacher.

In May, 1903, the church called R. J. Bateman, and he began his work with them on the first Sunday in July. At the time the church called him, Bateman was pastor in Milton. He had preached at Fayetteville Street in a series of meetings in April, and the editor of the *Recorder* had called him "a very promising man." W. P. Baker, in his unpublished history of Pullen Memorial Church, described him as

> a young man just out of College. A man of great power, mentally, spiritually and physically. He was a handsome man in the Pulpit with a great delivery, endowed with the spirit of love for the lost with great persuasive powers. 43 joined the Church by Baptism and 7 by letter. It was plain to see that this man on fire with God's Spirit was going far as a Minister of the Gospel. (p. 7)

Only a few weeks after he began at Fayetteville Street, the editor of the *Recorder* reported, "Rev. R. J. Bateman, the new pastor of the Raleigh Fayetteville Street Church, is a most excellent young man. He has from the first thrown himself into our denominational life, and his enthusiasm has succeeded in bringing his churches forward." (5/27/03)

Bateman represented a return to the evangelistic emphasis which had characterized most of his predecessors, but which apparently was not an emphasis of his immediate predecessor, A. A. Butler. He often preached in revivals in other churches in addition to conducting such services at Fayetteville Street. The *Recorder* reported on a meeting which he was conducting at Fayetteville Street and said "Large crowds and frequent manifestations of interest bear witness to the divine approval." (9/6/03) A month later, in commenting on a sermon which Bateman preached at First Baptist, the *Recorder* noted: "He has recently baptized thirty converts in his own church as the result of a revival conducted by himself. His people are delighted and the church was never in so hopeful a frame." (10/14/03) Thereafter the *Recorder* frequently reported on his evangelistic work both at Fayetteville Street and elsewhere.

Bateman actually served two terms as pastor of Fayetteville Street. He began his first term on the first Sunday in July, 1903, and ended it on the last of August, 1904, when he accepted the call of the Mount

Olive church. In April, 1905, he was back at Fayetteville Street to conduct a revival, and at the end of July he accepted the invitation to return as pastor. In congratulating Fayetteville Street on his return, the *Recorder* noted that the church "has a great field—half of Raleigh and the needier half at that." (7/26/05) In December of that same year Bateman resigned again, however, this time to accept the pastorate of Spurgeon Memorial Church in Norfolk. Apparently he saw himself primarily as an evangelist, and could not be satisfied long in any one place.

In light of Pullen Memorial Baptist Church's long and close association with Wake Forest University, as well as with Meredith College and North Carolina State University, it is interesting to observe that some twenty years after his service at Fayetteville Street Bateman became involved in the evolution controversy which focused on William Louis Poteat. At that time he was pastor of the First Baptist Church of Asheville. It was he who wrote the resolution on the controversy which was offered at the Baptist State Convention, meeting in Charlotte in 1925. The resolution was not bitter; it was not anti-Poteat; it was not overtly anti-evolution. Rather it affirmed a belief in "Genesis not as a myth, but as God's inspired revelation." In light of the strong feelings of the time, the resolution was remarkably mild and was not interpreted by Wake Forest as in any way limiting academic freedom. Friends of the College interpreted Bateman's resolution as one which, in the long run, protected the College from a far more serious attack.

Church statistics are notoriously unreliable. In this period of the history of Pullen, however, they are puzzling. According to Baker, when A. A. Butler was pastor the membership reached 232. In the interim between Butler and Bateman, he says, there were twenty additions to the church. Bateman, he reports, baptized forty-three and received seven by letter. Yet in the spring of 1904, according to the *Biblical Recorder* (5/4/04), the church had a membership of 216, with 171 in Sunday school. About the time of Bateman's departure at the end of 1905 there was a decline in membership; by the time for the annual report to be submitted to the Association in the fall of the year, there were only 159 members. The reasons for the decline are uncertain, but one of them may be the work at Caraleigh Cotton Mill Village. Members from Fayetteville Street were active in a mission Sunday school there, and some of them may have become a part of the church that was organized there.

After Bateman's resignation the church was without a minister for only four months. E. Y. Poole, who had been pastor in Sanford, began his work in May, 1906. In announcing his acceptance, the *Recorder* said:

47

> Bro. E. Y. Poole, of Sanford, accepts the call of our Fayetteville Street
> Church, which in recent years has taken on much strength, and which
> we hope will become a rival of her sister churches here. It is now a most
> useful institution. Brother Poole is well equipped for his task; not only
> a good preacher, but an enthusiastic pastor and leader. (3/7/06)

Perhaps the *Recorder's* appreciation of Poole was intensified by the
fact that every family in the Sanford church was receiving the
Recorder! Poole remained at Fayetteville Street for less than a year,
resigning in April, 1907. Apparently he resigned without having
received a call to another church, for the *Recorder* said:

> Bro. E. Y. Poole has resigned the pastorate of Fayetteville Street
> Church, Raleigh, after a term of devoted and successful service. He is
> an excellent preacher and a diligent pastor. We regret very much that
> he has left Raleigh, but hope that he will shortly take up a pastorate in
> our Convention. (4/17/07)

John Pullen's interest in denominational institutions apparently
continued to expand. An article in the *Recorder* for December 12,
1906, desribed one of his visits to Baptist Children's Home:

> Mr. John Pullen, the philanthropist of Raleigh, without a word of
> warning rolled in Thursday afternoon with candy enough for all. A
> hasty summons brought the children together and Mr. Pullen distrib-
> uted the candy and made the children one of his kindly, helpful talks.
> His coming was like a sunburst and left a sweet influence. He took the
> first train and glided away as quietly as he came. Blessings on the man.
> He must be very happy, because he brings so much happiness to the
> hearts of others.

About a year later Pullen's Sunday school class, the Baraca class,
decided to contribute $6.00 per month for the support of a child at the
Thomasville Orphanage. In addition, the church made a $33.00 cash
contribution to the Orphanage, along with a box of food and
clothing.

As usual in the periods without a pastor, Pullen was responsible for
the pulpit of Fayetteville Street Church. Often he had visting
preachers, some of whom were ministers and lay persons from
Raleigh. Others apparently were people whom the congregation was
considering for a call to the pastorate of the church. In this interim
Pullen also led the congregation in a small building program, adding
a class room in which Pullen's own class met. The seating capacity of
that room was a hundred and fifty. In announcing that construction
the *Recorder* called Pullen "a prince of teachers and Christian
workers."

The church was not long without a pastor. The Reverend P. G.
Elsom began his work at Fayetteville Street in the middle of September, 1907. While little background information about him is
available, he seems to have been one of the most colorful and charismatic individuals who ever served the church. He was pre-eminently

an evangelist, and his fourteen-month tenure at the church seems to have been one of continuous "protracted meeting." On September 25 the *Recorder* announced that "Pastor Elsom, of the Fayetteville Street Baptist Church began a series of revival meetings last Sunday." On October 9 it noted that "A great spiritual revival is going on in the Fayetteville Street Church in Raleigh under the leadership of its pastor, Rev. P. G. Elsom." On October 23 the *Recorder* reported that

> Revival of great power goes on at Fayetteville Street Baptist Church. Seventy-three persons have already united with the church, the majority of them strong young men. There have been fifty baptized up-to-date and fully 100 professions of religion. Sunday night the church was packed, and the pastor, Rev. P. G. Elsom, was asked by a vote of the Church to go on preaching in this revival.

The November 6 issue of the *Recorder* reported that the revival meetings had closed, and that there had been eighty-one additions to the church, fifty-six of whom had come by baptism. After that there were additions almost every week. In the first four months of Elsom's pastorate, ninety-seven persons were received into the membership of the church. In February of 1908 he conducted another revival in which sixteen persons joined the church. In July he was in a revival at Caraleigh, where ninety-six persons joined the church, seventy-three of whom were baptized. All of this activity was in addition to Elsom's evangelistic work outside the city.

W. P. Baker, author of the brief unpublished history of the first forty-five years of Pullen Memorial Baptist Church, had been baptized into Pullen Memorial on May 5, 1907, shortly before Elsom became pastor. He summarized Elsom's impact upon the church:

> He was an evangelistic [*sic*]. A man of deep and earnest convictions. He held several meetings. We would have a song leader and he doing the Preaching. One of these meetings lasted for six weeks. Over sixty people were saved. Our City was stirred under the dynamic Preaching of this Apostle. Other Churches joined in the meetings. It was a great blessing for our City. Hard and confirmed drunkards and many old people joined our Church for Baptism. The meetings in most cases would go on well beyond midnight. Mr. Elsom was not a strong man physically. When his energy would give out Mr. Pullen would do the Preaching. There ws a great deal of personal work, praying and visiting in the homes. Surely the windows of heaven were open. We could see the blessings of the Lord. A Prayer Answered. While whole families were saved. There was great activities in our Church. A Bible Class meeting every Friday night. Sunday School greatly improved and enlarged. 224 members. Total money raised $3,046.00 the first year. (Unpublished history, pp. 8-9)

Consistent with his concern for evangelism, Elsom had a great interest in missions. In June, 1908, he led the church in the observance of a "Mission Week" in which addresses were delivered by a number of denominational leaders, including E. L. Middleton, Livingston Johnson, J. W. Bailey, and Governor Glenn. One outcome of the week was the formation of a Mission Band comprised of people who agreed to "contribute every week toward the evangelization of the world." That line echoes the famous motto of the Student Volunteer Movement, "the evangelization of the world in this generation."

Elsom resigned on the last Sunday in October, 1908. His announced purpose was to "devote himself to evangelistic work with headquarters in Raleigh." Two weeks later, however, the *Recorder* announced that "A new Baptist Church was organized in Raleigh last Sunday afternoon, under direction of Rev. P. G. Elsom, no other pastors or churches co-operating, we understand." (BR, 11/18/08) The next issue of the *Recorder* carried further information:

> Rev. P. G. Elsom, the pastor requests us to state that no other churches were invited to participate and that the church was organized according to usual Baptist usage after adopting the customary articles of faith. Brother Sandridge, the leading member of the church, an earnest brother, and native of the same county in Virginia as Brother Elsom, also requests us to explain that the Baptist pastors in the city who were expected to participate were not present because they felt that the proposed organization was not wise at this time. (BR, 11/25/08)

The new church, called "Evangel Baptist Church," had ninety-two charter members. Its meetings were held in the court house, and they were, as might be expected, essentially evangelistic services. The *Recorder* regularly reported on the progress of the church, and on January 26, 1910, announced the church's purchase of a lot on the corner of Dawson and Davie streets. In March the congregation began holding their services in the residence that occupied that lot. On May 10, 1911, some two and a half years after its organization, without any further information as to reasons for the action, the *Recorder* announced "The Evangel Baptist Church of Raleigh recently disbanded. Pastor P. G. Elsom is giving himself to evangelistic work."

In a leather-bound notebook dated 1907 John Pullen recorded twenty-six of his sermons. The notes are written in Pullen's own hand and the fly-leaf contains the note, "Please Return to JOHN T. PULLEN — Raleigh, N.C." The book is well-worn, with many places where further notes were added to the original ones. Many clippings have been pasted in throughout the book, most of them illustrations which fit the sermons. As one would expect, the sermons are expository in pattern and evangelistic in content. Many are stern and moralistic. Typical titles are "Sin No More," "Conditions of Peace," "Flee the Wrath to Come," "Repentance toward God," "Wicked turned into Hell," and "How Shall we Clear Ourselves." A few are more inviting: "The Wondrous Works of God," "The Spirit Says Come," "The Master is Come and Calleth." All warn against the rejection of God. "John Pullen the preacher" seems quite different from "John Pullen the Philanthropist," and even from "John Pullen the friend of all kinds of people."

John L. Cooke, the successor of Elsom at Fayetteville Street, was very different in personality and in approach to ministry. He was called in April, 1909, five months after Elsom's resignation. The *Biblical Recorder* called him "a capable Northern minister, who had been spending some time at Southern Pines." (4/21/09) Baker's observations about Cooke are instructive: "He was a consecrated Man. He came at a time when we needed a Man of his type. He was easy going with a quiet disposition. He was a good Preacher with a thorough knowledge of the Bible." (p. 10)

During Cooke's short stay at Fayetteville Street there was only one *Recorder* report on his work. On July 28, 1909, after referring to the baptism of several persons into the church, the editor observed: "We are glad to know the church is prospering in every way and the Sunday school increasing. Besides the regular services of the church, open-air meetings and prayer meetings are frequently held at different places in the city." One year later, on July 20, 1910, the *Recorder* announced that because of poor health Pastor Cooke had resigned Fayetteville Street and would spend some months at his home in Ohio. "Those who have known Bro. Cooke love and esteem him most highly for his genuine worth," said the editor. "He is a royal Christian gentleman, and we are indeed sorry to lose him and pray for his recovery and return to the State."

Cooke was succeeded by L.E.M. Freeman, a man who was much like Cooke in temperament and in emphasis. Freeman was a native of South Carolina and a graduate of Furman University. He had studied theology at Newton Seminary, at Harvard, and at the University of Chicago. He completed his theological education at the Southern Baptist Theological Seminary, receiving the Th.D. degree from that institution. In the fall of 1910 he joined the faculty of Meredith College as Professor of Bible. In his early years at that institution, however, he also taught philosophy, sociology, ethics, and education. He was to remain at Meredith until his retirement in 1949. He accepted the pastorate of the Fayetteville Street Church in addition to his work at Meredith and began his ministry on September 1, 1910.

Freeman's chief contribution to the church, in addition to his preaching and pastoral work, was the improvement of the Sunday school. He gave considerable attention to its organization and operation, and it gained an approved rating with the Convention's Sunday School Board. In the spring of 1911 the church expanded its physical plant with the addition of twelve new Sunday school classrooms, borrowing the money to pay for them. Finding the demands of the pastorate too great for him to meet in addition to his work at Meredith, Freeman resigned at the end of April, 1911. He remained a member of the church, however, until his death in January, 1979.

During this period John T. Pullen continued his own unique ministry by preparing a series of brief articles on "Prayer and Its Answer," which was published in the *Recorder* in the early weeks of 1911. Later that series was expanded and published in book form. The material consists of brief quotations of scripture and devotional comments on those quotations. Some comments were simple, one-sentence statements; others were as long as two or three pages. The book concluded with his famous message on "Personal Work," and another sermon on the text, "Is Not My Word Like as a Fire? Saith the Lord."

Upon receiving Freeman's resignation in April, 1911, the church voted to call F. D. King. King, pastor in Jonesboro, had just been preaching in revival services at Fayetteville Street earlier in the month. In that series of services, according to Baker, forty persons had been received for baptism, twenty-seven had been received by letter, and three had been restored to fellowship. King began his work as pastor on the first Sunday in July, 1911. Apparently he had been called on the strength of his work as an evangelist, and the church continued to grow during his tenure. His chief contribution, however, was not in evangelism but in his emphasis on Christian education. Under his leadership the church organized its first Baptist Young People's Union. In April, 1912, the *Recorder* announced that Fayetteville Street had in its membership "three Blue Seal graduates of our Convention Normal Course." (BR, 4/24/12) That course was a Convention training program for church school workers. Even King's sermons often had what we would call an educational emphasis. In June, 1912, for example, he delivered two series of sermons, one in the morning services and one in the evening, which were essentially Bible studies. They dealt with such matters as "marriage, the sanctity of the home, amusement, business and religion, uses and abuses of the tongue, and the source of true holiness." (BR, 6/5/12)

Even though the Sunday school plant had only recently been enlarged, the need for more room was apparent and work was soon under way. An interesting side light is the notation in the *Biblical Recorder* for February 28, 1912, that the proceeds from the sale of John T. Pullen's little book, "Prayer and Its Answer," would be used to help pay for the $2500 improvements. When King resigned at the end of August, 1912, to work as an evangelist for the Home Mission Board, the *Biblical Recorder* commented on his achievements:

The church has recently been greatly improved, the church having spent fully $3,000 in improvements, which has all been paid. The church is now installing a new $1,600 organ. The prospects of the church are bright. Brother King's pastorate has been successful in every way. (9/11/12)

Unfortunately not a great deal of information about lay people in the church, other than John T. Pullen, has been preserved. Baker, however, has a paragraph on the death of one outstanding layman:

In May 1912 the Church suffered a great loss in the death of Mr. W. E. Fann. He and his Wife had been most faithful servants since they joined our Church by Baptism in February 1886. He was a man of great power and prayer. He constantly advocated prayer. His motto was "Prayer Changes Things." He was at his best in Cottage Prayer Meetings. Many was the time I have seen him come into the little meeting room at Fayetteville Crossing where a cottage prayer meeting was held every Thursday Night with an arm full of fire wood for the little stove. Other times he would bring sacks of meal and flour if he heard of anyone in need in the neighborhood. He entered into the rest that remaineth to the faithful during an afternoon nap. (pp. 10-11)

The same notice in the *Biblical Recorder* which announced King's resignation also announced A. V. Joyner's acceptance of the pastorate. Joyner came to Raleigh from Tarboro, where he had worked under the auspices of the Home Mission Board. He began his work at Fayetteville Street on November 1, 1912.

For several years the Raleigh *News and Observer* reported each Monday on services held in the local churches on the preceding day. Often those reports summarized the sermons. According to the reports on Fayetteville Street Church, Joyner was an able preacher who had considerable variety in his texts and topics. One report noted: "In his portrayal of the supreme sacrifice the preacher swayed his large audience which in spite of the heat gave strictest attention." (N&O, 7/13/14) The report for the next week began, "The services at this church were of unusually high order. The music was good and the sermons made each person who heard them wish for a better life." (N&O, 7/20/14) The following week the report concluded, "The preaching at both services was practical and spiritually quickening." (N&O, 7/27/14) On the next Sunday it seems to have been "business as usual" at Pullen, as at most other churches in the city, although war had just broken out in Europe. By way of contrast, the headline of the column next to the report on Pullen's services read "Peace Prayer at Tabernacle." (N&O, 8/3/14) On October 4, however, which was "Peace Sunday," Joyner did speak to the issue of the war.

Although the denomination's Baptist Young People's Unon originated in the latter part of the nineteenth century, the first documentary evidence of a B.Y.P.U. at Pullen is found in the *News and*

Observer for August 10, 1914. That item reports that the evening services at Pullen on the previous day "were conducted by the Baptist Young People's Union of the church," and that the subject of discussion was "The object of the B.Y.P.U." One speaker called the B.Y.P.U. "an extended function of the church, and declared it to be one of the greatest forces in bringing the young people to the front and preparing them for a greater work."

Joyner cooperated fully with denominational programs. On September 20, for example, he devoted the morning service to a consideration of state missions and had several members of the Woman's Missionary Society take part. His sermon dealt with "The History and Present Outlook of State Mission Work." In that same service he gave attention to "the place of State missions in the Baptist scheme for world evangelization, the church building fund and the Wake Forest church." (N&O, 9/21/14)

A notable event in the religious life of Raleigh occurred during the first two weeks in March, 1914. Ten Raleigh churches, including the three white Baptist churches, conducted simultaneous evangelistic meetings. This cooperative effort was lauded by the editor of the *Recorder*, who observed:

> Ten of our Raleigh churches have just united in a two weeks' evangelistic campaign which came to a close last Sunday. Each church had services each evening in its own house of worship and all came together each afternoon in a joint service. The idea was a very happy one and has worked out most admirably, promoting good fellowship among the Christian people of the city, committing due responsibility to each church, and resulting in a number of additions to the churches. (3/18/14)

The preacher for the services at Pullen was C. A. Jenkins, of Cavalry Church, Richmond, Virginia, and the church received twenty-two new members.

John T. Pullen died early in the morning on May 2, 1913. He had been ill for several weeks, although he had continued both his work and his church activities. At the annual meeting of the board of trustees of Meredith College, held on April 8, he had asked to be relieved of his duty as treasurer. On April 26 a revival meeting was begun at Fayetteville Street Church, and it is appropriate that Pullen died at a time when the church was engaged in the activity that, from his point of view, was the most important thing that the church did.

Pullen's importance in the Raleigh community would be hard to overestimate. The report of his death appeared on the front page of the *News and Observer* on the morning of May 2, 1913. Under the headline, "John T. Pullen Dies Suddenly," came the note "Banker and Philanthropist Passes at 2:05 This Morning." The brief news article stated:

Mr. John T. Pullen, president of the Raleigh Savings Bank and Trust Company died this morning at 2:05 o'clock at the residence of Mr. John W. Harden on Hillsboro Street.

Mr. Pullen's death came with shocking suddenness, he having been ill only since Monday and the fact of his illness being known only to a comparative few. Mr. Pullen was sixty years old in last December. He was generally known as Raleigh's best loved citizen and he had given aid to every charitable object in this city.

The next day the *News and Observer* eulogized:

The poor of Raleigh were never so poor as they are today.
John Pullen is dead.

The hand that was ever ready to help them in their helplessness, the voice that soothed them in their distress, the heart that beat with them in their sorrows—they are still; and those that knew him shall know him no more forever.

"There hath passed a glory from the earth."

Who shall measure the value of John T. Pullen to the city of Raleigh, not to mention the wider reaches of his influence? In business he achieved much more than most men do. He was president of one of our leading savings banks—He was in no small degree the heart of that bank. But the trophy of his business success is the least of the trophies that he now brings home with him. A greater trophy is that he managed to work out a great business career and at the same time led a life of ministry to the poor and the sorrowing that was unsurpassed by those of the most active ministers of the Gospel. And greater still is the inspiration of his example: John Pullen has been the standard in Raleigh—the standard of goodness for nearly thirty years. And he will be the standard for two generations to come. Mothers taught their sons to be "like John Pullen." Sunday school teachers and minister pointed to him as the living example of the practicability of the Christian ideal. There was in him the power of a genuine incarnation of the Gospel. He was the best representative of his Master this city has ever known. There was more radiance in his life, as there is more shadow in his death, than were possible of any other one man or woman.

It is not the purpose of this brief article to enumerate Mr. Pullen's good works. He was the founder and the chief human force in one of our most useful churches to which he ministered in the pulpit, in the Sunday school, in all its meetings, and in all its homes, with unfailing diligence. But this was not enough. He helped in all the churches upon opportunity. And he was besides the shepherd of the unsheperded masses of this city. Whenever death came, whether in the home of rich or poor, there soon was seen John Pullen. Whenever sickness or want befell there soon was he. Worthy and unworthy poor found in him a friend. It is not that he gave with an open hand—this he did as never did another here about—but that he gave also his life himself. He had a heart for all the world.

Some may say it is a slight matter, but probably the little girls and boys will miss his smile, his tender words and his little gifts—of picture cards and gospels—as much as any others. A slight matter compared with the more serious ministers of the man: but how beautiful and how beneficient!

Raleigh will never forget John Pullen—his name will be remembered here as long as sorrow and poverty shall make their calls on the human heart. She may not have had her greatest or her wealthiest man as yet, but she has had her best man and all her sons will be better because she has had him.

Intensely religious, the Christian in every fibre of his being, Mr. Pullen's mind and heart were ever fixed upon "the city which hath foundations whose builder and maker is God," and upon the central figure of that city, Jesus the Christ. One has no difficulty in imagining the scene as he entered into the gates of the City yesterday. One may almost see him smile as he found it all as he had believed—only a better place for himself and a far greater welcome for himself than he had ever expected.

Truly may we say of him: "For me to live is Christ; to die is gain." (5/3/13)

Funeral services for Pullen were held on Saturday afternoon, May 3, 1913. He had expressed his wish that his service be a simple one, and it was that. The pastor, A. V. Joyner, was assisted by Dr. T. W. O'Kelly, pastor of First Baptist Church; the Reverend Livingston Johnson, General Secretary of the Baptist State Convention; and the Reverend William McWhite, pastor of the First Presbyterian Church. At the church the choir sang "O Love That Will not Let Me Go," "Asleep in Jesus," and "Ten Thousand Times Ten Thousand." At the graveside they sang "Christian Goodnight" and "Face to Face." Both the service at the church and the graveside service in Oakwood Cemetery were attended by people from all walks of life. Baker noted that "Few men were ever followed to their grave in Raleigh by so representative people as Mr. Pullen was. The rich, the poor and the lowly hearted bowed low." (p. 14) In keeping with his desire for simplicity, Pullen's simple tombstone has on it, besides his name, the date of his birth, and the date of his death, only the words "Saved by Grace."

For nearly two weeks following Pullen's death each issue of the *News and Observer* carried tributes to him. Colonel Fred Olds, founder of the State Hall of History, wrote about him as a prison worker; Joseph Brown, president of the Citizens' National Bank, wrote of him as a banker; N. B. Broughton, of Edwards and Broughton, and a leading Baptist layman, wrote of his work for temperance; John N. Cole, a Methodist minister, wrote of him as a Christian worker; Charles Meserve, President of Shaw University, wrote of his "Deep Concern for the Colored People"; C. B. Edwards wrote of him as a citizen of the city and the state; and Hight C. Moore, editor of the *Biblical Recorder*, wrote of his work among Baptists. The long series culminated in the suggestion that a fund be established to create a memorial for Pullen. Contributions to that fund ultimately helped to provide a home for the nurses of Rex Hospital.

In conference on Wednesday, May 7, 1913, the congregation of Fayetteville Street Baptist Church adopted the following resolution:

> The members of the Fayetteville Street Baptist Church feel their loss too deeply to be content with the words we could speak in regard to our beloved Mr. Pullen. We can, from our hearts, extend sympathy to his relatives, and pray that the memory of his life may rest on them like a benediction.
>
> To those who will miss him most, those to whom he ministered, we would speak a word of comfort and point them to the Giver of every good and perfect gift.
>
> We would pray that some portion of his spirit may abide with us and help us to carry on the work that he commenced. We would that these broken expressions be recorded in our minutes as a record of our lasting appreciation of the gentle spirit who loved and labored among us.

Then a motion to change the name of the congregation from "Fayetteville Street Baptist Church" to "Pullen Memorial Baptist Church" was passed unanimously.

Pullen had willed to the church all of the real estate which he owned in the city of Raleigh. The appropriate paragraph of his will stated:

> I give and bequeath to the Trustees of the Fayetteville Street Baptist Church of Raleigh, N.C. and their successors in Office all of my real estate located in Raleigh, N.C. The said Trustees to use all the income arriving from the property for the benefit of the Church in carrying on the work. If at any time the Trustees with the consent of the Church Conference desire to purchase a lot and erect another church they are authorized to sell any or all of the property devised to them by this my will and buy the lot and erect the church. If the Trustees desire at any time to enlarge the present church they are authorized to sell a portion of the property to enlarge it.

The months following Pullen's death were crucial for the congregation. So closely were he and the church linked that to many his death was almost tantamount to the death of the church. Without intending to do so, he had dominated the church. His was the word of wisdom when any important decision was to be made. He was the one upon whom they could rely whenever they needed money. He was the great philanthropist and lay preacher-evangelist for whom Fayetteville Street Church was the base of operations. No pastor overshadowed him, and all depended upon him. Because he was the benevolent patriarch of the congregation, his death left the congregation at a loss like sheep without a shepherd.

One year after Pullen's death the church held a memorial service for him. The *News and Observer* for Monday morning, May 4, 1914, reported the event in full detail, including the following summary:

Special music was rendered by the Choir, including some of the hymns which were Mr. Pullen's favorites. The pastor read from Deuteronomy the account of the death of Moses, and a passage of Scripture from the book of Joshua, both of which were appropriate to the occasion. Talks were made by a number of the members of the church, and the pastor closed the exercise by a short talk on "How to Perpetuate His Memory."

T. W. Blake spoke of his "Personal Reminiscences of John T. Pullen," and W. I. Sawyer recalled "Mr. Pullen as the Friend of the Average Man." There were impromptu speeches by George F. Ball, Dr. C. F. Meserve, and S. A. Sutton. At the conclusion of the service the church decided "to make an annual affair of the memorial exercises in honor of the man whose life was spent in doing good and in befriending the poor of the city." (N&O, 5/4/14)

Although in the long run the property which Pullen had willed to the church was an asset, immediately it proved to be a liability. The houses were in bad repair and some were unoccupied because they were in such poor condition. The church borrowed $1500 to get them into shape, but, according to Baker, "There was no income ever realized from this property until it was sold." (p. 24) In addition to that added expense, for a variety of reasons the financial contributions to the church began to fall off.

The church had been established in a residential area and drew most of its membership from the white working-class people who lived there. In the second decade of the twentieth century, however, that area was in transition. Business establishments were beginning to expand and the white residents were moving out. By the time of Pullen's death most of them were gone. The people who continued to attend the services of the church came from widely scattered sections of the city.

Under the circumstances it is not surprising that the pastor would be open to a call from another church. On Monday, October 12, 1914, the *News and Observer* headlined its religion section with the news, "Rev. A. V. Joyner, Pastor, Resigns." The report included the observation: "His work here has been eminently satisfactory and he will be remembered in Raleigh as a young preacher of great power and promise. As a man he has made many friends and won a warm place in the hearts of many in his church and out of it." The *Biblical Recorder* for October 14, 1914, stated:

After two years of diligent, acceptable, and successful service as pastor of Pullen Memorial Church, this city, Rev. A. V. Joyner, on last Sunday morning tendered his resignation in order to accept the pastorate of our First Church in Waynesville. Not only the membership of his loyal flock, but also the people of Raleigh are very fond of Pastor Joyner and his wife.

The church was not long without a pastor. Walter H. Dodd, a native of Wake County who for several years had been doing evangelistic work in Georgia, accepted a call from the church and began his work early in March, 1915. In his sermon on Sunday morning, March 15, using Acts 10:29 as his text, he gave an indication of the kind of emphases which were to be expected from him:

I come to your call said the speaker and without asking questions as to what your ideal of a church and pastor is. Mr. Dodd declared that the whole plan would be a failure at this place without the prayers and support of his people. Mr. Dodd spoke strongly of the Womans' Missionary Society, the Baptist Young Peoples' Union and other auxiliaries, and stated that the great need of the church is the enlistment of its members in active Christian work co-operating with the pastor, and if this is done, said the speaker, the joys of the present are merely a foretaste of the perfect glory we will experience.

Dodd was at Pullen for less than a year, remaining only through December, 1915. In spite of the changed environment of the church, he seems to have tried to carry on the same kind of work that the congregation had been accustomed to in earlier years. The fact that he left without having received a call from another church suggests that the problems of the congregation had not been resolved.

During Dodd's tenure two of the leading members of the congregation died. George Ball, who died on July 4, 1915, had made a significant contribution through his work with the Sunday school, through music, and through recreational activities. Baker spoke fondly about his "most happy disposition and his love for Children and young people," remembering particularly his involvement in the annual Sunday school picnic. His description of these affairs gives a feel for the life of the church:

We would secure many vans, wagons, and buggys and bicycles. We would move up Fayetteville Street from the Church a singing happy band of people. It attracted the attention of our whole city. . . . The procession some time would be more than a mile long. We would go out to the river or some pond and there play games and many other attractions and Bro. Ball was at his best on these excursions. He ran a store on Smithfield Street. He roasted peanuts and sold them to other merchants. On these occasions he would load up his large covered wagon with small bags of peanuts to give away on the picnic grounds. Bro. Ball with his white apron, making lemonade and yelling for people to come and get it and all of it was free. In Heaven I am sure the Bro. Ball is still making people happy. (p. 25)

A year and a half later Thomas W. Blake died. Blake was one of the five charter members of the church and had always been involved in all aspects of the life of the congregation. Like John Pullen, he was a bachelor who found the church in a real sense to be his family. He was also active with both the Masons and the Odd Fellows. He was a charter member of Raleigh's volunteer fire department, and had been fire chief of the city of Raleigh. A merchant by occupation, he operated a jewelry store on Fayetteville Street, a half-block from the Capital. In reporting on his funeral service, the Raleigh *Times* called him "a man whom the city honored, irrespective of creed, and against whom no protest were ever raised, for he was man's friend and God's servant." (12/6/15)

Shortly after Dodd's resignation, Pullen Memorial called Lyman K. Dilts to become its pastor. On Wednesday, March 22, the *Biblical Recorder* reported:

> The call was extended last Wednesday night and the acceptance announced last Sunday. The new Pastor is a native of Summitville, Ind. He studied at Franklin College and at a Chicago law school. Some years ago he came to the Baptists from the Methodists. For two years he was pastor of the Baptist Church at Martinsville, Ind. He then served the church at Belleview, Ohio, for a time. Coming South he located a few months ago in Raleigh and engaged in the sale of law books. He supplied two or three Sundays at Pullen Memorial and the call resulted. He is married and has two children. He is hopeful in his new work.

Dilts was an impressive preacher, and the *News and Observer* often referred to his eloquence. The report on the February 27, 1916, sermon said: "The preacher, in words well chosen and at times surpassing eloquent, sketched the life of this Man of Sorrows." On the following Sunday "The preacher sketched with master strokes of word painting an outline of the hopeless condition of Jerusalem." On the next Sunday

> Mr. Dilts was greeted by two large congregations at the morning and evening services. His sermons have been inspiring and most interesting. Throughout the evening service there was the most rapt stillness and remarkable attention. The power of his preaching is being felt throughout the church life and the congregations grow larger at each service. (N&O, 3/13/16)

His sermon on June 30 was termed "powerful and convincing."

Apparently Dilts was not afraid to speak his mind on topics that might be controversial. At that time Billy Sunday, with his spectacular antics in the pulpit, was gaining national attention and his methods were being imitated by countless numbers of lesser lights. On Sunday, May 7, 1916, Dilts rapped "circus methods in the pulpit." According to the *News and Observer*, he "proceded to pay his respects, in no uncertain terms, to what he described as circus methods in the pulpit for purposes of notoriety." He went on to say:

> In this age there seems to be a tendency toward band-wagon methods in the churches and in the pulpits. What its purpose may be is not clear to my mind. Whether for the purpose of attracting crowds to the church or attention to the preacher I do not know, but this I do know—a band

wagon almost always leads to a circus if you follow it far enough, and usually it is preceeded and followed by a clown. The pulpit of the church of the Living God, as I see it, is the place for which His saving grace should be proclaimed to men; and when it is used as a platform from which to promulgate individual ideas on social problems, lectures on morality, individual codes of personal living or the preacher's personal ideas as to long faces or short skirts, it is missing its opportunity to a large extent.

Another example of Dilts' forthrightness was his speaking to what he considered a great injustice in a notorious murder trial. In Central Prison he visited two men awaiting execution and found some reason to wonder whether they were guilty. Perhaps his legal training prompted his interest in the matter. At any rate, he went to Graham county, where the murder had been committed, did some investigating of his own, and then examined the reports of the trial. He concluded to his own satisfaction that a grave injustice had been done to the men. He first expressed his doubts in a sermon at Pullen. Then in a public worship service at the Y.M.C.A. on the campus of State College on Sunday evening, September 24, he gave his reasons for believing as he did. Whether he met criticism for his public affirmation of his views we do not know. At the beginning of a revival meeting at Pullen on October 29, however, he declared:

God help the preacher who will preach only the gospel his congregation will allow. . . . When I can no longer be true to my call to the ministry and to the method God intended for me to preach the gospel, then I'm going to get clear out of it and go back on the road selling books. (N&O, 10/30/16)

Dilts remained with the church for a year. In spite of the large congregations who came to the services, the church was having such financial troubles that it could not pay the pastor. Dilts, therefore, found it necessary to resign and conclude his work with the church on January 1, 1917.

As the financial crisis deepened, the church leaders thought it wise to turn to the other Raleigh Baptists for help in deciding what to do. In April, 1917, a meeting was held at the Raleigh Y.M.C.A. to which the other Baptist churches were asked to send representatives. Approximately thirty people gathered to discuss the matter in detail. The group agreed to call for another session to be held two weeks later in Pullen Memorial Church. The church had already been discussing informally the question of whether it should move to another location. The entire congregation was, therefore, notified that at that second meeting that issue would be considered. One hundred and twenty-six members attended, and the question of a move was discussed in detail. Baker says that "It was consensus of opinion in this meeting that our Church should be moved to West Raleigh." (p. 28)

Dr. Rufus Hunter and Mr. W. N. Jones, representing First Baptist, suggested that First Baptist might give to Pullen for that purpose two lots in Cameron Park which their church owned. At that meeting no vote was taken, but clearly the sentiment for the move was not unanimous. The question of the use of the property then occupied by the church was raised. Some people suggested the possibility of maintaining a mission there after the church had moved. Finally a committee of representatives from Pullen and First Baptist was appointed to look into the entire matter.

After that meeting all members of Pullen Memorial Church were notified that a vote on the question of moving to West Raleigh would be taken at the next regular conference of the church. Approximately sixty persons attended that next conference. After lengthy discussion, those present voted unanimously to make the move. It was also decided at that time to sell the real estate that had been willed to the church by John Pullen and to use the proceeds for making the move. When that property was sold in 1918 and 1919 it brought approximately $28,000.

With these major decisions having been made, the future of the church seemed secure. According to Baker, several "influential families" joined the church in anticipation of the move. Baker named "J. J. Bernard and Family, R. L. Horton and Family, A. G. Nowell and Family, E. G. Green and Family, L. R. Gilbert and Family, W. H. Penny and Family." (p. 29)

The next step for the church was to call a pastor. The *Biblical Recorder* for June 6, 1917, reported:

> We are happy to say that Rev. R. D. Stephenson, of Mullins, S.C., has accepted the call to the pastorate of Pullen Memorial Church, this city, and is expected to enter upon his new work about the first of July. Brother Stephenson is a native of the West Chowan region and was brought up under the ministry of such men as Elder C. W. Scarborough, of Murfreesboro. He graduated at Wake Forest College a few years ago and we believe took a course at our Louisville Seminary. He is a strong, well equipped, consecrated young minister whom we are most happy to welcome back to the home State. We anticipate for him a very useful ministry in Raleigh.

Stephenson remained with Pullen for only nine months, however, leaving in March, 1918, to accept a church in Portsmouth, Virginia.

For a year and a half the church had no strong pastoral leadership. J. A. Davis, a student at Wake Forest College, preached for the congregation until September, 1918, but seems to have had no other responsibilities with the church. In January and February, 1919, the church had a series of outstanding public figures occupy the pulpit: Lieutenant Governor O. Max Gardner; Dr. Hubert Poteat from Wake Forest College; State Senator A. M. Scales; D. G. Brummitt, Speaker of the House of Representatives; and State Senator Joseph Brown. Who else occupied the pulpit is not known, but the lay leadership was strong enough to keep the church functioning.

In April and May, 1919, the evangelist "Cyclone Mack" McLendon conducted a five-week revival in Raleigh. His campaign was not a project of the local churches; like the other big-time evangelists, he planned his own itinerary and conducted his own campaigns entirely independently of the local churches. His advance people moved in to provide publicity, then he came and set up his tent on the corner of Lane and Bloodworth streets. And the people came by the thousands. Three weeks after he began his campaign the *News and Observer* reported:

> Two thousand yesterday morning, five thousand yesterday afternoon and ten thousand last night, a grand total of seventeen thousand men, women, and children, heard Evangelist McLendon on the opening day of his fourth week in Raleigh. Of this number, fifteen hundred made the pledge to stand with Jesus and fight on the winning side. (N&O, 4/18/19)

Mack was certainly aware of the criticism which was frequently leveled against him wherever he went. One evening, according to the *News and Observer*, he

> expressed deep appreciation for the encouragement he has received during the progress of the meetings here. He reminded the congregation that he had heard less criticism in Raleigh of his revival than in any of the many places he has held meetings. (N&O, 4/21/19)

If the numbers reported in the newspapers are correct, then surely everyone in Raleigh and the surrounding area must have attended at least one service. There is no evidence in the newspapers, however, that the local religious leadership in any way supported his campaign. Neither is there any tangible evidence that the churches were affected by those thousands of people who made decisions for Christ.

Beginning on Monday night, May 30, 1919, Dr. Charles E. Maddry, of the University Baptist Church in Austin, Texas, conducted an eight-day series of services at Pullen. Several of his sermons were reported in the *News and Observer*, and they seem to have been intended to renew the members of the church more than to win converts. Seven people, however, were baptized at the conclusion of that series. According to Baker, the church minutes for May 29 state: "Our church has been greatly edified, blessed and built up by the coming into our midst of Dr. Charles E. Maddry." Baker quotes them further: "The results of his coming cannot be recorded in words. The excellent soul stirring gospel sermons caused all who were Christians to desire to live better and more useful lives, caused the indifferent to want to live nearer their Savior, and many renewed their vows and many professed faith in Jesus Christ." (p. 29) This summary suggests that there were not the mass additions to the church that had characterized the revivals of earlier periods, and that many people had come to think of as the marks of success. That kind of result could not realistically have been expected, in light of the changed circumstances of the church. Maddry's impact upon the congregation, however, was to provide the kind of inner renewal which they needed at that time. So well did they respond to him that in a called conference held on the Sunday morning following his visit they voted to extend an invitation to him to become their pastor! (N&O, 6/9/19) While Maddry did not accept the invitation, the congregation's response to him is indicative of the turn that the church was beginning to take.

In a meeting held on Tuesday, August 6, 1919, J. A. Ellis was called by the church, and he accepted that call. He began his ministry at Pullen on the first Sunday in September. A native of Chowan County, he was a graduate of Wake Forest College and of the Southern Baptist Theological Seminary. He was pastor of the First Baptist Church of Dunn when the United States entered World War I. Although he had

J. A. Ellis
Minister 1919-1929

been there for only seven months, he volunteered for the army chaplaincy and the church granted him a leave of absence "for the duration of the war." (BR, 2/20/18) When he was released from the service, however, circumstances did not warrant his returning to Dunn.

Dr. Ellis' coming to Pullen was a propitious event. Almost immediately things began to look better. He was an able preacher, a good pastor, and an efficient administrator. Attendance at the services increased significantly, and new members came in imposing numbers. In October the church authorized a committee, consisting of the pastor, R. L. Horton, and W. P. Baker, "to draw up plans for the Cameron Park Church." The *Biblical Recorder* reported, seven months after Ellis' arrival:

> Pullen Memorial Church, Raleigh, is rapidly coming to the front. A few months ago the church collection was about 40 a Sunday. Now the collection is from $110 to $125 a Sunday. Dr. Ellis' salary was increased recently from $2,400 to $3,000. Since Dr. Ellis came to the church, about sixty members have been added. Mr. McMichael has been selected architect for the new church building in West Raleigh, and plans are now under consideration. The church music, superintended by Mr. Herman Senter, has been improved greatly. The services are attended by a great many. Dr. Ellis is preaching powerful sermons. The Sunday school, with the first Sunday collection, supports two orphans. This past Sunday there were 228 present with a collection of $41.50. R. L. McMillan, a young lawyer who has recently located in Raleigh, is suprintendent of the Sunday school. Mr. McMillan is one of Scotland County's "Sunburnt Boys." (BR, 3/31/20)

In 1919, following the meeting of the Southern Baptist Convention, the denomination launched a five-year program, known as "The Seventy-Five Million Campaign," to provide money for greatly increased support for all Southern Baptist missionary, educational, and benevolent work. It was an overly-ambitious plan with a goal which the Baptists did not reach. They did raise some $58 million, however. Pullen Memorial had sent Ellis to the Convention, and he returned full of enthusiasm for the plan. In October, therefore, the church asked W. P. Baker to coordinate the efforts to raise the $16,650 which it had accepted as its goal. On December 1, 1919, the *News and Observer* reported that, like the other Baptist churches in the city, Pullen Memorial "will meet its allotment."

At the end of 1919 the church was prospering under the leadership of an enthusiastic and able pastor and of some strong lay people. It was optimistically making plans for its move to a more suitable location. It was a part of a denomination that was looking to the future with a sense of a new mission in a world now "safe for democracy." Having recovered from the loss of its "patron saint," it had decided what to do about its own future.

Chapter 4
A Church With A New Mission
In An Era of Boom and Bust
(1920-1932)

While Pullen Memorial Baptist Church was confidently undertaking a new ministry in a different section of the city, the nation was troubled. President Woodrow Wilson had suffered a severe stroke on October 2, 1919, and almost died. Because of his inability to give leadership at the crucial moment, his political opponents carried the day and Congress refused to authorize American membership in the League of Nations.

Although the 1920's are generally characterized as "roaring," a better term might be "turbulent." The scandals of the Harding administration were accompanied by a peace treaty with Germany that actually laid the foundations for later problems in Europe. Coolidge gave the country honest government and efficient administration, but the masses of people felt no need to pay much attention to government. They were free to concentrate on making money, on amusing themselves, and occasionally on matters of race and religion. The Eighteenth Amendment had been ratified in 1919, and as of January 1, 1920, the domestic manufacture and sale of intoxicating beverages was prohibited. In 1920 the Nineteenth Amendment was ratified, at long last giving women the right to vote. Veterans of the Great War were organizing to win concessions from the government. At the same time, organized labor was suffering severe reverses, losing membership and, therefore, losing power.

On the international scene, the world was taking a new shape. Mussolini seized power in Rome in 1922. In that same year the Union of Soviet Socialist Republics was formed. The Irish Free State was proclaimed in 1921, the British protectorate over Egypt ended in 1922, and also in 1922 Mustafa Kemal became dictator of Turkey. Hitler began his rise to power in Germany in the early '20's. In the late '20's Chiang Kai-shek was emerging as the man in control of China. From 1929 Ghandi was conducting his civil disobedience campaign in India.

The United States experienced a business recession in 1920, but fairly quickly the nation recovered and the period 1922-29 was the "boom years." There was a phenomenal expansion in the automobile industry, in the production of electric power, in the manufacture and distribution of electrical equipment, and in transportation of goods and passengers by air. Entertainment became a major industry, and the names of radio personalities and movie stars became household words. It is estimated that in 1922 people in some three million American homes listened to broadcasts of music, sports, news, comedy skits, and "messages from the sponsor." At the same time weekly attendance at the movies reached an estimated 110 million. Attendance at professional sporting events set new marks every year. The publishing of novels and of periodicals boomed, with much of that literature devoted to "escape," but some representing a real flowering of American literature.

For the black population, the 1920's were not so gay. The NAACP had fought unsuccessfully to establish for blacks the right to vote and to secure federal antilynching legislation. Giving up on any hope for progress under the existing system, many blacks rallied round Marcus Garvey and his Universal Negro Improvement Association, which planned a wholesale movement "back to Africa." Black literary figures like Langston Hughes and James Weldon Johnson gave voice to a tremendous discontent, but few whites listened.

Meanwhile the Ku Klux Klan grew in membership and influence. While it had been revived as an organization in 1915, its greatest growth came in the early 1920's. By 1924 there were four million Klansmen in the United States. It had members all over the South and in many states outside the South. In many places some prominent political figures openly acknowledged their membership, and in few places did political figures dare challenge the Klan. Though its membership declined after 1927, it remained a force in the life of the South until the outbreak of World War II.

One movement of the 1920's deserves special attention. That was the campaign of the religious fundamentalists against the teaching of evolution in the schools. Anti-evolution bills were introduced in the legislatures of more than a dozen states, though only in Tennessee did one actually pass. Almost immediately after its passage, it was challenged by John Thomas Scopes, a high school teacher in Dayton, Tennessee. Legal action was taken against him, with William Jennings Bryan helping the prosecution and the American Civil Liberties Union employing Clarence Darrow to defend Scopes. Although Scopes was convicted, the Tennessee Supreme Court reversed the decision.

In religion, the decade of the 1920's was a period of change. Sharing the optimism of the period, churches erected new buildings by the hundreds. Radio preachers became well known, with Harry Emerson Fosdick, of Riverside Church in New York City, becoming the best-known minister in America. That was no small accomplishment, in light of the fact that Billy Sunday was still preaching to people by the thousands.

The churches reacted in different ways to the changing cultural climate in the United States. The Roman Catholic Church tried to resist challenges to traditional beliefs and practices by strengthening its parochial school system. It produced a new codification of canon law in an effort to guarantee unity in belief and practice. It launched a missionary movement in traditionally non-Catholic areas of the country, such as the South, and reached out to traditionally non-Catholic ethnic groups, such as the blacks.

The Protestant reaction to the changing cultural climate was divided, and a theological battle emerged between liberalism and fundamentalism. The liberals tried to come to grips with modern scientific thought by restating historical theological views, modifying their positions in such a way as to try to resolve any conflict between science and religion. Consequently they became less authoritarian in their view of the Bible, the church, and tradition, and more open to the methods of science, philosophy, and critical history. The social gospel movement, associated with theological liberalism, began to interpret the Kingdom of God as a sort of perfect social order which might be created in this world. The movement addressed both organized labor and the race problem. Its greatest attention, however, was focused on the problem of war, and many of the social gospel leaders were pacifist.

The other division of Protestantism was, in a sense, a reaction to the growth of liberalism. A number of church leaders, particularly among the Presbyterians and the Baptists, were convinced that the denominations had been captured by liberals whom they thought had abandoned the true gospel. In 1919 they had organized the World's Christian Fundamentals Association, under the leadership of three Baptist ministers: William Bell Riley, John Roach Straton, and

Jasper C. Massee. Massee had served in a number of Baptist churches in the South, including Tabernacle Baptist in Raleigh (1903-1908), before he had gone to Tremont Temple in Boston. Among Presbyterians the leadership was furnished by a layman, William Jennings Bryan, and by J. Gresham Machen, of the faculty of Princeton Theological Seminary.

The struggle between the liberals and the fundamentalists was nationwide, and all of the major denominations felt its impact. Its effect was not felt as profoundly in the South as elsewhere, however, perhaps because the churches in that region were essentially conservative. They had not been as much influenced by the liberal movement as had the churches elsewhere, and, therefore, the reactionary fundamentalism was not as militant. The one point at which it did become a factor in southern religious life was on the issue of the teaching of evolution.

By the end of the decade the American churches were experiencing a noticeable decline. One reason for the decline was the fundamentalist-liberal controversy. Another was the carefree attitude that characterized our nation just before the stock market crash. Yet another reason was a growing awareness that the sense of urgency which had taken thousands of missionaries into other lands might have been a reflection of American "imperialism," and that the dream of winning "the world for Christ in this generation" was totally unrealistic.

The story of Raleigh in the 1920's is the story of the nation writ small. Like the rest of the union, Raleigh experienced a period of prosperity, growth, and general optimism. Large-scale construction projects were undertaken, new businesses were established, and the population grew by nearly fifty percent. Government mushroomed and new buildings were erected to house new services. The public school system was expanded and improved, N.C. State grew in size and in status, and Meredith College outgrew its facilities and moved to a new campus on the edge of the city. By the end of the decade there were half a dozen movie houses in Raleigh, and in 1926 the first commercial radio station in the city went on the air.

The bubble burst in 1929. The stock market crash was followed by years of the most serious depression the nation has ever known. All of America was affected by it, and Raleigh was no exception. The building industry virtually disappeared. Even before the crash there had been a consolidation of some banks and the closing of others. The ones that survived were in danger by 1930. Manufacturing declined, retail sales declined, unemployment shot up, and Raleigh, like the rest of the nation, was in deep trouble.

The churches were not immune to the distress felt by all other social institutions. Budgets were significantly reduced and rarely met. Programs were curtailed or eliminated. Some local churches that had never been strong were forced to close. The main-line denominations suffered more than the smaller ones, partly because their well-being was more tied in with the economic system and with "the American way of life." The smaller sects, on the other hand, because they were more closely identified with the poor and disinherited, tended to multiply. They were able to function without spending a great deal of money. In addition, in a time of despair their escapist theology held out hope for a better world to come.

Jack Ellis had begun his work at Pullen Memorial Baptist Church in September, 1919, at the beginning of the "boom" era. A little more than a year after his arrival the church building was destroyed by fire. The alarm was sounded at 10:45 p.m. on April 22, 1921, and Raleigh's entire fire fighting force and equipment were brought out to battle the blaze. The fire spread to the Wake County Clinic next door, but the firemen managed to extinguish that blaze before significant damage was done. Within forty-five minutes after the fire was discovered the church building was gone. The loss was estimated at well over $25,000.

The fire forced the church to implement at once a decision that had been made some four years earlier. The church had decided at that time to move to west Raleigh. The John Pullen estate had been sold in 1918 and 1919 with the expectation that the proceeds from the sale would be used to implement the decision. Ellis had come as pastor expecting in due season to lead the church in its building program. The period after his arrival had been one of renewal and growth. Attendance at the services had improved, membership had grown, and the offerings for the work of the church had increased significantly. The church was proceeding deliberately, perhaps even slowly, in making preparations for the move. Then came the fire and the church was forced to find a place to meet.

The church received a number of offers of temporary quarters where it could hold its services. For two Sundays the congregation met in the Centennial School building, just across the street from the ruins of their old sanctuary. Then, to be near the location where they were to erect their new building, they began on May 8 to hold services in Pullen Hall on the campus of State College. They remained there until they moved into their new building two years later. The *News and Observer* reported on Monday, May 9, 1921:

> The Rev. J. A. Ellis, pastor, states that plans for the new building are proceeding rapidly, and that a campaign for funds will be started in the near future. The services in the memorial hall yesterday were largely attended, there being several additions to the church membership.

Meanwhile, the proposal for the operation of a mission at the old site was implemented. A committee from Pullen Memorial, Tabernacle, and First Baptist churches was appointed to draw up plans for the work "in the southern part of the city formerly served by the Pullen Memorial Church." The committee dreamed of somthing other than a traditional church. According to the *News and Observer*, "Plans for the structure may include recreational and community work as well as religious work. Plans are under consideration for using the building somewhat on the order of a community center as well as a religious center." (N&O, 6/6/21) It was expected that all three of the Baptist churches would maintain the mission. Pullen Memorial, however, expressed greater interest in the project than did the others. Not only did the congregation pass another resolution favoring the establishment of the mission, but even though the congregation was holding its regular services at Pullen Hall on the campus of State College, it also maintained a Sunday school in the Centennial School building. When time came to erect a facility for the mission, consideration was given to other sites. The decision was made, however, to build on the same spot. According to Baker (p. 37), it was thought that that site was "the most convenient location for the white people in that section." Pullen Memorial Church donated the lot and provided $5,000 toward the construction of the new building. Baker noted (p. 32) that "This building (is) to be used for religious purposes only." That was Pullen's response to the idea of building a community center.

As we have observed, not all of the members of Pullen Memorial Church had approved the decision to move from Fayetteville Street. That fact certainly influenced the decision of the church to make such a large contribution to another group building on the spot which Pullen had just vacated. The *News and Observer* reported on February 12, 1923, that

> After the Pullen Memorial congregation voted to abandon the site of the church established by the late John T. Pullen and to erect a fine church building in Cameron Park or West Raleigh, a few members of the old church, going beyond the plans for a mere mission at that point, established a church, gave it the name of the Southside Baptist Church, and called to its pastorate Dr. W. D. Hubbard, a minister well known in Southern Baptist circles.

On Sunday, April 23, 1922, just one year after the fire, and nearly a year before Pullen Memorial entered its new building, the mission began services in its new building. Within a few months it was organized as the "Southside Baptist Church," and years later its name was changed to Calvary Baptist Church.

71

Pullen Memorial Baptist Church
1923

Pullen Memorial Church continued to hold services in Pullen Hall on the campus of State College until Sunday, February 11, 1923. On that day the church held its first service in its just-completed Sunday school plant, located on the corner of Hillsboro and Cox streets. The lot, which had belonged to the L. T. Yarborough family, was purchased with the proceeds from the sale of the two lots in Cameron Park donated by the First Baptist Church. Nelson and Cooper, the architects for the new building, had designed a facility to which the sanctuary could later be conveniently added. The church owed only $20,000 on the new building which had cost a total of $75,000. The *News and Observer* described the new building:

> The church structure will eventually join the blank wall that now faces Hillsboro street. The Sunday school wing, three stories with a sub-basement, has an auditorium which will seat 300 persons and will be used for both Sunday school and church purposes until the completion of the main auditorium. In all, thirty-five Sunday school rooms provide for all classes. (N&O, 2/12/23)

The plans for constructing a new sanctuary, however, did not materialize for many years. It was not until 1938 that serious efforts were made to undertake the project, and those efforts were cut short by the entrance of the United States into World War II.

After the move to Hillsborough Street, the membership of Pullen Memorial Church grew significantly. When Ellis became pastor in 1919, the church had lost some members to other churches, and there were only 101 active members. Soon after Ellis' coming, as we have seen, there was such an increase that the church's letter to the Association in 1920 reported 220 members. Thereafter there was steady growth, and in the last year of Ellis' pastorate the membership had risen to 417. After Ellis' departure and the coming of Edwin McNeill Poteat, Jr., as pastor, the membership leveled off, generally fluctuating between 400 and 450.

The Sunday school also experienced significant growth during the period. In 1919 the enrollment was only 168, lower than it had been at any time since 1906. But in one year it rose to 318, and thereafter grew steadily until it reached a peak of 659 in 1928. For several years after that it was usually in the 600's. For eight years during that period of growth, beginning in 1920, R. L. McMillan was superintendent of the Sunday school. Baker says that J. Henry Highsmith was "Educational Director" in 1920, although he gives no details of Highsmith's work. (p. 31) Then he says that "In January 1922 Mr. C. H. Warren began his work as Educational Director." (p. 33) He does not report how long Warren remained in that capacity.

Another organizational development was the formation of a Boy Scout troop. The troop was organized on November 23, 1923, with W. P. Baker as Scoutmaster. Charter members were Henry Craven, Rupert Lechner, Floyd Rigsbee, William Baker, Clarence Horton, Dan Stewart, Tom D. Cooper, Luther A. Wood, and Jonathan Lane. This troop is still in operation and is the oldest in the Oconeechee Council.

Pullen Memorial Church moved to its new location on Hillsborough Street with a definite commitment to a ministry to college students. In June, 1950, E. McNeill Poteat, Jr., then pastor at Pullen, prepared a document to be used in requesting help from the Baptist State Convention for the completion of its sanctuary. In summarizing the history of the move of the church to Hillsborough Street Poteat wrote:

> The records concerning the initiation of the proposal of the State Board of Missions for the establishment of a church at Hillsboro Street and Cox Avenue to provide a spiritual ministry for the students of State College are sketchy. It was in the mind of Dr. Walter N. Johnson when he was State Secretary but it had its active beginnings under the leadership of Dr. Charles E. Maddry in 1920.
>
> The first minutes from the Executive Committee of the State Convention occurs April 26, 1921:
>
> "The Secretary was authorized . . . to aid Pullen Memorial in all the difficulties of moving."

That the project was well advanced in the minds of the Executive Committee and was a part of a similar program at Chapel Hill and the Woman's College in Greensboro is clear from the minutes of the Convention as printed on page 95 of the 1922 Annual. The paragraph referring to Pullen Memorial follows:

"The Pullen Memorial Church of Raleigh decided to move to West Raleigh and built a church and Sunday School house adequate to care for the spiritual needs of the great number of Baptist students in A. & E. College. The Executive Committee to whom the matter was referred by the Board of Missions made an appropriation of $16,000 on the Sunday School unit of the church. The Pullen Estate paid some $35,000 toward the cost of this building, the State Board $8,000 and the local church some $25,000. The building is well arranged for student work and will take care of the needs of A. & E. College, until we can complete the building at a later date." This last statement makes it quite manifest that the Board of Missions was committed to the project and to the eventual completion of the entire plant.

From the time of the decision to move, the church has functioned with a definite awareness of its mission to the academic community. Jack Ellis was well-equipped to speak to that community in his sermons and in his total ministry. He preached on contemporary issues and represented a religion which was not threatened by the expanding frontiers of truth. His successor, Edwin McNeill Poteat, Jr., widely recognized and acclaimed as a scholarly young minister, was to enlarge on that kind of ministry.

Shortly after moving into its new building, Pullen Memorial Church strengthened its ministry to students by employing a specialized minister to work with them. On June 25, 1923, Dr. Ellis announced that R. M. Warren had been employed in that capacity. At the end of his summary of the work for 1924, Baker stated, "The work of Brother Warren among the students of Meredith, State College and the Blind Institute was very effective." (p. 33) Baker, whose history concludes with the year 1930, did not refer again to Warren or to any other person in the capacity of student worker.

During the 1920's two significant developments took place in connection with the Board of Deacons. The first was the decision, made in 1927, to institute a rotation in the service of the deacons. Until that time a person who was elected deacon served for life. In 1927, however, the practice was begun of electing persons to serve four-year terms. The recommendation for the change came from the Board of Deacons, of which Dr. Z. M. Caviness was chairman. (Church Minutes, December 11, 1927) Pullen was not the first church to adopt this plan, nor was it the last. Lifetime deacons seem more appropriate to a small congregation, where the number of persons from which to choose leaders may be limited. Furthermore, as long as John Pullen and those stalwarts who had worked with him in establishing the church were alive, the rotation of leadership—except in the office of pastor—would hardly have seemed feasible. The growth of the church, however, and the passing of time, made it apparent that the church would benefit from the contributions of a greater number of persons serving in that capacity.

The other change, which was more radical, was determined in the same church conference on December 11, 1927. That was the election of women to the Board of Deacons. After reporting the approval of the plan for the rotation of deacons, the minutes note that

> A further recommendation was that women be elligible [*sic*] to office as deaconness. This was adopted.
>
> Next the election was entered into. Some fifty men and women were nominated. The previous recommendation of the deacons was that six-teen deacons be elected. On motion only one ballot was taken, those receiving the highest vote to serve for four years, next highest three years, third highest two years, fourth highest for one year.

In that election one woman, Mrs. Gilbert T. Stephenson, was chosen. At the next conference, however, Mrs. Stephenson resigned. The official minutes state no reason for her resignation, but the secretary's notes from which the minutes were written reveal, in a phrase scratched out, that she was sensitive to the fact that she was the only woman chosen. Dr. Ellis led the ordination service for the other newly elected deacons, and in that service Dr. C. E. Maddry spoke on "the duties of deacons." In that address "He also stated that he thought we should have deaconesses, that all modern churches were electing women to this office." (Minutes, December 21, 1927) The minutes of that same session add:

> After Dr. Maddry's talk it was thought by some that we should elect some of the women to the office of deaconess, and after considerable discussion motion passed that the four ladies receiving the highest votes in the preceding election be named as deaconesses.

Those women were Mrs. Gilbert T. Stephenson, Mrs. L. S. Madison, Mrs. Z. M. Caviness, and Mrs. G. H. Ferguson.

Revival services continued to play a significant part in the life of Pullen Memorial during this period, although they ceased to be a regular activity. In the earliest years of the church they had occurred frequently, sometimes two or more in a year. During Ellis' pastorate that was not the case. The immediate increase in membership after his coming was not the result of any special evangelistic campaign. There was a revival meeting in March, 1923, in which Dr. Charles E. Maddry did the preaching, but there are no records of its impact upon the church. There was another in October, 1924, five years after Ellis became pastor, in which Dr. Zeno Wall, then pastor of the First Baptist Church of Goldsboro, preached. The *Biblical Recorder* reported on that meeting:

Dr. Zeno Wall, pastor of the First Baptist Church of Goldsboro, recently held a ten days' meeting with Pullen Memorial Church. He preached twice daily and I do not hesitate to say that it was one of the very best series of sermons that I have ever heard. Dr. Wall . . . is a close student of the Bible and is preeminently a Bible preacher. His sermons come out of the Book. Dr. Wall is a lover of people and along with his own eagerness to live on a high spiritual plain he seeks to lead his hearers into closer fellowship with the Christ. . . . The number of additions were not large, there being but few in attendance who were not church members. Ten have been added to our membership thus far. We shall receive members along through the months as a result of this meeting. (BR, 11/19/24)

Evangelism at the church's new location was different from what it had been on Fayetteville Street. Never again was the traditional "revival" to play a part in the life of Pullen.

A new approach to the Christian witness adapted to the academic community was represented by a series of lectures delivered in 1927 by Dr. W. L. Poteat, President of Wake Forest College, on "A Scientist's View of Religion." In that series Dr. Poteat spoke forthrightly as a Christian who knew the scientific method and was entirely at home with the scientific world view. His message was intended for the academic community, and it was well received by that community.

During his decade at Pullen, Jack Ellis distinguished himself as a preacher. At that time the Raleigh *News and Observer* carried each Monday rather full reports on sermons preached in local churches on the preceding Sunday. The paper reported on Ellis two or three times a month, and sometimes more frequently. Almost always he used a New Testament text as the basis for his message; out of seventy-five announced texts, only eight came from the Old Testament. The Gospel of John apparently was his favorite book, for fourteen of his texts came from it. The general tone of his messages was positive, a discussion of the Christian life rather than a denunciation of sin. Repeatedly as he talked about the Christian life, he specified how he thought Christian love might validly be expressed. He placed strong emphasis on works as a necessary expression of Christian faith. He also had a strong devotional element in his messages, with ideas about the life of the spirit frequently appearing.

One theme which permeated Ellis' sermons was the worth of the individual and of the possibilities of individual action. On June 8, 1924, he preached about helping the person who is "down" or "in the wrong." On July 21 of the same year he preached on the text, "How much, then, is a man of more value than a sheep" (Matt. 12:12). On May 25, 1925, he preached on the text, "Let him who is without sin cast the first stone" (John 8:9). Such individualism is consistent with traditional Baptist theology. Ellis, however, consistently made an

76

emphasis that turned the attention of his hearers away from themselves and toward the worth of and the needs of other persons.

Frequently Ellis spoke to contemporary issues, almost always taking a liberal stand. On June 15, 1924, for example, at the time when the Ku Klux Klan had its largest membership in history, and when its campaign of intimidation and violence made the news constantly, Ellis preached a sermon on the basis of Philippians 3:7 in which he said, "Excessive race pride unfitted Saul of Tarsus for large service to mankind." He went on to say:

> One of the dangers that imperils the white race is the feeling of superiority, and along with that our failure to remember that where much is given much is required, and that unusual gifts and talents impose great responsibilities upon either an individual or a race. It took Christianity to give Paul the correct estimate of himself and to bring him into the right relations with his fellows. When this had been done he became the servant of mankind. Christianity and that alone will bring the white race, the most richly endowed of all the races, to a sense of obligation to the rest of mankind. (N&O, 6/16/24)

Ellis often spoke about war, urging his congregation to inform themselves on international issues and to devote themselves to "the things that make for peace." He was an ardent admirer of Woodrow Wilson, and on a number of occasions referred to him in his sermons. On July 20, 1924, for example, he said:

> Men have not been lifted to higher conceptions of the sacredness of human life, and to greater visions of the rights of mankind since Jesus was in the world than they were lifted by Woodrow Wilson. He thought of men as of more value than sheep. He pointed his fellows to the better way, but even his own America was too narrow minded, low visioned and selfish to follow his leading. (N&O, 7/21/24)

At the beginning of his sixth year at Pullen, on September 7, 1924, Ellis spoke on Haggai 2:4, "Work: for I am with you, saith Jehovah of hosts." At one point in his sermon he said that the words of this text

> are spoken to those groups of peoples, churches, civic organizations, states and nations when men and women unite their hearts, their minds, their hands in that sublime effort of making this world a better place for those who come after us. Would that America, our America, were sitting yonder as a member of the League of Nations today instead of talking about 'Mobilization, Preparedness, and Defense.' (N&O, 9/8/24)

On December 21, 1924, Ellis spoke on the subject of "Peace."

> The greatest question that now faces the human race is the outlawing and abolition of war. . . . The greatest curse that has afflicted mankind is the plague of war. We passed out of the recent deluge of blood declaring that it was a war to end war, but during the six years since its close

77

greater inventions have been perfected, and more death dealing instruments made for wholesale slaughter than in any like period in the history of the world. Games more deadly than any dreamed of in former years, and means more perfect for their spreading than ever before are now available. There are experts working on the idea of spreading disease germs among the soldiers and the civilians of the enemy that would possibly be more widely destructive than gases.

A bit later in that sermon he said:

Jesus did not come into the world to accept or approve the evils that existed, but to make all things new. The mission of Christianity is not to accept and endure the evils that afflict mankind, but to challenge and destroy them.

Let this war to end war begin in the home and the schools. Let the text books be disarmed. Let us cease to glorify war and write of war as though it were a glorious thing. Let the horrors of war, the unspeakable tragedies of war, the desolation that follows in the wake of war be known. Let there be a rule among the nations that those who are most responsible for the conditions that lead to war be the first sent to the front. For the older men to create the conditions and bring on the conflict and then remain in safety while the smooth faced lads are sent into the jaws of death to give their lives to settle a dispute the creating of which they had nothing to do, this is tragically wrong. Let the first draft be for men above forty, let the burden fall heaviest upon those who are responsible. (N&O, 12/22/24)

On Sunday afternoon, November 8, 1925, Ellis, who was a chaplain of Raleigh Post No. 1 of the American Legion Auxiliary, addressed that group in a public meeting. The *News and Observer* termed his address "a stirring appeal for the abolition of war." (N&O, 11/9/25) He reiterated his support for the World Court and the League of Nations by saying, "All honor to those nations which are struggling to find the light, and all shame to this country who has absolutely failed to give the assistance that counts." Speaking of the idea that war is sometimes necessary to defend the weak, he called attention to "the millions who die, the millions who were wounded, and the millions of refugees and orphans whose present state was brought about through war." He declared that "War is not to defend the weak . . . it only multiplies the weak and unfortunate." (N&O, 11/9/25)

Reporting on a sermon which Ellis preached on Sunday, February 6, 1927, Nell Battle Lewis wrote:

Members of the congregation of the Pullen Memorial church yesterday morning heard the gospel of Jesus Christ preached to them by their pastor, the Rev. J. A. Ellis. Mr. Ellis repudiated the attitude of the vast majority of Christians today, that herd attitude which in time of war makes the church scarcely less militaristic than the army. He turned from this completely in unequivocal allegiance to the supreme Pacifist, and with the sword of the Lord and of Gideon he went to war on war.

The first denunciation of the monstrous wickedness of war by a Christian minister in Raleigh ever heard by the writer during a life spent in this city of churches was that by the Rev. Mr. Ellis about eighteen months ago. This same man yesterday gave a thrilling revelation of zealous faith, and bravely and directly expressed again the message of peace and good will his Lord died to bring.

"War," Mr. Ellis quoted, "is everything that Christ is not!"

Ellis stood in that theological camp which believed that it was possible for Christians to be open to new scientific developments without endangering their faith and without challenging the validity of the Scripture. In the midst of the national furor over the teaching of evolution in the public schools, Ellis proclaimed:

> Can a Christian continue to study and seek knowledge? The present civilization that all are now enjoying is due to men who have been seekers after knowledge. The men who use the microscope and telescope need not forsake God but should combine their strength with His. Man alone is a very weak creature but if he and God are working together then there is a combination that can not be beat. (N&O, 5/31/26)

That statement was consistent with what Ellis had been doing in his own efforts to give leadership to the church. On March 16, 1924, a year before the Scopes trial, he had had W. L. Poteat, the biologist who was President of Wake Forest College, preach at Pullen. In the aftermath of the Scopes trial in 1927 he had Poteat deliver his series of lectures on "A Scientist's View of Religion."

Ellis was much in demand for services in places other than Pullen Memorial Church. He preached in a number of revival meetings: at Broadway, Holly Springs, and Baptist Chapel in Moore County; at Coats; at Mebane; at Meherrin near Murfreesboro. In addition, he spoke at civic and at community meetings: a commencement sermon at Sanford High School; a thanksgiving service sponsored by the Baptist churches in Raleigh; the dedication of a new building for the YWCA; a graduation address to Rex Hospital's School of Nursing; the Amerian Legion Auxilliary.

When Ellis was absent from the pulpit of Pullen Memorial Church he often had well-known religious leaders supply for him. Twice he had Dr. J. A. Campbell, founder and president of Campbell Junior College, speak at Pullen. Twice Dr. R. T. Vann, president of Meredith College, preached for him. Once he had W. D. Weatherford, president of the Southern Y.M.C.A. College in Nashville, address the congregation. Once H. H. McMillan, missionary to China, occupied the pulpit. A frequent guest minister was Dr. Charles Maddry, General Secretary of the Baptist State Convention of North Carolina and a member of Pullen.

On Sunday, December 9, 1928, Dr. Ellis announced his resignation from Pullen Memorial Church and his acceptance of the pastorate of the First Baptist Church of Sherman, Texas. His statement to the congregation was quoted in full in the *News and Observer* for Monday, December 10, 1928:

On August 22, 1919, Pullen Memorial Church did me the honor of calling me to this pastorate. On the first Sunday in September, following, it was my privilege to begin what has been to me a most happy relationship. At an appropriate time I hope to have opportunity to express, in some small measure at least, the gratitude I have to the members of this church and congregation for these years of unfailing loyalty and faithfulness to a work and a cause that have lived so close to our hearts. Today I come to return to this church the trust committed to me more than nine years ago. I came not only in response to your call, but at what I then believed, and believe as firmly today, to be the call of our Lord. I shall leave in response to what I believe to be the same high call. I now place before this church my resignation as pastor with a view to accepting a call recently extended by the First Baptist church at Sherman, Texas. In order that the work there may be begun at an early date let me request that I be released from this church not later than the second Sunday in January of next year.

In commenting on Ellis' resignation, the *News and Observer* stated:

Dr. Ellis has made an enviable record in Raleigh in building up his church and in work among the young people, especially the students of State College. His campaign against the militaristic attitude, including controversies with E. E. Spafford, while he was National Commander of the American Legion, and with General A. J. Boley while he was commandant of Fort Bragg, and his arguments against compulsory military training at State College gained for Dr. Ellis considerable attention during the past several years.

The same article also noted that Dr. Ellis would be moving from the leadership of a congregation numbering between four and five hundred to the leadership of one numbering nearly seventeen hundred. In reporting on Ellis' last sermon at Pullen, preached on January 13, 1929, the *News and Observer* called him "the dean of Baptist ministers in the city."

Throughout most of Ellis' pastorate Dr. Charles E. Maddry was a member of Pullen Memorial Church and was actively involved in a leadership position. Dr. Maddry was elected Corresponding Secretary of the North Carolina Baptist State Convention in 1921. At the time he was no stranger to Pullen. A native North Carolinian, he had been pastor of the University Place Baptist Church in Austin, Texas, for several years. He had maintained his North Carolina contacts, however, and in May, 1919, had preached in revival meetings both at Tabernacle Church and at Pullen Memorial. Without a pastor at the time, Pullen had tried unsuccessfully to get him to accept the pastorate of that church. In announcing his appointment as Corresponding Secretary, the *Biblical Recorder* stated, "Dr. Maddry is a native of North Carolina, a gráduate of the State University, and of the Louisville Seminary. He is a good preacher and a man with a great heart who will fill the office admirably." (BR, 1/5/21) In another item in that same issue the *Recorder* noted that "In joining the Pullen Memorial Church, rather than one of the strong churches in Raleigh, Secretary Maddry exhibited the true missionary spirit." Maddry remained a member of Pullen until 1932, when he moved to Nashville, Tennessee, as Executive Secretary of the Promotion Committee of the Southern Baptist Convention. After only a few months in that position, he became Executive Secretary of the Southern Baptist Foreign Mission Board in Richmond, Virginia.

Maddry's denominational work naturally required him to travel throughout the state. At the same time, however, he managed to be quite active in the life and work of Pullen Memorial. He was a member of the Board of Deacons. Both in Board meetings and in congregational meetings his judgment was often sought and always respected. He frequently filled the pulpit for Ellis when the latter found it necessary to be away.

Another member of the church throughout Ellis' pastorate, and for many years afterwards, was R. L. McMillan. Beginning his service as Superintendent of the Sunday school in 1920, he continued in that office through 1927. The *Biblical Recorder,* in a statement about progress at Pullen in Ellis' first few months, stated, "R. L. McMillan, a young lawyer, who recently located in Raleigh, one of Scotland County's 'sunburnt boys,' is superintendent of the Sunday school." (BR, 3/31/20) Commenting on his work in that office, Baker said:

> For 9 years Bro. R. L. McMillan had served very efficiently as Supt. of Sunday School. Our Sunday School has grown from a membership of 168 to 659 during his administration. There had been many conversions all along from the Sunday School into the Church. Bro. McMillan is a consecrated, zealous Christian worker. He has the ancestral background of great Baptist leaders. His Brother Hud McMillan has been a missionary in China for many years. Another Brother, Jim Arch McMillan is a minister and for many years Editor of the "Charity and Children" at our Thomasville Orphanage. The McMillan Family have truly been outstanding in Church and Religious Work. (p. 36)

Edwin McNeill Poteat, Jr., became pastor of Pullen Memorial Baptist Church on September 15, 1929. Poteat was born November 20, 1892, in New Haven, Connecticut, the son of Edwin McNeill and Harriet Gordon Poteat. He was a graduate of Furman University, where he received the A.B. in 1912 and the A.M. in 1913. He then studied at the Southern Baptist Theological Seminary, where he received the Th.M. in 1916. For a year after his graduation from the seminary he was a traveling secretary for the Student Volunteer Movement. Then he went to China, under the auspices of the Foreign Mission Board of the Southern Baptist Convention, serving there from 1917 until he came to Pullen in 1929. During the last three years of his work in China he was associate professor of philosophy and ethics at the University of Shanghai.

Poteat was a member of a family well-known in the Baptist denomination and in educational circles, particularly in the Carolinas. His father had been pastor in Chapel Hill, had taught ancient languages at Wake Forest College, had served as pastor in several New England churches, and had been president of Furman University. After resigning from Furman in 1918, he had worked successively with the Laymen's Missionary Movement, the Northern Baptist Convention, and the University of Shanghai. Returning to the United States, he had been pastor first of First Baptist Church in Richmond, and then of Second Baptist in Atlanta. He had returned to teaching, working at Mercer University for three years and then at Furman University. He was at Furman at the time of his death in 1937.

Poteat's uncle, William Louis Poteat, was a biologist on the faculty of Wake Forest College from 1878 until 1905, and was president of Wake Forest from 1905 until 1927. His aunt, Miss Ida Poteat, was head of the art department at Meredith College from its beginning in 1899 until her death in 1940. His brother, Gordon Poteat, was a long-time missionary in China.

At the time of his call to Pullen, McNeill Poteat was in China, teaching at the University of Shanghai. He was thoroughly committed to the cause of missions, and he maintained that commitment throughout his life. He was not entirely at home with the philosophy of the Southern Baptist Foreign Mission Board, however. More sensitive than most of his peers, both among Baptists and among missionaries of other denominations, to economic and political conditions, he understood the instability of China. He was aware that Christian missionaries might not be permanently welcome there and, therefore, urged the Foreign Mission Board to transfer leadership to nationals as quickly as possible. The Foreign Mission Board, however, was unwilling to take the steps which he thought necessary. That difference was certainly one factor in his willingness to leave China.

We are not sure exactly how Poteat's name came before Pullen as a prospective pastor. The nomination may have come from his father, who had returned from China in 1927 and had preached at Pullen on May 29 of that year. At the time of Ellis' resignation, the elder Poteat was pastor of the First Baptist Church of Richmond. Furthermore, McNeill Poteat had family and friends in the area. Pullen's pulpit committee must have been in contact with him when the following news item, quoted from the *Baptist Courier*, appeared in the *Biblical Recorder*:

> Rev. McNeill Poteat is now a professor in Shanghai College, China. He knows as much about the Chinese situation as any man that we have in that great country. You will be interested in this paragraph which we

clipped from a recent private letter to a member of his family. "Whatever may be said of the period of comparative peace that envelops this land just now, it cannot be gain-said that it is the longest period that we have had in nearly a dozen years. I am coming to think that with the exception of inevitable flares up in local quarters there will not come a period of nationwide revolution again for many years—perhaps never. This means that there is at least an opportunity for constructive developments. . . . Our work here in the college has been quite successful. The Chinese president is very much on his job. He is coming to the Southern Baptist Convention this year. Last month I baptized nine students. This is the first time that there have been open confessions of Christ here in the past two years. The times of disturbance have, somehow, taken the minds of the students away from such matters, and I think it can be safely said that it indicates a change in atmosphere when so large a group comes out into the open. (BR, 4/3/29)

The *Biblical Recorder* for May 8, 1929, announced that Pullen had extended a call to "Dr. E. M. Poteat, Jr., of Shanghai, China," and by cabelgram he had notified the chairman of the committee that he had decided to accept the call. In the June 26 issue the *Recorder* again spoke of his coming, saying "Dr. E. McNeill Poteat, who has spent several years in China as missionary, was called to the pastorate of the Pullen Memorial Church, Raleigh, some time ago, and has written that he accepts the call."

The *Recorder*'s references to the communication prompted Poteat to write to the editor:

May I ask your cooperation in a small matter? I am not "Doctor" Poteat. No doubt the numerous doctors Poteat in your mind make it difficult to think of one Poteat as plain and undeserving of such rank. Such however is the case, and I would prefer to be known as the quite unadorned person I actually am. (BR, 7/31/29)

Not everyone agreed that Poteat was quite so "plain and undeserving" as he indicated, for ultimately he was to receive honorary doctorates from Wake Forest, Duke, and Hillsdale.

Poteat served as pastor from September 15, 1929, until September 15, 1937. Continuing its practice of reporting every Monday on several church services held in the city on the preceding day, the *News and Observer* often summarized Poteat's sermons. His first several sermons were basically expository. On August 24, as a visiting minister, he preached a sermon in which he said that "The final proof of religion is in the heart of man." On September 22, his second Sunday as pastor, he began a series of sermons on "The Temptations of Christ." In November he delivered a series on "Seeing Jesus through the Eyes of His Contemporaries." Beginning in January, 1930, most of his sermons were efforts to bring the gospel to bear upon the issues of life, both personal and social, but with a concentration on the social. A list of the ideas with which he dealt, as reported in the *News and Observer*, is instructive:

January 5, 1930: a New Year's sermon based on Abraham's venturing out on faith, citing areas in our life which call for faith.

January 12, 1930: the nation is suffering from "a multiplication of moral and legal codes," and is therefore more Pharisaic than Christian.

February 2, 1930: Jesus' followers have restricted him.

February 9, 1930: The Great Progress in our Society is due to the Social and Moral Influence of Jesus.

February 23, 1930: "And God saw that it was Good."

March 2, 1930: Cowardice and Ignorance are Responsible for our not Following Christ.

March 16, 1930: Jesus Saves from Ignorance.

March 27, 1930: The Christian Attitude Toward Truth is to be Open to it.

June 1, 1930: "Glorious Freedom"—Must not be Confused with Unrestraint.

June 29, 1930: Parable of the Good Samaritan.

July 6, 1930: We would Change this City if We were to take Christ Seriously.

July 13, 1930: Attitudes toward Trouble.

July 20, 1930: "Thinking is Dangerous."

July 27, 1930: "A Cure for Pessimism."

November 23, 1930: "Love and Personal Quarrels."

December 7, 1930: Condemnation of Industrial Oppression.

December 14, 1930: Against Military Training for Students.

December 21, 1930: The Meaning of Christmas has been Lost.

January 11, 1931: Does Religion bar Progress?

January 18, 1931: Anti-alcohol.

February 8, 1931: Property Rights are often Oppressive of Humanity.

February 15, 1931: Nationalism is Unchristian.

February 22, 1931: Our Shame is that We are no longer Morally Indignant at Corruption.

March 8, 1931: Parable of the Good Samaritan, with the theme, "Get the Robbers!"

March 22, 1931: Christianity is the Solution to our National Economic Difficulty.

May 17, 1931: Peace. (At the conclusion of this service, the congregation adopted a resolution asking President Hoover to work for peace and brotherhood.)

September 6, 1931: Labor has the Right to Work.

November 8, 1931: Three levels of Religion: Physical, Social, Spiritual.

November 29, 1931: America has a Heathen Aim: The Quest of Material Gain.

December 6, 1931: "The Threat of Insecurity" (he spoke of social, not personal, insecurity).

December 13, 1931: "Slaves to Alcohol?"

December 20, 1931: Peace.

December 27, 1931: Barriers to Human Relationships.

April 4, 1932: Skepticism is Needed.

July 24, 1932: Capitalists Need to be Converted.

September 11, 1932: A Denunciation of Patronage and Privilege in Politics.

As expressed in his sermons, then, Poteat's major concern was with what is termed "Social Christianity." Even when he spoke on subjects that seem to be basically personal, he usually saw also a social application. In the sermon on January 5, 1930, speaking about venturing out on faith, he cited areas needing attention. First he called attention to the international friction centering in China, India, and the Near East, and to the questions of "debt settlement." Then, at the national level, he spoke of financial depression and law enforcement. Next he spoke of the local economic problems of farm and industry. He concluded with a statement about individual concerns: "the pressure of hard times, the indifference to the claims of higher values in life; and the widespread contempt for traditional moral restraints." In another sermon preached on March 2, 1930, on Peter's denial of Christ, he said:

> We don't know where He is going, and we are afraid to follow as far as we can see Him. . . . We have been content to follow him to church, to young people's societies and presumably to heaven, but we don't follow Him to business, to the voting precinct, to the Houses of Congress or to international conferences, because we think that He has never preceded us there! (N&O, 3/3/30)

Poteat always dealt with contemporary issues. He was thoroughly biblical, basing his messages upon scripture appropriate to the subjects with which he dealt. Frequently he found in the biblical passage implications which more traditional preachers did not discover. His knowledge of contemporary issues was extensive, for he read widely, with materials ranging from the morning newspaper to ancient philosophy. He believed that it was possible to build a better society and that the teachings and example of Christ were the guides to accomplish that goal.

Poteat was much in demand as a visiting preacher, particularly in colleges and universities. On Friday, January 31, 1930, he delivered the annual Founders' Day address at Meredith College. So impressed was the editor of the *Biblical Recorder* with that address on "Creativity" that he printed it in full in the February 19 issue. In March, Poteat was in a week-long series in Danville, Virginia. In April he was the featured Religious Emphasis Week speaker at the University of Richmond, where his theme was "The Adequacy of Jesus for the Life and Thought of Today." In June he conducted services for a week at Blue Ridge. In July, apparently sensitive to the fact that he was spending a great deal of time away from the church, he asked the deacons for an official statement. The minutes noted: "The pastor asked permission of the Board of Deacons to have leave of absence not to exceed once each month to make contact speeches with colleges, by which he has been invited to speak. His request was granted on the condition that he did not leave Pullen Church at the first opportunity which might present itself." (Minutes, 7/7/30) In October of that year Poteat delivered a series of nine addresses at Georgia Tech, where his stated aim was "to impress upon the students the claims of Jesus as an adequate moral guide in the twentieth century." (BR, 11/5/30) In October also he was at Wake Forest College to deliver a series of lectures on the subject of human behavior, dealing with the question, "Why Should a Man Behave Himself?" (BR, 10/28/31) In the spring of 1932 he preached the baccalaureate sermon at Coker College. A few weeks later he addressed the Federation of Women's Clubs in York, Pennsylvania, on the subject, "The International Mind." He had received the invitation to deliver that address on the basis of some women having heard his radio sermon on the subject of "Nationalism and Church Obligation." In June, 1932, he was on the faculty of "The Preachers' School," held at Meredith College. (BR, 4/27/32)

In November, 1930, the annual session of the North Carolina Baptist State Convention was held in Raleigh at the First Baptist Church. In that meeting a great deal of attention was paid the fact that the Convention was celebrating its one hundredth anniversary. Poteat wrote the words and music for the "Centennial Hymn," which begins with the line, "Backward our glance surveys the road we've trod." The fourth stanza summarizes Poteat's spirit:

Forward we move in hopefulness to gain
Crosses and crowns throughout the coming age;
Thy Kingdom comes through passion and through pain,
Thou art our hope and Thou our heritage.

Poteat's first book, *Coming to Terms with the Universe*, was published in 1931. It was written during the early years of his pastorate at Pullen, and incorporated many of the ideas which he had developed in his addresses at the colleges and universities where he had spoken. It represents his serious and continued effort to retain basic Christian convictions in light of the new information which science was daily bringing, and to present Christian faith as the necessary ingredient for life in the scientific age. It was not so much an attempt to reconcile science and religion as it was to understand them as complementary to each other and as necessary each to the other.

From the scattered minutes of church conferences and deacons' meetings between 1927 and 1932, some interesting information about the institutional life of the church in this period can be gathered. On December 4, 1929, the church approved the following recommendations from the deacons:

That all present church officers except the church clerk be re-elected—retiring deacons excepted. New deacons to be elected at a later meeting for that purpose. In case of the church clerk, they recommend that the office be combined with that of secretary to the board of deacons, for obvious good reasons, thus automatically making the church clerk a member of board of deacons.

That retiring deacons be eligible to re-election and may succeed themselves in office.

That elderly male members of church may be elected deacons for life.

On December 9, 1931, the deacons voted to recommend to the church that the number of deacons be increased from sixteen to twenty. To those minutes was appended a notice dated December 16, 1931, that the recommendation was approved and additional deacons were elected.

The minutes of the deacons' meeting for 1930, 1931, and 1932 indicate offerings had declined every year, falling from $12,540 in 1926 to $7,363 in 1929. In 1930 they were up by $300, but in 1931 they were down again to $6,090. In 1932 the church was in a dangerous financial situation, with all offerings totaling only $1,561. In December the deacons authorized the use of money from the building fund to pay current expenses. In light of the national economic situation the decline is not surprising. Yet the deacons were worried. Minutes for the meetings in February, April, July, and October, 1930, and two meetings in October, 1931, reflect their growing concern. There were frequent references to such details as Pullen's share in the cost of bus transportation for Meredith students to attend the churches in Raleigh. (2/3/30; 2/24/30; 4/2/30; etc.) The Sunday evening services were being broadcast, and inevitably the question arose as to whether the church could afford to continue to pay for that practice. The question was raised at the January 7, 1931, meeting, and "A motion by Mr. Maynard to tell Mr. King to continue as long as funds were available was passed." The August minutes state that "The pastor reported for the broadcast committee that there was money in hand for the broadcasts through November, December and perhaps January from 7:30-8:30 in the evening on Sundays."

At one point, Poteat "discussed the order of the service and asked for criticisms, favorable or unfavorable. There were some of both." (Deacons, 10/13/30) Apparently Poteat thought that more discussion was needed, for the matter came up again in the November meeting. He may have received some suggestions, but "it was decided to leave the order of service to the pastor, the chairman of the Board of Deacons, and the President of the Woman's Missionary Society." (Deacons, 11/3/30)

Another matter was brought up in the October 13, 1930, meeting of the deacons which was a foretaste of things to come: "Motion was made and carried to recommend to the church in conference that 'foreign baptism' (immersion) be accepted by this church." Unfortunately, no record exists of the church's action on this issue, but later practice makes it clear that the action must have been ratified.

As might be expected of one who had served in China, Poteat maintained a strong interest in missions. The minutes of the Deacons' meeting for January 6, 1930, report that "Mr. Poteat and Mr. Browne were asked to cooperate with Mrs. Maddry and Mrs. Allen in regard to the week of missions." They did indeed cooperate, and on February 16-21, 1930, the church observed "missionary week," with the opening address being delivered by Dr. W. L. Poteat, of Wake Forest College. (BR, 2/12/30) The *Biblical Recorder* described the sessions:

> The Pullen Memorial Church, Raleigh, under the capable leadership of pastor E. McNeill Poteat conducted a School of Missions last week. Each evening at 6:30 lunch was served; then there were sectional meetings, story telling for the little folk, biographical sketches of missionaries for young people, and a discussion of the missionary enterprise by the pastor. After these meetings each evening there was an inspirational address by some capable person. Those who attended these meetings regularly declared this the best meeting for the discussion of missions they have attended. Few people have such a grasp of this great subject as pastor Poteat. (BR, 2/26/30)

As Poteat's pastorate progressed, this emphasis upon missions was to continue and to grow.

In November, 1932, America chose a new president, Franklin Delano Roosevelt, a man who promised the nation "a new deal." Anyone who looked beyond the borders of our nation might have seen something of the trouble brewing in Japan, in Italy, and in Germany. Few people, however, saw much further than the poverty and the unrest in our own country. In the midst of the Depression, they looked with a hope born not of optimism but of desperation to the new president. In that setting, Pullen Memorial Baptist Church was responding to the leadership of a pastor who had a hope based not on desperation but on an optimistic faith.

Chapter 5
A Church With A Conscience
In An Era of Crisis
(1933-1941)

When Franklin D. Roosevelt was elected President of the United States the nation was at its lowest economic ebb in history. Thirteen million people were unemployed, one out of every four persons in the labor force. Jobless and homeless, a million or more people wandered across the nation searching day by day for food and shelter, not knowing from one day to the next what luck they might have. The hobo and the bum and the pencil peddler were familiar sights. Many employed people survived on drastically reduced income, often piling up debts and constantly afraid that they might lose their jobs. As Roosevelt had campaigned he had found the nation desperately afraid. While he did not spell out his policies during his campaign because he had not worked them out, he did promise to involve the federal government in resolving the problems. He won overwhelmingly, and at his inauguration in March, 1933, he announced, "First of all, let me assert my firm belief that the only thing we have to fear is fear itself."

Immediately after his inauguration Roosevelt began to take drastic steps. Some of his programs were highly successful; some much less so; and the constitutionality of some was ultimately tested in the courts. He met strong resistance, much of it in the South which he had declared "the nation's number one economic problem." He was re-elected in 1936, however, and the national recovery continued.

During Roosevelt's first eight years the world was moving inexorably toward war. Hitler came to power in Germany in 1933, the same year in which Roosevelt began his first term. In 1934 Hitler and Mussolini had their first meeting. In 1935 Hitler proclaimed a number of anti-Semitic laws, and in the same year Mussolini invaded Ethiopia. The Spanish civil war broke out in 1936. In 1937 the Japanese began an undeclared war against China. In 1938 Hitler took Austria and Czechoslovakia. In 1939 the German invasion of Poland led to the Franco-British declaration of war. By the time of the Japanese attack on Pearl Harbor, on December 7, 1941, Hitler had overrun Norway, Denmark, the Low Countries, and France, and was bombing Britain. He was defeating the British in North Africa and was marching through Russia toward Leningrad. The Italians had failed in their attempt to take Greece, but the Japanese, who had joined the Axis, had occupied most of Indochina. In spite of the fact that many Americans opposed our involvement in the wars of Europe and Asia, the attack on Pearl Harbor was merely the percipitating factor for our inevitable involvement.

Throughout the country the churches, as voluntary institutions, suffered severely during the Depression. Many had entered extensive building programs in the late 1920's and were heavily in debt. Between 1930 and 1934 church offerings were cut in half. Inevitably such a curtailment of financial resources meant not only trouble in paying off mortgages but also cuts in salaries and the curtailment of programs. In addition, it meant reductions in contributions to denominational programs. The records of churches at both the local and the denominational level are the story of struggling to make ends meet.

Between 1930 and 1940 the growth rate of the churches was only half what it had been in the previous decade. Attendance at worship services declined and organizational programs for young people, men, and women all dropped at an unexpected rate. Only the smaller sects, and particularly those of the Pentecostal and Holiness theology, experienced any significant growth.

Despite their limited resources, the churches made a valiant effort to do their part in feeding the hungry. Most churches made some provision to help at least a portion of those who came to their doors seeking shelter or pleading hunger. The problems, of course, were far too great for them to deal with; only drastic action by the national government was to suffice, and that effort took a great deal of time. The churches, however, helped many, assuming that the fact that they could not do it all did not excuse them from doing what they could.

Among Southern Baptists during the decade of the thirties there were no major developments. The youth organizations and the educational programs which had been devised in earlier years did take more precise form. Most of the attention of the denomination, however, was given to dealing with its financial crisis. So severe was the problem, in fact, that there was a temporary reduction in the denomination's missionary force in other countries. Southern Baptists did manage, however, to expand their work with blacks. That was not a direct mission work but cooperation with blacks in providing higher education both at the college and at the seminary level. Of particular importance were efforts in support of a theological seminary for blacks.

The problem of the approaching war troubled the Christian conscience deeply. Christians had supported American involvement in World War I as a "holy crusade," but after that war they were much less sure that the nation was blameless. Many ministers became avowed pacifists in the thirties. In a 1931 poll of nineteen thousand Protestant ministers, twelve thousand stated that they would disapprove of any future war, and over ten thousand said that they would refuse to take an active part in one. A similar poll taken in 1934 produced essentially the same results. Yet the church could not be indifferent to what was going on in the world, and many Christians saw war as sometimes the lesser of two evils. As Christian theologians debated the moral issue, however, the international crisis grew, war broke out in Europe, and inexorably the United States was drawn in. The churches were confronted not with the possibility of war but with its reality.

E. McNeill Poteat, Jr.
Minister 1929-1937

91

During the early part of this period Edwin McNeill Poteat continued to preach sermons that stressed the social responsibility of the Christian. On Sunday, June 18, 1933, for example, he preached a sermon based on the Parable of the Great Feast (Luke 14:16-24). He began by saying that "Most of the mischief of the world had not been caused by bad people but by sincere people who are misguided." He then made the point that "it is not enough to be sincere; we must be right." He added: "We have accepted Jesus as our Lord. We have accepted Him not as someone to call Lord but to follow in every part of life. Yet most of us have agreed to that declaration with a proviso that there may be something else more important. That attitude is the final infidelity. It is the unpardonable sin if there is one." (N&O, 6/19/33)

In another sermon, based on Jesus' warning against covetousness, Poteat attacked the profit motive:

> Our bravado in defying and our cleverness in rationalization have not saved us from the fate which has overtaken covetousness. The socioeconomic order, capitalism, is planted squarely upon the profit motive. And, the church has shared in the whole business by extolling the virtues of thrift while it fattened on the largess of the successful profit-seekers.
>
> The amazing exposures of the munition makers are evidence of the moral insensitiveness that the quest for profit can produce. It is not too much to say, in the light of recent exposures, that in obedience to the profit-motive, there are men who will not stop short of setting the torch to a world conflagration.
>
> Rarely has the world been faced with the penetration of this ancient warning as it has been in the past 20 years. Russia has established a new nation as a protest against it. Our own NRA started out with a denunciation of the money changers in the temple of American business.
>
> And yet, have we seriously understood the matter? There is little point in condemning munitions makers for making profit when our social order assumes the need for munitions in order to secure its permanence. Why complain of code breakers when even under the codes the consumer can be exploited by business for profit? (N&O, 4/7/34)

One week later Poteat warned against the possibility of our nation being drawn into a "nationalistic bog." (N&O, 4/16/34) In another sermon he declared that "the so-called natural law of private ownership of land is an illusion" that must be corrected by the insight of Christ. That illusion, he said, "undergirds our present life, individual and social. It insists that human nature—a composite of instinctive and rational powers—contains by divine creation the ground for selfishness. It is not called that. It is called 'the acquisitive instinct.'" (N&O, 4/12/37)

Poteat expressed his social concerns not only in his sermons but also in activities outside Pullen Church. He had broad contacts in the black community, both in Raleigh and throughout the South, at a time when such contacts were rare. On April 25, 1934, the *Biblical Recorder* announced:

> In the annual meeting on April 18 in Atlanta Dr. E. M. (sic) McNeill Poteat, Jr., pastor of the Pullen Memorial Baptist Church, Raleigh, was elected president of the Interracial Commission. This is a wise selection as Dr. Poteat is especially equipped for this work.

There is little evidence of how "the person in the pew" at Pullen responded to this kind of involvement. Had there been vigorous opposition, however, it surely would have been reflected in church documents. One action of the deacons suggests a degree of support by the church. On June 14, 1937, they passed a motion that "Mr. Poteat be authorized to invite a colored speaker to occupy the pulpit on June 27 in connection with the Negro Educational Conference to be held in Raleigh." While that action may not have been unique, it was certainly a radical one for the time.

A little more than a month later, in an address at Ridgecrest, Poteat accused Southern Protestants of standing by complacently "as constitutional rights are denied millions of fellow citizens" and called upon them to "accord the Negro his civil title and discontinue racial segregation in public worship." In a lengthy editorial, the editor of the *Biblical Recorder* took vigorous exception. He began:

> Dr. Poteat is to be commended for his humanitarian zeal, but with the facts before us we cannot subscribe to his conclusions. To do so would be to indict our Southern people of neglect of their colored people among us, of a criminal disregard of their rights as citizens, and of an un-Christian attitude towards the Negroes which has stood in the way of their religious and moral development. So far as our observation and knowledge extend this is far from being the case. (BR, 8/18/37)

The editor went to great lengths to insist that no constitutional rights of blacks were being denied and that segregation in the churches "came with the consent and good-will of white and colored members." He concluded with a thoroughly familiar line of reasoning:

> Here is one other matter that deserves serious consideration: the sitting together of whites and colored in the same house of worship Sunday after Sunday would inevitably lead to a mixture of the races; white men would soon be mating with Negro women and white women with Negro men, if they should meet and mingle at the services of the churches. We think that is self-evident. Anything else would be contrary to nature. Is miscegenation, or amalgamation, desirable? Those who argue against 'racial segregation in public worship' should face this issue squarely. If miscegenation is desirable, they are justified; but if miscegenation is not desirable, they are wrong. A general mulatto population in the South is what abandonment of 'racial segregation in public worship' would result in.

Poteat also used the written word as a vehicle to express his views. In 1934 he published his second book, *Jesus and the Liberal Mind*. The next year he produced a lighter work, *Rev. John Doe. Thunder Over Sinai* appeared in 1936, and *The Social Manifesto of Jesus* in 1937. He was also writing poetry, and over the years many of his poems appeared in *The Saturday Review of Literature* and in *The Christian Century*.

Poteat also used the media nearer home. On April 3, 1935, the *Biblical Recorder* printed his response to "The discussion recently carried on in the columns of the *Biblical Recorder* regarding war and the mind of Christ." His contribution was prompted by the announcement of planned Naval maneuvers to be held in May near the Aleutian Islands, only two hours flying time from Japan. He stated:

> Whatever we may think of war as a philosophy of action, here is a demonstration of war as a state of mind. And this sort of thing needs the summary rebuke of all patriotic Christians. We should like to propose that the Christian conscience that surely detests all sabre-rattling whenever it is indulged, become vocal in protesting to our representatives in Washington, and to the President himself. We have a right, nay an obligation, to dispute the need and the wisdom of such a stupid, costly and highly provocative display of our Navy in waters so near to Japan.

In 1935 Poteat was chairman of a special commitee of the Southern Baptist Convention that recommended the establishment of a denominational "Bureau of Social Research." The Bureau was to have a paid staff and was to be outside the control of any denominational agency. Its responsibilities would be the study of such social changes as those cited at the beginning of the committee's report:

> We are living in a time of great social unrest. The amazing confusion of the public mind on liquor, the increasing laxity of moral imperatives, the recrudescence of mob-violence in lynchings and labor disputes; the changes in the ideals of the home and its increasing disappearance as a place of discipline and instruction; unemployment and the efforts to correct it by the government and business, impress us with the fact of the confusion and uncertainty of our social life. (Reported in BR, 5/20/35)

Because of "division of opinion," action on the report was delayed for a year. A convention-wide discussion ensued, with opposition to it dominating. The *Recorder* carried articles on both sides, but the editor opposed the proposal. The chairman of the denomination's Social Service Commission circulated an article in which he supported the recommendation. The Raleigh-Central Association of Baptist ministers endorsed it.

Aware of the tide of opinion against the proposal, the Committee revised it by recommending that the Board be incorporated into the

Social Service Commission. Even that compromise was inadequate, however. When the Convention met in May, 1936, the report was tabled. The editor of the *Recorder* observed that "The Convention did itself an injustice even as it did Mr. Poteat, in not allowing a discussion of the report. The tabling of the report was an error." (BR, 5/27/36) In that same editorial, however, he insisted that "The Convention did not vote against social service" but against "a proposition to establish an agency to investigate certain social problems."

The defeat of the proposal was a severe blow to Poteat. The idea had been his, and he had done most of the work of the committee in drawing up the recommendation and in trying to gain support for it. Its passage would have placed the Convention in the company of other major denominations, nearly all of which were giving official recognition to the social implications of the gospel. By defeating the proposal the Convention reaffirmed its allegiance to that individualistic emphasis which had served it well during the nineteenth century, but which could not adequately cope with the problems of the complex social order of the twentieth century.

The blow may have been softened by a significant recognition which came to Poteat from outside the denomination. Hard on the heels of the decisive vote at the Convention, Duke University awarded him an honorary doctorate. The editor of the *Biblical Recorder* observed, on June 24, 1936, that "In conferring upon him the D.D. degree the University honored itself, as well as Poteat and the denomination with which he affiliates."

Poteat continued to be a popular speaker in places beyond Pullen Memorial Church. In May, 1933, he preached the baccalaureate sermon for the Raleigh high schools. In June he spoke at the commencement exercises at Crozier Seminary. In July he delivered a dedicatory speech for the opening of a new girls' gymnasium in the Carolina Pines area. In October he spoke in support of prohibition at a public meeting in Chapel Hill. In February, 1934, he was Founders' Day speaker at Salem College. In February, 1935, he spoke to the Meredith students in their "Week of Deeper Religious Thinking." In July, 1935, he delivered the baccalaureate sermon at the University of Virginia. A news note in the *Biblical Recorder* for October 16, 1935, listed his October itinerary:

> Dr. E. McNeill Poteat, Jr., of Raleigh, has a very strenuous campaign immediately ahead of him. He spoke at the Tidewater Association, Norfolk, Va., on October 7. His subject was "Jesus and the Ethical Absolute." He is to preach a sermon for the Woman's College of the University of North Carolina in Greensboro, October 27. On October 28 he is to preach at the Union Theological Seminary in New York. He is to deliver four addresses at a Mission Conference and the Baptist State Convention of Massachusetts, at North Adams, Mass., on October 29-31.

On October 14, 1935, Poteat was one of three Baptist ministers attending the organizational meeting of the North Carolina State Council of Churches. A year later, at his suggestion, Pullen Memorial Church included in its budget for 1937 an item of $25 for that organization and a like amount for the Federal Council of Churches.

With all of these outside activities, however, Poteat worked closely with the deacons of Pullen Memorial Church. He was almost always present at their meetings and participated freely in their discussions. One topic with which the deacons dealt at almost every session, and to which Poteat frequently spoke, was that of finances. The church was still having a hard time financially, and the deacons struggled with setting the budget, raising the money, and approving expenditures. They debated repairs to the property, the cost of insurance, the fair share of the church in providing transportation for college students to the church, and the expenditure for music. They were disturbed that the church was not doing enough for missions, but were unable to find a way to do more. They debated the issue of canvassing the membership for pledges to the budget, and they discussed ways of reminding the people of their obligations to the church. At no time did the church seem in danger of not paying its bills, nor even of failing to make its promised contribution to denominational causes. Contributions totaled over $6,000 each year in 1933, 1934, and 1935. In 1936 they were $7,700, and in 1937 they were $8,400. Yet at all times there was an intense awareness of the necessity of spending the limited funds in the wisest way possible.

While the minutes of the deacons' meetings do not reflect any controversy on the subject, they do show that from time to time concern was expressed about the procedure for admitting new members to the church. At the meeting for February 8, 1933, for example,

> Mr. Bryan suggested that the doors of the church be opened regularly on Sunday mornings. Mr. Poteat stated that he would prefer opening the doors of the church once a month and that the service be made more impressive, but that until a plan could be worked out, the doors would be opened each Sunday.

Other deacons thought that the church was not sufficiently evangelistic. In the meeting on October 10, 1934, someone evidently raised the question of a revival, for one note in the minutes reads: "McMillan: 'Revival,' remarked that church is being revived." In the spring of 1936 the question of a revival came before the board again. On March 4 the deacons approved Poteat's plan to have a series of visiting speakers on the five nights before Easter. In addition, the minutes report, "The Board also expressed a wish that some form of evangelistic services be held soon after the close of schools." On May 6, 1936, "Motion made and carried that Mr. Poteat, Mr. Browne, Mr. Abell constitute a committee to make plans for an evangelistic meeting, which was suggested by the Board at the March meeting." On September 20 the deacons approved the committee's recommended date of "November 29-December 6 immediately following the National Preaching Mission." In addition, a new committee was appointed "to arrange for our participation in the special preaching mission and also in our follow-up program." On October 7 "Mr. Poteat reported for the committee on the evangelistic meeting that he had made contact with six men, all of whom had declined, and that others were being considered." On November 4 the committee reported on plans, without mentioning the name of the preacher, and "the Board authorized two meetings per day during the week of services." Although the next session of the deacons was held on December 9, three days after the closing date of the revival, the minutes do not refer to it.

In 1933 the church adopted a membership policy of major significance. At the meeting of the deacons on April 12, 1933, Dr. Caviness raised the issue of "our policy on baptism" and made a motion that "associate membership be permitted." No action was taken on that motion. In the church conference on April 26, however, on a motion by R. L. McMillan, the congregation voted that "Those who have not been baptized by immersion may be rece ved as associate members, having all the privileges of active member nip except to vote and hold office." An amendment which would have accepted such persons as full members was voted down.

The deacons frequently gave attention to matters having to do with the worship services. One of those matters was music. The minutes for November 5, 1931, report the resignation of the choir director and the appointment of a committee "to ask Mrs. Wallace to take charge of the music and direct the choir." Thereafter there were frequent references to the work of the music committee. A significant action was recorded in the minutes of the deacons' meeting on February 10, 1937:

> 1. Report of Music Committee—Committee expressed the idea that more elaborate music would be better, and that it had been reported to them that it was difficult to get outside help for special music. The committee reported its action in the matter, and asked that the Board ratify the action of the music committee. It developed in the discussion that the cost would be more than the am't in the budget, but several members expressed the opinion that the extra amount could be raised by outside contribution. The action was approved by the Board.

The question of evening services was frequently discussed in the deacons' meetings. Early in Poteat's ministry the evening services had been well attended and had been broadcast by the local radio station. When the broadcasts ceased is not known, and when attendance began to decline is not known. By mid-1933, however, Poteat was trying to find some way of dealing with a changing situation. At the regular meeting of the deacons on June 8, 1933, "The pastor brought up the question of the Sunday evening service with the suggestion that the young people's work be more closely aligned with the Sunday evening service." On February 7, 1934, "The matter of Sunday evening services when the pastor is away was discussed. It was decided that services will be held, and the deacons designated their intentions to come when the pastor is absent." Does that latter statement suggest that the deacons were not always present at the evening service? Or does it suggest that they tended to stay away when the pastor was not there? At any rate, the problem continued. At the meeting on September 7, 1936, Poteat sought and received approval for a plan "to enliven the evening service." That plan must not have succeeded, for the minutes of the deacons' meeting on April 7, 1937, report: "Mr. Poteat raised the question, What shall we do about the evening services? After much discussion, it was suggested that the services be continued through the school term and plans would be made regarding the continuance of the evening services in the fall."

During these years the church continued to hold weekly prayer services. One note in the minutes of the deacons' meetings suggests that there was strong sentiment to continue them, even though attendance apparently was quite limited: "Mr. Poteat stated that he had taken leave to call off the evening prayer service during the remainder of the summer." Upon motion, the Board authorized the pastor the [*sic*] announce the time of meeting of the next evening prayer service in the fall."

Poteat often secured the approval of the deacons for the use of the worship service for special events. On December 9, 1931, for example, they approved his extending an invitation to a Jewish Rabbi "to speak some Sunday evening after Jan. 1st." On April 6, 1932, at his request, they approved his inviting "the Shaw University Choir to occupy evening hour some Sunday." On June 14, 1937, they authorized him "to invite a coloured speaker to occupy the pulpit on June 27."

The minutes of the deacons' meetings contain some hints that Pullen people were not universally enthusiastic about Poteat's ministry. On January 6, 1932, for example, without any hint of an earlier discussion of the matter, a motion was passed "that we have communion service once each quarter instead of once each month." On February 8, 1933, a motion to encourage the deacons to give better support to the Sunday school was amended "to ask the members of the Board not to walk out on the pastor at the preaching service." One of the most provocative notes in the records is an action of the deacons on October 4, 1933. According to the minutes, "Mr. Poteat was asked to write the Britts a friendly letter in behalf of the Board of Deacons, expressing the friendly feeling of the Board for the family and best wishes for them in their new church home." On the next day Poteat wrote:

Dear Friends,

I was requested last night at the meeting of the Board of Deacons to write you a letter, expressing the regret of the Board that conditions were such as to make you feel it wise to move your membership elsewhere in the city. This was, however, no word of criticism. It was on the contrary, with a feeling that you had made the wise decision, in the light of the circumstances. Furthermore, the members of the Board wished it made a matter of record that they had appreciated both the services of Brother Britt as a Deacon, and the activities of Mrs. Britt and the girls in the life of the church while with us.

The hope, that you will find in your new church allegiance happiness and usefulness, was also expressed, and you were most warmly commended to the fellowship of the Tabernacle Church. It was a pleasure to have you a part of our organization, and you will be distinctly missed, both as a family, and as officers and helpers in our work.

With the cordial regards of the whole church family and the Board of Deacons in particular, I am,

Very sincerely yours,

Although the letter was written on behalf of the deacons, it does seem surprising that Poteat gave only the slightest hint that he personally shared the regret of the deacons in the Britt's departure.

As already noted, Poteat was constantly speaking to both religious and community groups all over the South and often outside the South. The minutes of the January, 1934, meeting of the deacons report that "The pastor asked to be permitted to accept several invitations to hold special services out of town during the Spring. This request was granted." Two years later, however, a definite limit was set upon the number of invitations Poteat was to be free to accept. The deacons passed a motion that the Pastor be allowed a total of eight Sundays away from his pulpit, including the vacation period. (3/4/36)

On the whole, the church members were aware that Poteat was a man of great ability and were supportive of his ministry not only within the local congregation but also to the wider community. It basked in the reflected glory of an outstanding preacher who had a national reputation for his scholarly insight and for his forthright public proclamation of the gospel. They came close to losing him in the spring of 1933, when he seriously considered a call from the Chapel Hill Baptist Church. It was known to the congregation that he had received that call, and in their May 3 meeting the deacons unanimously adopted the motion "that the Board expressly say to the pastor that it hopes he can see his way clear to remain at Pullen Memorial Church. Dr. Caviness suggested that the Board pledge its more loyal support of the pastor." On the following Sunday Poteat announced his decision to decline the call to Chapel Hill. In commenting on his decision the editor of the *Biblical Recorder* said:

> In the judgment of many people who are informed of the situation there is no man who could better serve the Chapel Hill Church than Mr. Poteat. But it is also true that he is just as much needed at Pullen Memorial where he has the opportunity to serve the students of State College, Meredith College, and other colleges of Raleigh. The people of Pullen Memorial Church and Raleigh are greatly pleased at his decision to remain in Raleigh.

Throughout Poteat's first term as pastor of Pullen Memorial Church the deacons were constantly giving attention to the Sunday school. Their attention, however, was focused not so much on the quality of work that was done but on the practical matters of providing adequate space. That was particularly true in the years 1929 through 1934. After 1934 there were fewer references to the matter, not because adequate space had been provided but because people simply accepted the limitations.

Figures reported to the Raleigh Baptist Association show that during these years enrollment in the Sunday school fluctuated a great deal. Enrollment had reached an all-time high of 659 in 1928. Between 1929 and 1937 it ranged between 635 and 502. The reason for the fluctuation cannot be determined, but it is reflected in frequent changes of leadership. During that nine-year period six different superintendents held office. There was a particularly sharp drop in 1937, the year that Poteat left Pullen, from 564 in 1936 to 502 in 1937. It might be noted that in that period the membership of the church also dropped, from 395 to 338.

The minutes of the deacons' meetings of the thirties are notably lacking in references to the work of the Women's Missionary Society. Pullen Memorial's Missionary Society had been organized in 1904, and thereafter had functioned effectively in missionary education and in fund-raising. Among its early leaders had been Mrs. Fred Senter, Mrs. R. D. Stephenson, Mrs. W. P. Baker, Mrs. R. L. McMillan, Mrs. G. H. Ferguson, and Mrs. Z. M. Caviness. During the depression years the church maintained its interest in missions, as budget discussions in the board of deacons show, and the activities of the W.M.U. played no small part in keeping that interest alive. In 1937, the year in which Poteat left Pullen, the church's total contribution to all mission causes was $1,642. Of that amount, the W.M.U., of which Mrs. Caviness was president, raised $551.

On Sunday, July 18, 1937, Poteat announced his resignation, to become effective on September 15. For some months, according to the *Biblical Recorder*, he had been considering a call from the Euclid

Avenue Baptist Church in Cleveland, Ohio. (BR, 7/28/37) After giving a brief summary of Poteat's career, the *Recorder* observed: "Dr. Poteat is one of the most brilliant men of the Baptist State Convention of North Carolina, and many friends are expressing regret that we are to lose him from the State." This statement preceded by only three weeks the editor's long and heated attack on Poteat's Ridgecrest statements on race.

Poteat preached his farewell sermon on Sunday, September 5, 1937. His text was John 12:32: "And I, if I be lifted up from the earth, will draw all men unto me." His plea was "that Christians steadfastly hold to Jesus as their one guiding 'polar star' against the dangers of world political movements which would crush individualism." He spoke of Communism, Facism, and Naziism as today's "terrors of the world," and of loyalty to Christ as the Christian's only defense against them.

In conference on Friday, September 3, 1937, Pullen Memorial Church adopted the following resolution:

> Whereas, Dr. E. McNeill Poteat has been pastor of Pullen Memorial Baptist Church for the past eight years; and
>
> Whereas, during Dr. Poteat's pastorate he and the members of his family have endeared themselves greatly to the members of our church and to the people of Raleigh generally; and
>
> Whereas, throughout Dr. Poteat's pastorate at this church he has consistently preached Christian messages of an extraordinarily high and challenging order, which have brought national recognition to him and to our church; and
>
> Whereas, Dr. Poteat has accepted a call to the Euclid Avenue Baptist Church, of Cleveland, Ohio:
>
> Now, therefore, be it resolved,
>
> First, That the members of Pullen Memorial Baptist Chruch hereby express their deep regret and feeling of keen personal loss at the resignation of their pastor, realizing how fortunate they have been in having the inspiration which comes from his personality, his teaching, and his leadership.
>
> Second, That the members of the Euclid Avenue Baptist Church, of Cleveland, Ohio, are congratulated for securing as their pastor one of the ablest preachers in the country today, a man of remarkable ability and versatility, at home in any group, community, or land: a pastor who, by his life and teachings, interprets a living Christ in terms of our needs today.
>
> Third, That a copy of these resolutions be presented to Dr. Poteat and a copy forwarded to Euclid Avenue Baptist Church, in Cleveland, Ohio, and a copy be forwarded to the denominational and the daily press.

After Poteat's departure the church was not long without a pastor. No official records name the members of the pulpit committee, but the committee lost little time. They were in almost immediate contact with Lee C. Sheppard, pastor in Blacksburg, Virginia. On October

12, 1937, the deacons approved a recommendation that Sheppard be invited "to meet with the Board of Deacons and leaders of our Church for consultation." That meeting was held, and on November 6, 1937, the "Committee for new pastor presented name of Mr. Lee Shepherd [*sic*] as the new pastor. Recommendation was accepted by the Board." On December 6 Mrs. Gordon Middleton "reported for the committee who went to Blacksburg to extend the Church's call to Mr. Sheppard." On December 8 the *Biblical Recorder* announced: "Rev. Lee C. Sheppard, of Blacksburg, Va., has accepted a call to Pullen Memorial Church, Raleigh, and expects to begin his pastorate the first of the year."

Sheppard was a native of Georgia and had a degree from a business college there. He served for three years as educational director of the First Baptist Church, Columbus, Georgia. Then he earned his B.A. from the University of Richmond, and during his student years was on the staff of the First Baptist Church. In 1933 he was granted the B.D. degree by Yale University Divinity School, and during his years at Yale he was associate pastor of the Union Memorial Church, Glenbrook, Connecticut. His first pastorate after graduation from Divinity School was the Blacksburg, Virginia, Baptist Church, where he served from 1933 until he came to Pullen.

Lee C. Sheppard
Minister 1937-1947

In calling Lee Sheppard, Pullen Memorial Baptist Church secured a man who would continue the tradition of prophetic preaching which had been firmly established by Ellis and Poteat. The Raleigh *News and Observer* was still reporting each Monday on sermons preached in local churches on the preceding day. Its favorite preachers were Newton Robison, pastor of Hillyer Memorial Christian Church, and Carl Voss, pastor of the United Church. Even Poteat did not make the paper as frequently as those two. Voss left Raleigh at about the same time as Poteat, and was replaced at the United Church, and in the favor of the *News and Observer*, by Allyn Robinson. Sheppard never became a favorite, for there were only occasional reports of his sermons. Those which were reported, however, were on timely topics and stressed the social responsibility of the church. In his Labor Day sermon in 1938, for example, he declared that not merely "the lazy panhandler," but also "the idle rich" needed to be put to work. Inherited wealth, he said, is no justification for idleness. Then, according to the *News and Observer*, he declared:

> The laboring man has certain definite rights and we might say that only the laboring man has any rights. Yes, slavery is over and man has the right to have a word as to what wages he will accept and under what conditions he will labor.
>
> We need to re-think the philosophy of our wage system. Do we pay what the market demands? If we say we pay a man what he is worth, how do we go about determining how much he is worth? In accordance with the value of what he produces? Who is to determine what the laboring man is to receive for his work? The employer alone? The laboring man alone? The Government? Why not all three? (N&O, 9/5/38)

Another example of this type of preaching was his sermon delivered on January 15, 1939, in which he called for the abolition of capital punishment in North Carolina. In supporting this position he stated:

> We cannot believe in capital punishment because we do believe in life. Dress it up how we may, punishment is closely allied with the idea of vengeance and in the practice of vengeance there is always a measure of sadistic perversion.
>
> Capital punishment as a method of dealing with criminals is nothing more or less than a hold-over from our barbarous past. . . .
>
> Fundamentally my objection to capital punishment grows out of my interpretation of the character and disposition of God. God has said Let there be life and life came surely for some purpose. When an individual or society takes a life, there is destroyed that which only God can create. (N&O, 1/16/39)

As pastor, Sheppard took an active interest in all phases of the life and work of Pullen Memorial Church. In the annual business meeting held in January, 1939, he presented a report on church activities of the first year of his pastorate. His statements were quite optimistic. Sunday school attendance had passed four hundred, marking "the largest attendance our Sunday School has had in some time." There had been regular monthly teachers' meetings "and a steady program of Bible study." He observed that the weaker departments were the Young People and the Adults. There were only two adult classes, and he expressed the belief that there should be five or six. There were Training Unions for Juniors, Intermediates, and Young People. The strength of these programs, Sheppard noted, was due primarily to the work of the assistant pastor, Laurence Fox. A well-attended Daily Vacation Bible School had been held during the summer, and plans were under way for one to be held in the summer of 1939 in cooperation with West Raleigh Presbyterian Church and Fairmont Methodist Church. He commended the continuing "full activity" of "the circles of the Woman's Misssionary Society," particularly for "keeping alive the spirit of missions" in the church.

In that same report Sheppard noted that during the year the church had received twenty new members by baptism and forty-eight by letter. He suggested that the church could realistically expect a net increase of a hundred members a year for several years. He reported also that the church's financial situation was good, and that the prospects for 1939 were even better. Pullen had raised $7,000 in 1938, and "In all probability we shall raise during this year about $10,000, for all purposes. Even though the church had no wealthy members, he said, its "capacity to give is not being strained."

Sheppard made a systematic effort to strengthen the organizational structure of the church. At the first meeting of the deacons after he became pastor he recommended that church conferences be held quarterly, and that recommendation was adopted. He encouraged the holding of "Fellowship meetings"; he encouraged the deacons in their plans for regular visitation of church members; and he encouraged the deacons to consider the establishment of a Junior Board of Deacons. He emphasized denominational relationships, and the minutes of the deacons' meetings suggest that they became more important to the church.

In 1939 a significant change in the organization of the Board of Deacons was made. On March 6, 1939, the board voted to recommend to the church the election as "life members to the Board of Deacons" persons who had served as many as three terms of four years each, who had reached the age of sixty-five, and who were recommended to the church by the board. That proposal was approved and Dr. Lineberry was the first person to be recommended for life membership. The next year Dr. Z. M. Caviness and Mr. T. E. Brown were made life deacons.

At the meeting on February 2, 1941, Sheppard asked the deacons to consider the adoption of a church covenant, and a committee was appointed to work on the matter. With the pastor as chairman, the committee worked for several months. On October 5, 1941, the deacons approved for recommendation to the church a covenant modeled after one in common use among Southern Baptists. In conference on October 22, 1941, the church formally adopted it. It read:

> Having been led, as we believe, by the Spirit of God, to receive the Lord Jesus Christ as our Savior, and on the profession of our faith, having been baptized in the name of the Father, and of the Son, and of the Holy Ghost, we do now, in the presence of God and this Assembly, most solemnly and joyfully enter into covenant with one another, as one body in Christ.

> We engage, therefore, by the aid of the Holy Spirit, to walk together in Christian love; to strive for the advancement of this Church, in knowledge, holiness and comfort; to promote its prosperity and spirituality; to sustain its worship, educational, training and missionary endeavors; cheerfully and regularly to bring in our tithes and offerings in support of the ministry, the expenses of the Church, the relief of the poor, and the spread of the Gospel through all nations.

> We also engage to maintain family and secret devotions; to educate our children; to pray and work for the salvation of our kindred and acquaintances; to walk circumspectly in the world; to be just in our dealings, faithful in our engagements, and exemplary in our deportment; and to be intelligently zealous in our efforts to advance the Kingdom of God.

> We further engage to watch over one another in brotherly love; to remember each other in prayer; to aid each other in sickness and distress; to cultivate Christian sympathy in feeling and courtesy in speech; to be slow to take offense, but always ready for reconciliation, and mindful of the rules of our Savior to secure it without delay.

> We moreover engage that when we remove from this place we will, as soon as possible, unite with some other church, where we can carry out the spirit of this covenant and the principles of God's Word.

To the copy of this covenant found in the church files there was appended a note: "A copy of this covenant to be provided each new member on his admission, and that it be read at stated intervals as a part of the regular church service."

Almost immediately after Sheppard's arrival, Pullen Memorial Church turned attention to the question of constructing the long-desired sanctuary. Although there had been a building fund for some time, it had never grown very large. In February, 1939, less than $500 was in the account. Sheppard had come to the church anticipating launching a building campaign. On March 7, 1938, he read to the deacons a letter from Mr. King, a church architect from Richmond, who had inspected the building. After commenting on this, he stated that he thought he would be prepared at the next meeting to recommend that the church pass a resolution looking toward the building of an auditorium as soon as possible.

The minutes note that "There was general discussion to the effect that we proceed with caution." At the next meeting the pastor "stated that at the next meeting of the church conference he would be prepared to make some specific recommendations to the church relative to the planning and building of a church auditorium when and if we are able to do so." Because we have no records of the church conferences we do not know when the proposal was presented to the congregation. December 5, 1938, however, the deacons approved sending a letter to M. A. Huggins, General Secretary of the Baptist State Convention, requesting help in the construction of the sanctuary. The basis on which they asked for that help was the Convention's interest in reaching the students at North Carolina State through Pullen Memorial Church. On July 3, 1939, Sheppard announced "that he attended the meeting of the committee of the State Mission Board, and that the committee committed itself to a recommendation to the Convention of $25,000 to be paid over a period of years, on condition that Pullen Memorial raise $50,000."

A fund-raising campaign was launched in early 1940, and the building committee began to discuss the kind of sanctuary to be erected. In 1941 a space for designating contributions to the building fund was provided on the card used in the annual every-member canvass. The committee was in constant touch with M. A. Huggins regarding the anticipated help from the Convention. At the meeting of the deacons on April 6, 1941,

> Mr. Baker reported in detail for the Building Committee. Dr. Caveness reported on a consultation with Mr. Huggins to the effect that Mr. Huggins would recommend to the State Board a series of payments on our building program consisting of 2500 in 1941, 5000 in 1942, 5000 in 1943, 5000 in 1944, and 6500 in 1945, and in addition that the interest on the deferred payments would be paid by the board also.

By May, 1941, plans were almost complete, and the church was prepared to proceed with construction early in 1942. The *Biblical Recorder* announced the plans on May 21, 1941:

> Pullen Memorial Church, Raleigh, Rev. Lee C. Sheppard, pastor, plans to begin construction within the next few months on its new auditorium. The entire building and remodeling project, according to a recent report, will cost $60,000, of which amount $25,000 will be paid by the State Mission Board. It is anticipated that $14,000 will be raised in the near future from members and friends of the church and the rest of the amount will be financed over a period of years. In addition to

$4,000 already in the church treasury, a number of church officers and others concerned in the building program have made cash pledges totaling $5,047, thus bringing the total cash fund now available to approximately $9,000. The auditorium as planned will accommodate around 700 people and will be built so that additions can be easily made when occasion demands. The Sunday school building will be remodeled to accommodate comfortably the seven departments, with adequate classrooms for 1,200. W. P. Baker is chairman of the building committee, and W. E. Jordan is chairman of the building finance committee.

Construction was to be long-delayed, however, because of the entrance of the United States into World War II.

Another matter to which the church gave attention shortly after Sheppard's arrival was the need for additional staffing for the church. A part-time secretary was employed in September, 1938. In the fall of 1939 Laurence Fox was employed as "part time assistant to the Pastor," to serve for the rest of the calendar year. In December the deacons agreed to receommend to the church that Fox be employed for a period of six months "subject to approval of the pastor." In January, 1940, however, that action was reconsidered, and the deacons decided to recommend that Mr. Fox be employed for only two months. Fox resigned immediately. After that there was no action on an assistant to the pastor until October 5, 1941, when the deacons recommended the employment of "Mr. Wilbur E. Campbell, State College student, to help with our young peoples' program."

Yet another matter given attention shortly after Sheppard's arrival was a retirement plan for the pastor. The Southern Baptist Convention was just instituting a retirement system for ministers of the denomination. On February 6, 1939, Sheppard discussed the plan with the deacons. The minutes note, "Mr. Canaday stated that he had studied the plan and was in favor of it. Mr. Wilson made a motion that a committee be appointed to make a detailed study of the plan and report back to the board. After being seconded, the motion carried." The plan was discussed in March and in April, and in May the board voted to recommend to the church that Pullen participate. In January, 1940, the church took the appropriate steps to enter the plan.

During the first four years of Sheppard's pastorate the church had an active music committee. It made frequent reports to the deacons and received instructions from them concerning such matters as the possible purchase of a Hammond organ, the purchase of new hymn books, the appropriate location of the choir, and so on. On Monday, March 18, 1940, the *News and Observer* reported on the Easter Cantata which the choir had presented on the previous day. After naming

Miss Helen Sharp, a member of the Meredith College music faculty, as director, it listed the members of the choir:

Eva Cotner, Frances Dixon, Lena Futrelle, Mrs. W. E. Jordan, Mrs. J. D. Paulson, Mary E. Parris, Rachel Senter and Mrs. T. W. Steed, sopranos; Florence Botick, Mrs. Carlyle Campbell, Mary Ann Canaday, Alma Carlton, Sarah Lovette, Mrs. George Norwood and Mrs. J. A. Rigney, altos; Jarvis Adams, J. P. Harrington, W. C. Orders, E. N. Peeler, and S. F. Teague, tenors; Dr. Carlyle Campbell, E. F. Canaday, L.E.M. Freeman, T. E. Gerber and M. A. Wilder, basses.

The deacons often discussed the Wednesday evening services. Those services continued to be poorly attended during Sheppard's pastorate, as they had been during the latter part of Poteat's tenure. Yet the deacons were reluctant to terminate them. At their first meeting after Sheppard became pastor there had been "general discussion pro and con on the advisability of Sunday evening and mid-week services." (1/3/38) On two separate motions the deacons had voted that both services "be resumed immediately." Presumably that was done. In September, however, the deacons decided "that the pastor and the chairman of the board of deacons should confer on the subject of the mid-week meeting." In July and August, 1940, they discussed the topic again, and again decided "to have a mid-week prayer service." Sheppard asked for suggestions as to "the desired method of conducting these meetings." He received some suggestions, but the problems of involvement were not resolved.

The church was much aware of its opportunity to minister to the college community. The students at Meredith were required to attend church services, and many attended Pullen. The church helped finance the bus transportation of Meredith students to the church. Many students from N.C. State also attended, some coming for the worship service only, but others being involved in the Sunday school program as well. In September, 1939, the church sent letters to all incoming freshmen at State and Meredith, inviting them to Pullen. In July, 1940, the deacons authorized the placing of an advertisement in the N.C. State Y.M.C.A. handbook. In February, 1941, they approved a small appropriation of $25 to help finance the work of the Baptist Student Union at State.

In his first year at Pullen Sheppard began holding classes with "Junior and Intermediate boys and girls" to discuss with them the meaning of Christianity and of church membership. From the first, those sessions were held just prior to Easter. In 1938 he also began the practice of holding special services the week before Easter. It was his judgment that the Easter period was a particularly appropriate time both to encourage young people to make their initial Christian commitment and to encourage other people to reaffirm the commitments which they had already made.

In his first year the success of Sheppard's program was demonstrated by statistics. Nineteen people were baptized and twenty-seven were received into the church by letter. Because of losses by death and transfer of membership, the net increase, however, was only five. Sunday school enrollment increased by twenty over the previous year. In subsequent years, however, the number of baptisms was not nearly so great: seven were baptized in 1939, none in 1940, and ten in 1941. Additions by letter increased, with thirty-one coming in 1939, twenty-eight in 1940, and thirty-eight in 1941. For some reason Sunday school enrollment dropped to just over four hundred. The church did not seem destined to grow as Sheppard had suggested that it might.

On December 7, 1941, the deacons held their regular meeting. According to the minutes, they received a report of the election of new deacons; they received a report on the every-member canvass; they elected their officers for the next year; and they appointed a committee to nominate church and Sunday school officers. Then "The closing prayer was led by Dr. Middleton." Only a few hours earlier the Japanese had bombed Pearl Harbor. If the deacons had heard the news of that attack they had as yet learned none of the details. They could not possibly have envisioned the future of Pullen Memorial Baptist Church in a world at war.

Chapter 6
An Ecumenical Church
In An Era of Hostility
(1942-1954)

While Cordell Hull sat in his office on Sunday morning, December 7, 1941, awaiting an answer from the Japanese envoys to his latest proposal to maintain peace, the Japanese planes were already near their target at Pearl Harbor. A crowd of nearly four thousand people sat in Raleigh's Memorial Auditorium and heard a 234-voice chorus sing Handel's *Messiah* while the battle raged. After listening to that magnificent message of hope, they went out to find their city in shock with the realization that the nation had been plunged into war.

Life for all Americans was drastically changed immediately. Already registered for the draft, men were conscripted by the millions. In addition, some two hundred thousand women joined the armed forces as nurses or in some auxiliary. The draftees were quickly—and often inadequately—trained and rushed off to the battlefield. They did not go into battle with the idealism that had characterized World War I, a war to make the world "safe for democracy." Rather they fought with the grim desire for survival, with the belief that the dirty job should be finished as quickly as possible so that life could return to normal. Nearly half a million lost their lives, and millions were wounded.

The people at home were at war too. To produce the goods necessary to the war effort, women entered the labor force by the millions. Not only did they take white-collar jobs, but also they went into the aircraft plants and the shipyards and the munitions factories. Families moved from rural areas and from small towns into industrial centers. More than twenty-seven million people moved during the war. Wherever they lived, they were asked to conserve power, to save tin cans, to collect scrap metal, to donate blood, to buy war bonds. They were required to live with the rationing of gasoline and sugar and coffee and shoes. The production of new cars ceased as the automobile plants were converted to the production of planes and tanks. Public transportation—planes and trains and buses—was crowded. Cigarettes were hard to come by, and liquor even more so. Some people were frozen in work considered essential to the war effort. In one way or another, almost everyone was involved in the war.

The war effort made a tremendous impact upon the race situation in the United States. In search of employment in the new war industries, blacks moved from the South into other sections of the country. They did not escape the problems of discrimination, however. They were housed in segregated sections of the cities and were served by segregated social institutions. Often their work applications were rejected even though jobs went unfilled. When they gave blood to the Red Cross their blood was kept separate from the blood of whites and was not to be used in transfusions for whites. It is not surprising, therefore, that black discontent grew during World War II. One significant expression of that discontent was a rising tide of support for the National Association for the Advancement of Colored People, with a five hundred percent increase in membership in the four years following Pearl Harbor. Another, radically different, expression of that discontent was the outbreak of race riots in Detroit, in Los Angeles, in Beaumont, and in Harlem.

Like the rest of the nation, Raleigh did not take long to gear up for the war effort. Beginning on Monday, December 8, there was a rush of men to enlist in all branches of the armed services. A Citizens' Defense Corps was formed with more than 4,500 citizens of Raleigh ultimately involved. Although Raleigh was not an industrial center, a few local small industries won government contracts. Hundreds of people had "Victory Gardens," and thousands gave blood and saved scrap metal and bought war bonds. They followed the war news by reading the papers and listening to the radio. They were anxious about the events of the war in Europe, in Africa, and in the Pacific. They were relieved when victory came in Europe in May, 1945, but they knew that the war was not over. They were stunned by the news of the atomic bombing of Hiroshima and Nagasaki in August, and there was unrestrained rejoicing when the announcement was made that Japan had surrendered on August 14.

Before the United States went to war Lee Sheppard had established himself as a preacher who dealt with vital issues and who brought the gospel to bear both upon current events and upon the daily life of the individual. During the war that kind of preaching was even more characteristic. In hardly a sermon, at least among those seventy or so reported in the *News and Observer*, did he fail to refer to current events. A number of his sermons focused on the war. On January 24, 1943, for example, he spoke on "God at Work in a World in Crisis." On March 14 his subject was "Establish our Christian Front." The next Sunday he spoke on the Christian "World-Wide Strategy." On June 13 he preached on "The Church Victorious." Twice he used the topic, "Christ or Chaos," using different texts and making different points each time. On September 16, 1945, a few weeks after the end of the war, he preached on the duty of the church to cultivate peace.

A recurring theme in Sheppard's sermons was the centrality of Christ. On February 14, 1943, his topic was "Whither Shall We Go," and his answer was Peter's affirmation to Jesus, "Thou hast the words of eternal life." On March 7, he dealt with the question, "Mad-Man or God-Man?" On September 12 he spoke of Christ as the only adequate answer to the universal human need to have an object of faith. He preached later on "The Mind of Christ," on "The Anger of Jesus," on "Christ as Guide," on "Life Through His Name."

Sheppard saw the church as the indispensable instrument of Christ's work in the world. On June 13, 1943, he preached on "The Church Victorious." On January 2, 1944, his topic was "This Church— Now and Future." On January 30 he dealt with the question, "Does the Church Make a Difference in the World?" On May 14 his subject was "The Church in Thy House." His view of the church was a broad one, and he often spoke in terms of Christian unity. In his communion sermon on "The Imperishable Church," preached on October 4, 1942, he said:

> All over the world today, Christian groups are gathering around communion tables. . . . In the main, the same words will be spoken, the same prayers intoned, the same songs sung. There will be a reaffirmation of faith in Jesus Christ as Savior and Lord and a rededication of disciples of the Nazarene to the unfinished task of spreading the gospel throughout the world. . . . This is an expression of the unity of all Christian believers.

On January 17, 1943, he made the point that "We are Christians first and Baptists second." On November 21, 1943, he preached on "The Communion of the Saints."

In a number of his sermons Sheppard expressed the concept of the oneness of the human race. On January 10, 1943, he made that point in his sermon on the "Dignity and Worth of Man." On July 11, 1943, he preached on "Danger Spots in the American Scene," and called for a recognition of our unity with all persons. On March 12, 1944, he declared that Christians must ignore all barriers between people. And in his sermon on "The Faith by which Democracy Lives," preached on October 1, 1944, he declared that "There is but one God and all men are brothers." In his conclusion he stated, "There is one God; one world; one mankind. We are all bound together in a living together."

Several generalizations might be made about Sheppard's preaching during this period. First, his sermons were almost always timely. His titles reflect his awareness of contemporary events. Furthermore, when he dealt with a more general topic he gave an up-to-date treatment to the subject. Second, he always used texts from the New Testament. He was thoroughly familiar with the Old Testament, and sometimes cited or quoted it in his sermons. For him, however, the Old Testament seems to have been only background for the New. And third, he sometimes took controversial positions. He spoke, for example, about a proper Christian attitude toward the enemy, about race divisions, about the improper identification of Christianity with democracy, about personal morality.

Sheppard continued his ministry beyond the local church. In 1942 he was one of two featured speakers at Religious Emphasis Week at Vanderbilt University. Also in 1942 he preached the baccalaureate sermons at two high schools and was a conference leader at Blue Ridge Assembly. He published two articles in the *Biblical Recorder*, one on the subject of faith and the other on religious literature. In 1943 he was a member of the North Carolina Baptist State Convention's Committee on Social Service and Civic Righteousness. And in 1944 he preached the baccalaureate sermon for the Raleigh high schools.

Sheppard's ecumenical interests were shared by the church. Each spring Pullen Memorial participated with the other churches in West Raleigh in an Easter sunrise service, held in the outdoor auditorium of the Raleigh Little Theater. With West Raleigh Presbyterian Church and Fairmont Methodist Church, Pullen conducted Vacation Bible Schools. During the summer months the congregation joined with the other West Raleigh churches in evening "union services." On May 6, 1945, Sheppard distributed to the deacons copies of the proposed constitution of the Raleigh Council of Churches, and the deacons voted to recommend to the church "that we become a member of this Council." Church minutes for 1945 are missing, but apparently the church voted to affiliate with the Council.

The denominational connection of Pullen Memorial Church was by no means neglected. The church was regularly represented at the

Assocational meetings and at the meetings of the Baptist State Convention. It contributed to the support of the missionary of the Raleigh Central Association. Some efforts were made to have the church represented also at the meetings of the Southern Baptist Convention, but that was not always possible.

One denominational concern of particular significance was a proposal to merge Meredith College with Wake Forest College. Early in 1944 Meredith had launched a campaign to raise $565,000 to erect new buildings and to increase the endowment. The campaign had gone well for several months. But in October, 1944, seven prominent ministers in the area proposed that Wake Forest College and Meredith College be merged into a single university to be located on the Wake Forest College campus. That proposal gained considerable support, and the possibility that it might be approved effectively halted Meredith's fund-raising campaign. The matter was of special concern to Pullen for two reasons. First, Pullen saw itself as having a special ministry to college students, and the proposed merger would remove a significant segment of the college population from Raleigh. Second, a number of Meredith administration and faculty were members at Pullen, including President Carlyle Campbell; Mary Yarbrough, head of the Department of Chemistry; L. E. M. Freeman, head of the Department of Religion; John Yarbrough, head of the Department of Biology; Dorothy Park, teacher of philosophy and psychology; Lillian Parker Wallace, head of the Department of History; and many others.

For the next month the proposal was debated state-wide. In anticipation that a decision would be made at the Convention which was to meet in Charlotte on November 14-16, Sheppard discussed with the deacons the importance of the church sending its quota of messengers. Like many other people, Pullen's messengers went to the Convention expecting a heated discussion. Instead, however, they heard a resolution "prepared by the proponents and opponents of the proposal" which called for the maintenance and strengthening of the two colleges as separate institutions. Two of the framers of the proposal for merger spoke in favor of the recommendation. When the question was called, the recommendation was passed unanimously. Sheppard reported at the next meeting of the deacons, on December 3, that "The Meredith question is probably settled now for a long time."

From time to time several other denominational activities were discussed by the deacons. Three times they talked about Pullen's financial responsibilities to the Cary Street Mission. Twice they discussed contributions for the new chapel at Wake Forest. In 1945 there was discussion in the Raleigh Association about the establishment of a new church in West Raleigh, and that topic naturally came before the deacons of Pullen Memorial. When that church was organized, on Sunday, August, 1945, at Forest Hills Baptist Church, some of the charter members came from Pullen.

During the war years the deacons gave a great deal of attention to business matters. Hardly a meeting went by without their making some decision about repair or improvements to the church property. They were constantly concerned about the financial situation and were seeking ways to encourage the church members to fulfill their responsibilities to the church. They debated and finally took action on the need for secretarial help for the church.

In spite of the wartime difficulties, the church determined early in 1942 to proceed with its plans to remodel the building which it had occupied in 1923. For some time many people had been making contributions to the building fund. Work was begun in the spring, and on April 5, the chairman of the Board of Deacons reported that "at the present rate of contributions approximately $10,000 will be collected for the Building Fund by the end of the year." The total cost of the project was expected to be about $15,000. The project was completed in the fall, and on September 12 an impressive service of dedication was held. The sanctuary had been enlarged to increase the seating capacity to 700. The floor had been carpeted, and new pews, a new communion table, and new offering plates had been provided. Four new Sunday school rooms had been added, bringing the total to 25.

On February 7, 1943, the board was alarmed by a report that the church might not receive the help which it had anticipated from the Baptist State Convention for constructing the sanctuary. The chairman appointed a committee to contact M. A. Huggins, General Secretary of the Convention, "to let him know that this church is definitely planning to continue with the original building plans and is expecting the State Mission Board to make its contributions as scheduled." On May 2, "Mr. Jordan reported on a visit to Mr. Huggins' office in regard to our building fund. The check which will be forthcoming in a few days will more than pay our remaining indebtedness. Our own collections in the future will be toward our future building program." With that problem resolved, the church continued to think in terms of building the sanctuary. At the October meeting of the deacons the pastor suggested "that the State Board will probably be more sympathetic to continuing the building fund payments if we ourselves raise $2000 to $2500. Several members were in favor of increasing pressure to obtain more funds for building."

A new problem associated with the contribution from the State Convention came up in January, 1944. The treasurer reported that $2750 was received from the State Mission Board instead of the $5000

Mr. Huggins had promised. "There was considerable discussion of the ways and means of obtaining the full amount, and it was finally moved and carried that a committee of Messers Baker, Caviness and Rackliffe be appointed to see Mr. Huggins in this connection." For months after that the minutes contain no reference to the contribution from the Convention, so there is no clue as to what success the committee had. The next reference, on January 7, 1945, is the last one during the war years. It still does not answer the question. The minutes simply state: "Correspondence with Mr. Huggins relative to the contribution of the conference to the building fund was presented. A copy is attached." But the copy is missing.

A major concern of the church was the acquisition of an organ. In 1942 the congregation toyed with the idea of purchasing a used electric organ but decided against it. On August 4, 1943, Sheppard brought to the attention of the deacons a different possibility:

> He mentioned the possibility of getting partial installment now and adding to the organ as funds and new building plans permit. Dr. Campbell suggested Mr. T. H. Shinn [sic] had done a good job of putting in an organ at Meredith which was made of parts from organs being replaced or torn down.

On his own, Sheppard wrote to T. H. Sheehan and in September he read the response in which Sheehan said that he could install a small organ for around $3,200. The deacons asked the music committee to communicate further with Sheehan. Negotiations proceeded, though some questioned the wisdom of starting an organ fund "in the light of a recent expression by Mr. Huggins that the present building fund was not for such purposes." (3/5/44) Sheppard observed that the organ fund was separate from the building fund, and that Huggins could impose no restrictions on funds which the church itself raised. The church went ahead with its plans, and on November 5, 1944, the deacons heard Sheehan's proposal. The minutes report:

> The pastor presented a letter from Mr. Shehan [sic] which stated that he had or could get materials to install an organ for $3500 plus $500 for Vox Humana pipes and a concert harp, and that he could probably begin installation around the first of the year if a contract were drawn reasonably soon. The pastor submitted a set of recommendations, a copy of which is attached, which briefly were that the church proceed to have the organ installed and solicit contributions to pay for it over and above the regular contributions. It was moved and carried that the board go on record as approving the idea of putting in the organ and that the matter be turned over to the business board for study and action.

The Business Board acted quickly, took the matter before the church at its next regular conference, and the church approved the plan. A campaign to raise the funds was launched immediately. By the end of March $2500 had been pledged and the order for the organ was placed with Mr. Sheehan. Then came disappointment: Sheehan canceled the contract because he could not get the materials. No other organ company could be found which could do anything until after the war was over. The church had to wait.

Meanwhile changes were taking place in the leadership of the choir. From October, 1940, until June, 1943, Miss Ethel Rowland was choir director. After she resigned, "Mrs. Steed and Mr. Peeler" were asked to work with the choir on an interim basis. At the end of the year, however, they asked to be relieved. On February 6, 1944, "The music committee reported that Miss Geraldine Cate had been obtained to direct the choir at the same salary as we had been paying the previous choir director." At the next meeting of the deacons "There was some discussion of the work of the choir, after which it was moved and carried that the Board express to Miss Cate and the choir their appreciation of the fine music being rendered." (3/5/44)

Miss Cate was a member of the faculty of St. Mary's College. A native of Columbia, South Carolina, she earned a Bachelor of Arts degree from the University of South Carolina and a Bachelor of Music degree from Westminster Choir College. After her studies at Westminster she went to Silliman University in the central Philippines, organized the music department there, and remained for five years. She came home on furlough in 1939, knowing that she probably would never return to her work in the Philippines. She spent a year at Columbia University earning a Master of Music degree, and joined the faculty of St. Mary's in 1940. Although the church was not aware of it at the time, in securing her services in 1944, it resolved the problem of leadership in its music program for many years to come. Under Miss Cate's leadership the Pullen choir soon became widely recognized for the high quality of its work and for its integration of music into the total worship service.

More than at any earlier period in the history of the church, the minutes of the deacons' meetings during the war years reflect a concern for matters other than the business affairs of the church. At the meeting on May 3, 1942, "There was a very fine, frank discussion of the spiritual welfare of the church and ways and means of improving the general spiritual morale." In the meeting of March 7, 1943,

> The chairman suggested that he and Dr. Mumford go over the church roll and get a list of the names of the members who have become indifferent and that these names be distributed among the board of deacons. It was felt that a real need exists for aggressive action by the board in building the spiritual morale of the church and that contacting indifferent members would be a good place to start.

At the next meeting

> Mr. Rackliffe again suggested that a list of new families moving into the community be made up as a working basis for increasing the church membership. It was suggested that the names be given the secretary at each meeting. The board members could then volunteer to visit them. The pastor suggested making these visits especially to invite all newcomers to the special services during the week preceding Easter.

Although no vote was taken, the suggestion was implemented, for at the next meeting "Reports on visiting were heard from various members. The Chairman read a list of other names to be visited." The August 4 minutes note that "The list of 'possibilities' was reviewed and four new names added." In December, 1943, just before the election of deacons, "Mr. Jordan suggested that the board of deacons ask the pastor to lead them in a study of a book on being a deacon by Mr. Burroughs." On April 7, 1944, "Mr. Sheppard discussed what it meant to be a deacon." On September 16, 1945, at the beginning of the meeting, "Mr. Sheppard stated that originally the duties of the deacons were (1) to look after the widows (2) to distribute bread and wine. In addition to these two duties deacons are now considered to be spiritual leaders in the Church and examples of Christian living."

The support of evening services was a continuing problem during the war years. As had long been the case, the deacons were unwilling to discontinue them; yet apparently few were willing to participate in them. On May 3, 1942, the deacons talked about "the spiritual welfare of the church and ways and means of improving the general spiritual morale." In that discussion Dr. Caviness and Mr. Sikes "urged greater support of the evening services." At the meeting of April 4, 1943, "Dr. Mumford entered a plea for more faithful support of the mid-week services by the deacons." On October 3:

> Dr. Caviness suggested that this group lend greater support to the evening and prayer services of the church. Dr. Mumford pointed out that this board has voted several times for the continuation of the prayer meetings, but very few have supported it by their presence. Mr. Baker recalled a recent visit to a country church in eastern North Carolina which had 60 odd people at their prayer services even though no pastor was available. Several other comments were made along this line and many expressed a desire to see the prayer service reinstated.

The word "reinstated" suggests that they had been discontinued, if not by deliberate decision then by default. Were they reinstated? Was there any greater interest after that discussion? The next hint is found in the minutes for September 2, 1945, two years later, when the pastor included in his report on church activities the statement that "Greater emphasis will be placed on evening services."

The war did not prevent the church from continuing its efforts to minister to college students. Each fall it contacted incoming students at State and at Meredith, and those contacts met with some success. On June 4, 1944, the deacons appointed a committee "to look into the possibilities of getting additional help in handling student and Sunday School work." That committee acted quickly and recommended that "a student worker be employed from the Meredith College student body" for the 1944-45 school year. The recommendation was approved, and the pastor and the chairman of the Business Board were given the power to act. Miss Doris Gene Bowman was employed and began her work in September. The next year Miss Elizabeth Murray became church secretary and student worker.

In 1942 the deacons gave a great deal of attention to the organizational structure of the church. The minutes for January 4 report the suggestion for the appointment of two new committees, a coordinating committee "to act as a laison [sic] group between the board of deacons and the various branches of the church" and a community service committee to be responsible "for whatever community services that may be required of the church as a community organization." On February 1 Mr. Baker volunteered to call a meeting of the church committee chairmen at which they might "outline and coordinate the activities and duties of their respective groups." At the next session of the deacons he reported that the meeting had been held and suggested that "it might prove very advantageous for the chairmen of the various committees to hold more or less regular meetings and that the chairmen be called on periodically for a report to the executive council."

The organizational concern came up also in connection with the church financial structure. On May 3, 1942, Dr. Caviness proposed the establishment of a committee that would have authority to receive and disburse funds. A committee was appointed to consider the matter, and on June 7 it presented a proposed organizational structure. On July 5 the deacons voted to approve the plan and to recommend to the church that it be adopted. The matter was presented to the church at its regular conference on October 1. While the minutes of that conference have been lost, it is apparent from passing references in later minutes that the recommendation was approved. The most conclusive reference is found in the minutes for January 7, 1945:

> Mr. Rackliffe, as chairman of the Business Board, presented an outline of the organization of the Church as approved in 1942. The Board of Deacons suggested that the outline be reconsidered in relation to recent changes. The suggestion by the business board to retain the members of the service board and the business board for a two year term was to be thought over.

A question was raised in one of the meetings of the deacons about how long an individual should serve on the board. On December 20, 1942, Dr. Caviness asked that "some action be taken to devise a system of retaining deacons on the board so their advice and talents will not be temporarily inaccessible to the church." A committee was appointed, with Caviness as chairman, to consider the question and report to the board "as soon as possible." Nearly a year later, on November 7, 1943, the committee reported:

> Mr. Wilson reported for the committee which was appointed to review the present system of requiring deacons to be elected for a 4-year term, after which they must become inactive for one year before being eligible for reelection. The report recommended that every deacon duly ordained by the church be kept in active service unless some just reason arises for discontinuing his services. A copy of the full report is attached. Mr. Wilson moved the adoption of the report and it was seconded. Dr. Caviness defended the report on the following grounds: (1) It is the scriptural method, (2) There has been or could be underhand methods of getting men elected to the board under the present system, (3) Those duly ordained deacons who are not re-elected are considered embarrassed, (4) This could be the reason for this church not having grown in the past 15 years. After further discussion the motion carried.

A committee was then appointed to draw up rules for the election of deacons, to be used if the church approved the recommendation. What happened to the recommendation? There are no church minutes for the period. The minutes of the deacons' meeting on February 6, 1944, speak of a question as to "the interpretation of the rules for eligibility to the board as a life deacon." A committee asked to deal with the matter reported on April 7 with the recommendation "that the rule be construed to mean that a man must have served 12 years as a deacon in this church." The recommendation was approved. Then, at that same meeting,

> There ensued considerable discussion as to the desirablity of retaining offices of life deacon and the rules of eligibility for such an office. It was moved and seconded that the board recommend to the church that it rescind rules of eligibility for the office of life deacon. A substitute motion was offered and carried that the board recommend to the church that the present rules be rescinded and that the board appoint a committee to offer a substitute for the present rule.

Although the committee was appointed, no later minutes refer to any report from it.

During the war years Pullen Memorial Church was trying to maintain a normal church life for its people. The pastor's sermons were full of references to the way things were going in the world. While we have no information about what went on in the Sunday school and in the organizations of the church, it is highly unlikely that current events were ignored. The most complete records of church activities during that period are the minutes of the deacons' meetings. Those minutes occasionally refer to the war effort, to Pullen members who were in the armed services, and to limitations under which the church had to labor because of the conflict. The deacons seem to have felt that the church should carry on as best it could until things returned to normal. That attitude is well reflected in the concluding statement in the minutes for March 4, 1945: "Mr. Sheppard made some remarks emphasizing the need for building on a solid rock particularly in preparation for the return of the members of the armed forces."

The end of the war came in September, 1945. Few people had the insight of General Douglas MacArthur into the implications of what was called "the ultimate weapon." From the *Missouri*, where the peace treaty with Japan was signed, he broadcast to the American people:

> A new era is upon us. . . . Men since the beginning of time have sought peace. . . . Military alliances, balances of power, leagues of nations, all in turn have failed, leaving the only path to be by the way of the crucible of war. The utter destructiveness of war now blots out this alternative. We have had our last chance. If we do not devise some greater and more equitable system, Armageddon will be at our door.

The United Nations was organized in 1945, and it is impossible to assess fairly its effectiveness in promoting peace. In spite of its efforts, however, in the first ten years of its existence old national hostilities were revived and new ones came into being. Germany was divided and occupied by the Four Powers. The West busied itself with War Crimes trials, with the reconstruction of war-torn areas, and with defense pacts directed at Soviet expansionism. The United States implemented the Marshall Plan for European recovery, spent billions on foreign aid and other billions on "Point Four" economic assistance to undeveloped nations. The Soviet Union consolidated its control of Eastern Europe. The Reds in China proclaimed the People's Republic, Indonesia became independent, Vietnam was partioned, and there were continuing disputes between India, Pakistan, and Red China. The Arab League was formed, Israel became an independent nation, African countries were torn by terrorist activities, and Greece was disrupted by a civil war.

For three years, 1950-1953, the United States was involved in the fierce war in Korea. At the close of World War II Korea had been partitioned at the 38th Parallel. On June 25, 1950, the forces of the People's Democratic Republic of Korea (North Korea) crossed the line to attack the Republic of Korea (South Korea). The United Nations committed itself to the defense of South Korea, and although eighteen countries sent troops to the area, the United States carried the main burden of that commitment. In the battle that raged back and forth across the 38th Parallel some two million men were killed or wounded. The nation had been ill-prepared for involvement in the war, and at the outset most Americans had approved of our intervention. Everyone expected it to end earlier than it did, however, and Eisenhower's promise to bring it to "an early and honorable end" was a major element in his campaign for the presidency. When the cease-fire agreement was signed, on July 27, 1953, the boundary was drawn at almost exactly the same place where it had been at the beginning of the conflict.

In the United States the struggle for civil rights was taking shape. In December, 1946, President Truman appointed a Committee on Civil Rights to study the situation and to make recommendations. Its report, issued ten months later, urged a federal anti-lynching law, new laws against police brutality, equal opportunity to vote, equal educational opportunity, and federal action to end segregation. It further recommended the establishment of a permanent federal commission on civil rights. Truman began immediately to try to implement some of the recommendations. He persuaded the Democratic National Convention to adopt such a strong civil rights plank in its 1948 platform that some southern Democratic leaders bolted and formed the States Rights Party. Between 1946 and 1948 the civil rights provisions governing federal and military employment were strengthened. In 1948 the Supreme Court ruled against racially restrictive covenants in housing. The National Association for the Advancement of Colored People was challenging various kinds of discriminatory practices throughout the country and was winning many of its court cases. Then, on May 17, 1954, the Supreme Court handed down its momentous decision that "separate but equal" provisions for blacks in the public schools were unconstitutional.

In the late '40's and early '50's the United States was victimized by a Communist scare that affected almost every area of life. It was touched off by the disclosures made by former Communists Elizabeth Bentley, Louis Budenz, and Whittaker Chambers. They named as Communist spies, among others, Alger Hiss, a former governmental official; and Julius and Ethel Rosenberg. Ultimately those three were convicted on a variety of charges and sentenced to prison terms. In 1950 Senator Joseph R. McCarthy began his climb to power as chairman of various Senate investigating committees. He first attracted general attention by accusing the State Department of harboring Communists. After that, until 1954, he was constantly in the news with his accusations of other people, many of them in government. A growing number of people came to consider him irresponsible and dangerous as more and more people were subjected to arbitrary investigation and untold numbers were victimized by unfounded rumors.

In the rapidly expanding "Communist hunt," prominent church-men, educators, movie stars, scientists, civil rights activists, and others were brought under suspicion. In some states, including North Carolina, the legislatures passed "speaker ban laws" which prohibited Communists from speaking in state-supported institutions. Suspicion and fear raged across the nation. In 1954, however, the Army-McCarthy hearings suddenly brought an end to McCarthy's effectiveness and prepared the way for a more realistic understanding of the Communist presence in this country. That change did not come, however, before a great deal of damage was done both to many individuals and to the civil liberties of American citizens.

In the decade following the end of World War II the United States experienced a significant religious revival. Church membership grew steadily, rising from about fifty percent of the population in 1940 to approximately two-thirds in 1955. On a typical Sunday in 1955 approximately one-half of the nation's people attended some religious service. All major denominations shared in the growth; all engaged in programs of constructing new buildings; all overhauled their religious education and youth programs; all took a new look at their worship services; and all found an increasing number of people seeking seminary training.

The best-known person associated with this revival of religion was William F. (Billy) Graham. Graham's early work in the "Youth for Christ Crusade" launched his evangelistic career. In 1949 he conducted a large-scale revival in Los Angeles, the success of which propelled him into full-time evangelism. He conducted campaigns in the United States, England, Scotland, Continental Europe, the Middle East, the Far East, and Africa. In 1950 he started a radio program, "The Hour of Decision," and soon after that was making use of both television and the movies. He built a large and efficient organization and was soon counting "decisions for Christ" by the thousands. Although he was a Baptist, his campaigns were never denominational. He preached a traditional evangelical message and always tried to secure broad church support in every city in which he preached. He always had careful plans made by an interdenominational group of churches before he went into a city; he trained people to serve as counselors at the meetings; and he tried to get the people who made decisions to establish contact with local churches.

Another less-heralded facet of the renewal of interest in religion was a search by many people for inner peace and serenity. That search was expressed, and perhaps aided, by a religious literature which drew upon the insights of popular psychology. In 1946 Rabbi Joshua Loth Liebman published his widely read *Peace of Mind*. Two years later Norman Vincent Peale, minister of the Marble Collegiate Church in

New York, published *A Guide to Confident Living*. His later book, *The Power of Positive Thinking*, published in 1952, became a long-time best seller. On the Catholic side, Fulton J. Sheen published in 1949 his popular *Peace of Soul*. Both Sheen and Peale became well-known television personalities by teaching popular psychology with religious overtones.

Roman Catholicism shared in the benefits of the general religious revival, and between 1940 and 1960 its membership doubled. Some growth came from continuing immigration and some from an increasing birth rate, but some also came from the winning of converts. There was also an internal stirring as the Church became more open to new trends in biblical scholarship, in theological discussion, and in liturgical developments.

It would not be correct to say that the Roman Catholic Church and the Protestant churches were antagonistic toward each other. It would be correct to observe, however, that certain tensions persisted and that they became apparent at a number of points. When President Roosevelt had named a "personal representative" to the Vatican many Protestants had been disturbed. When President Truman proposed to name an ambassador to the Vatican overt opposition emerged, particularly in the founding of an organization named "Protestants and Other Americans United for the Separation of Church and State." That organization, of which McNeill Poteat was one of the leaders, concerned itself not only with the issue of diplomatic relationships with the Vatican but also with the use of tax money for parochial schools.

A major event in twentieth-century Christianity was the organization of the World Council of Churches at a conference held in Amsterdam in 1948. The basis for membership in that group was the acceptance of "our Lord Jesus Christ as God and Saviour." Twenty-eight American denominations, including the Northern (later American) Baptist Convention, affiliated with the Council. Southern Baptists, however, did not join.

Two years after the organization of the World Council, the National Council of the Churches of Christ was formed. Some thirty American denominations, which had been cooperating through the Federal Council of Churches and through several other missionary, educational, and social service causes organizations, created this new comprehensive Council. Included in the group of participating denominations were the main line white Protestant denominations, the five major black churches, and four churches of the Eastern Orthodox background. Three Baptist denominations were in the group, including the Northern Baptists. Again the Southern Baptist Convention did not participate.

Post-war Raleigh was not significantly different from other parts of the country. There was a rapid growth in population and there was a resurgence of building. In 1940 the city had just under forty-seven thousand people; in 1950 the population topped sixty-five thousand. Some growth came as the boundaries of the city were expanded, but most came when people from rural areas moved to the city. Automobiles again became available, and like the rest of the nation the people of Raleigh loved their cars. There was, consequently, an immediate need for road and street construction. A belt line to speed traffic around the city was proposed in 1946. Raleigh began to experience urban sprawl as industrial centers and housing developmetns and apartment complexes were constructed. State government expanded, bringing more people to the city and requiring more buildings. City government expanded also, bringing still more new buildings and more people. Newspapers thrived and radio stations prospered. The churches grew and renewed their plans for building new facilities.

Pullen Memorial Baptist Church, as other churches, renewed her efforts to implement delayed projects. As the financial situation of the church improved, the deacons began to think about reviving the plan to construct the new sanctuary. They first discussed that matter in 1946. In the spring of 1947 they considered it again, but decided that it would be best to wait. The need for an organ came up again, and the deacons frequently discussed the possibility of acquiring one. Authorized by the deacons to investigate, the music committee reported on October 5, 1947, "that we should be able to obtain an organ this month." Again, however, the deacons decided to delay action.

For a brief time after the war the church had an assistant to the pastor. At their meetings the deacons spoke appreciatively of the work of Miss Elizabeth Murray, who held that position. She had begun her work, which included both educational and secretarial responsibilities, in 1945. In the spring of 1948 she requested a leave of absence through August, and her request was granted. At the first of August, however, she presented her resignation. After that the church was to have no other assistant to the pastor until 1954.

Late in 1948 Mrs. Betsy Wooden was employed as part-time secretary. Mrs. Wooden had grown up in Pullen Church, the daughter of Fred and Bessie Ball Senter. She had graduated from Hugh Morson High School, had attended Meredith College, and had secured secretarial training at Hardbarger's Business School. Before coming to Pullen she had worked for a time with the state legislature, and for a time with the State Department of Public Instruction. Her husband had been killed in the invasion of Normandy in June, 1944, leaving her with two small children. Her employment at Pullen was initially part-time, but soon became full-time, and she was to remain in that position until her retirement in 1980.

To help finance its student ministry, the church received assistance from the Baptist State Convention, though there was constant uncertainty about how long that would last. On April 14, 1946, the deacons appointed a committee to "inquire of Mr. Huggins when the $1200 on the secretary's salary will be paid." At their next meeting, they heard that there was "no action from Mr. Huggins as yet." In early October, however, Huggins wrote the pastor:

> Following our conversation, I have looked at our records and I find that our committee voted sometime ago to provide $500 to help Pullen Church in keeping Miss Murray this year, it being understood that this was done to help until such time as a Student Secretary for the City of Raleigh should begin work. Check in that amount is enclosed herewith, being made to your treasurer, Roy Medlin. It appears this will be all we can do this calendar year. As for next year, contact me along toward the end of the year in order that we may have this in mind in making up the budget. It may be that the Board will feel that we can help some particularly in view of the fact that you are taking care of so many of the students from the State School for the Blind in addition to the students from State College.

In the fall of 1946 the deacons considered the question of recommending that women be elected to the Board of Deacons. No woman had served on that board since those first four who were elected in 1927. Informal discussion must have taken place prior to the meeting of August 4, for at that time, "After considerable discussion it was decided to obtain an expression from the W.M.U. as to the placing of women on the Board of Deacons." The question was taken to the circle meetings, and the records show reports from five circles. Four approved, though in one of them the judgment was not unanimous. The other reported that it did not matter whether deacons were male or female, "just so they were qualified." At a called meeting of the deacons, then, held on August 11, the deacons made a surprising decision. In spite of the fact that they had taken the initiative in the discussion, and in spite of the fact that the responses of the women were overwhelmingly favorable, they decided not to take a recommendation to the church. The minutes report: "Motion defeated that a recommendation go to the Church that the same number of deacons be elected and either men or women be elected. Motion passed that we drop the matter until the women request election on the Board."

In December, 1945, Lee Sheppard was involved in a serious controversy. Throughout his ministry at Pullen he had been quite forthright in his statements on the race issue, and was clearly more progressive than some, though not all, of the members of Pullen Memorial Church. Apparently there had been no serious criticism of him for any position he had taken. On Monday, December 7, 1945, the Raleigh *Times* reported and editorialized upon a statement that

Sheppard had made in an address to the Progressive Voters League at Shaw University. In that article he was referred to as the "president of the Committee for North Carolina of the Southern Conference of Human Welfare." The article attacked James Dombrowski, executive secretary of the Southern Conference of Human Welfare, as a "consort of Communist bigshots and a man whose political jingoism had brought him under surveillance of the Dies Committee on Un-American Activities." It also claimed "that the Human Welfare Conference, wittingly or unwittingly, is a political arm of the Communist party; that through Dombrowski and persons of his ilk is a means of agitating in favor of the Fair Employment Practices Committee; that it provokes ill will between the races and foments discontent—at least in the South." Most of the comments on Sheppard came near the end of the editorial:

> In his speech, the Rev. Sheppard recalls the story of the Negro who was asked what he considered a fitting punishment for Adolph Hitler. The Negro, according to the pastor, replied, "Just change his skin to black and make him live in the South—that will be punishment enough."
>
> This story is an insult to the Negro race. For a man of the cloth to give it circulation is deplorable. Does the Rev. Sheppard expect to contribute to a sensible solution to the race problem by publicly voicing this libel upon every white Southerner?
>
> Incitements such as this can set at naught the progress being made toward a solution of the race question. Certainly the recounting of the story was ill-advised, for it presents the sorry spectacle of a minister with one foot in the pulpit and the other upon the soapbox, exhorting not to Christian reasoning but bracketing the Southern Negro with Adolph Hitler.

Although no further statements appeared in the newspaper, the matter was widely discussed in the community and among members of Pullen Memorial Church. On Wednesday, December 19, 1945, Sheppard addressed the following letter to the deacons:

> In view of certain recent news articles and editorials appearing in *The Raleigh Times* concerning the Southern Conference of Human Welfare, the North Carolina Committee thereof, and, directly and indirectly myself, I should like the opportunity of relating to the Board of Deacons, and to other interested members of the Church, the information I have concerning these organizations, and my connection thereto.
>
> After conference with the chairman, A. J. Rigney, I am calling a special meeting of the Board at the Church, Friday evening, December 21, 7:30 o'clock. Please feel free to bring with you any other members of the Church who would like to come.

The discussion in the meeting was free and sometimes heated. Sheppard defended both the Southern Conference and his own statements. Some of the deacons were in strong agreement with the *Times*; others fully supported Sheppard and his right to speak. At least two deacons recommended that no issue be forced, with the expectation that the matter would soon be forgotten. No motion was made in that meeting, and no action taken; Sheppard had called the meeting to invite discussion and to present his position, and that objective had been achieved.

At the next regular meeting of the Board of Deacons on January 6, 1946, however, most of the discussion dealt again with Sheppard's association with the Conference and his statement at Shaw. The matter had not died down, but had been discussed both by church members and by the community at large. When the issue came up in the deacon's meeting, Sheppard said, according to the minutes:

> Nothing further to say that hasn't already been said and a mountain has been made out of nothing. He said he wished the members would stand behind him as the folks out in town have done. Anything he can do to help and encourage the negro people he will do. He is a child of God and a member of the human race.

One deacon expressed a judgment shared by several: "The matter should be settled or it will hurt the church." Some thought that the deacons should settle it among themselves; others thought it should be taken to the church. At one point Sheppard "Stated he would present his resignation anytime 5 members of the board decide it would be best and present their reasons. He wants it clarified here or will bring it to the church." Thereupon another deacon said that "He did not believe the problem should be brought before the church. Thought the pastor should apologize for the statement. Sheppard in the committee work is looked on as the pastor of Pullen Memorial Church and may be related to communism." After further discussion Sheppard stated: "I'm not going to resign although the board has a right to fire. I have an obligation to stay with this church and preach the gospel that all men are of one blood." The final statement of one deacon sounds a bit folksy: "Folks talk too much. Nobody is as much worried about this as we are. Trouble with the church is lack of leadership in the board of deacons."

The matter did not come before the deacons again. At the church conference on January 9, 1946, the "Annual Report of Chairman of Board of Deacons" contained no direct reference to the problem. The minutes for the rest of the time that Sheppard was pastor reflect a good working relationship between the pastor and the deacons. Furthermore, Sheppard does not seem to have felt that his freedom was in any way restricted by the controversy. On Sunday night, December 1, 1946, for example, he reported to the congregation on the meeting of the Baptist State Convention, focusing on the Convention's action "in regard to racial segregation in Baptist churches." On May 18, 1947, he

128

reported on the meeting of the Southern Baptist Convention and called attention to the statement which that Convention had adopted on race relations. The church clearly did not intend to impose any restrictions upon its minister.

Sheppard's preaching during those post-war years, therefore, was a continuation of the same type that had been characteristic of the war years. Between September, 1945, and December, 1946, the *News and Observer* summarized forty-one of Sheppard's sermons. All were based on New Testament texts, and most on texts from the Gospels. He stressed the importance of the church, the necessity of the individual following Christ, and the necessity of the believer working through the church for the cause of world peace. He was concerned with the need for reconstructing the war-torn world, for working for peace between people, for setting a proper sense of values. He believed that evil in the world would be overcome by the power of God working through people who responded to the leadership of Christ.

Near the end of 1947 Lee Sheppard resigned from Pullen to accept a call to the First Baptist Church of Columbia, Missouri. Exactly when he presented his resignation to the church we do not know, but he ended his pastorate on October 31. On November 12 the *Biblical Recorder* published the statement of appreciation which had been drawn up by the deacons and adopted by the church:

> Pullen Memorial Baptist Church records with keen regret the resignation of its beloved pastor, the Reverend Lee C. Sheppard, who has felt called to accept the pastorate of the First Baptist Church in Columbia, Missouri. We are grateful, however, that for almost ten years he has lived and served among us. Through the coming years we shall recall our delightful fellowship with him, the vitality of his Christian experience as reflected in the pulpit and in the discharge of his civic responsibilities, and his effective leadership in the continually expanding program of our church.
>
> Mr. Sheppard, his gracious and capable wife, and children will have our abiding devotion. We pray God's richest blessings may attend them and all of their interests in their new field of service.

At the recommendation of the deacons, the church approved a pastoral search committee comprised of three members from the W.M.S., three members from the Sunday School, the church Pulpit Committee of three members, and three persons selected from the board of deacons. Dr. Z. M. Caviness was chosen chairman, and the committee began work immediately. On Sunday, August 1, 1948, upon the unanimous recommendation of the committee, the church voted to invite Dr. E. McNeill Poteat to return as pastor.

Poteat had ended his first pastorate at Pullen Memorial Baptist Church in September, 1937. From that time until the end of 1943 he had been pastor of the Euclid Avenue Baptist Church in Cleveland,

Ohio. In February, 1944, he had assumed the presidency of Colgate-Rochester Divinity School in Rochester, New York. He did not find administrative responsibilities entirely to his liking. Furthermore, his health suffered seriously from the pressures of that situation. The *Biblical Recorder* had reported on July 21, 1948:

> Dr. Edwin McNeill Poteat, president of the Colgate-Rochester Divinity School since February, 1944, has presented his resignation to the Executive Committee of the Board of Trustees of the school, to take effect not later than September 30 of this year. In his letter of resignation Dr. Poteat stated that his recent serious illness made it imperative that he give up administrative responsibilities in the interest of complete physical recovery. The Executive Committee has acceded to his request and has appointed a committee to secure a successor to Dr. Poteat. Dr. Poteat's many friends in this section of the country are much interested in his welfare and hope that he will make a complete recovery rapidly.

During the years at Euclid Avenue and at Colgate-Rochester, Poteat had continued to write and had published six books: *Centurion*, a narrative poem, in 1939; *These Shared His Passion* in 1940; *These Shared His Cross* in 1941; *Four Freedoms and God* in 1943; *Over the Sea, the Sky*, a collection of poetry, in 1945; and *Last Reprieve?* in 1946. *The Christian Century* had continued to publish his poetry. For that same journal he had written in 1939 an article entitled "Searching for Greater Loyalties," the sixth in a series by eminent theologians on "How My Mind Has Changed in This Decade." (*Christian Century*, February 22, 1939) And in 1943 he had published in that journal an article entitled "Logic or Life?" and subtitled "A Baptist View of Church Federal Union." (*Christian Century*, April 28, 1943).

Poteat was one of a small group of Protestant churchmen who, on January 4, 1948, organized "Protestants and Other Americans United for the Separation of Church and State." The precipitating factor was President Harry Truman's proposal to appoint an ambassador to the Vatican. They were also concerned about the use of tax funds to provide transportation for pupils to parochial schools. They stated in their "manifesto" that they had no controversy with the Roman Catholic Church, but that they would oppose any move to use government funds in direct or indirect support of the activities of any religious group. Along with Poteat, the founders were Methodist Bishop G. Bromley Oxnam; Louie D. Newton, President of the Southern Baptist Convention; John A. Mackay, President of Princeton Theological Seminary; and Charles Clayton Morrison, former editor of the *Christian Century*. (N&O, 1/12/48)

After he left Pullen in 1937, Poteat maintained his connections in the area and was often back for a variety of engagements. With Lee Sheppard presiding, he preached at the West Raleigh vesper services

E. McNeill Poteat, Jr.
Minister 1948-1955

on July 11, 1938. An excerpt from one of his sermons was published in the *Biblical Recorder* for December 6, 1939. He was at Pullen again on January 14, 1940. In March he was in Raleigh to address the North Carolina Education Association. In June, 1941, he preached to the graduates of Woman's College in Greensboro. In January, 1942, he spoke at the Raleigh United Church's annual Institute of Religion, and on the occasion of that visit he preached at Pullen. In December, 1942, he preached at Duke Chapel and spoke at the evening service at Pullen on the same day. In June, 1943, he preached the baccalaureate sermon at North Carolina State. After he became president at Colgate-Rochester his visits to Raleigh were less frequent, but they did not cease altogether. It must have taken a great deal of grace on Lee Sheppard's part to welcome so frequently to Pullen the former pastor who was so well-known and so much-appreciated by the congregation.

Before he accepted the call to return to Pullen, Poteat put into writing his understanding of what would be expected of him and what he woud expect of the church. He wrote:

In the light of my knowledge of the people and the general situation at P.M.B.C., if I were to be invited to accept its pastoral leadership, I should be inclined to ask for agreement by the Church to several propositions.

1. *My main responsibilities would be:*
   a. *General supervision of the Church* life, in terms of organizations, and long and short range planning.
   b. *The ministry* of preaching and worship.
   c. The pastoral and counseling responsibility.
2. *The main responsibilities of the Church* — as represented both by chosen officers and the congregation at large
   a. *To support the pastor* in the maintenance of a free pulpit from which the moral and spiritual dynamics of the christian faith can be constructively and boldly proclaimed.
   b. *To provide the minister* the opportunity of maintaining such national and denominational (State and Nation) contacts as will contribute constructively to the preaching of the Christian Gospel and the growing interests of the P.M.B. Church and the Kingdom at large. The minister will agree to a maximum number of Sunday absences during the year, exclusive of vacation of six weeks.
   c. *To provide financial* support to the program agreed upon by the Church. This will include
      (1) the compensation of the pastor
      (2) the provision of a home (details to be agreed upon)
      (3) the maintenance of the Annuity Benefits under the Southern Baptist Convention for the pastor, and provisions for attendance on Baptist Conventions — State and Southwide.

It is further contemplated that within such a time as is necessary for careful planning, an Associate Minister shall be secured who will exercise supervision over certain agreed on administrative responsibilities, and give particular and major concern to the development of a student program in connection with the Church.

Concerning the item "b" under "1," (Ministry of preaching and worship), there will be only one formal, regular preaching worship service per Sunday. Such activities as may be organized for Sunday evenings, in which the pastor shall have responsibility for planning and administration, shall be devoted largely to young peoples group meetings, vespers, etc.

A mid-week service for devotion and Bible study and church fellowship activities shall be the pastor's responsibility.

Poteat expected to begin his second term with Pullen on the first of November, 1948. On his way to Raleigh, however, he became seriously ill and his arrival was delayed until December. When he did arrive he returned to a church which he had never fully left and was welcomed by a congregation many of whom remembered with great appreciation his first tenure as pastor. All of the congregation were aware that their new minister was a man of unusual abilities who had an international reputation for his accomplishments.

Like Sheppard and Ellis, Poteat never considered his ministry to be limited to the church of which he was pastor. He was in great demand as a speaker in college and university circles. Between January, 1948, and May, 1954, he spoke at Meredith two or three times each year, sometimes in chapel, sometimes at the Religious Emphasis Week, and sometimes as Founders' Day speaker. He addressed various organizations on the campus of North Carolina State almost as frequently. He spoke at other colleges: Campbell, Sweet Briar, Hollins, Coker. Several times he preached in the Harvard chapel. He was the finals speaker at the conclusion of the first year of Southeastern Seminary's operation.

In his first term of service at Pullen, Poteat had experienced a serious defeat at the Southern Baptist Convention in 1935, when his proposal concerning a Bureau of Social Research was rejected. Upon his return to the South, however, the denomination frequently called upon him for committee work and for public statements. Almost immediately upon his return to Pullen he was made a member of a committee to investigate and publicize the plight of Baptist displaced persons in Europe. In July, 1950, he was the keynote speaker at the meeting of the Baptist World Alliance in Cleveland. In September, 1950, he was the speaker at the organizational meeting of Longview Baptist Church. In 1950 he was a member of the Baptist State Convention's Committee on Social Service and Civic Righteousness. In 1953 he was chairman of the Baptist State Convention's Committee on Religious Liberty.

Poteat's ministry beyond Pullen was not limited to work with the Baptist denomination. In June, 1949, he addressed the annual conference of the United Church of Canada. He continued to be active in P.O.A.U., and was often a speaker at its meetings. Twice he preached at the presentation of the "Lost Colony." In 1952 he addressed the North Carolina Press Institute. Always active in politics, he took a particularly strong part in the campaign of Frank Porter Graham for election to the Senate. His state-wide, and even nation-wide, involvement in religious and civic activities was recognized by the Raleigh *News and Observer*, which featured him as "Tar Heel of the Week" on October 22, 1950. He continued to write, publishing several articles in the *Biblical Recorder* and a number of poems in the *Christian Century*. He published three more books: *Parables of Crisis* in 1950; *God Makes the Difference* in 1951; and *Mandate to Humanity* in 1953.

Poteat excelled in the pulpit. He made the same social emphasis that had characterized his first term as pastor, and he brought to that emphasis sound biblical scholarship and broad knowledge of what was going on in the world. In addition, he had the maturity that was enriched by experience as pastor in a different setting and as an administrator of a theological school. He was knowledgeable about such a wide variety of fields that he was able to preach effectively to the intellectual community at large, and in particular to those college and university people who regularly participated in the services at Pullen. He always prepared carefully and spoke eloquently. A careful listener did not always agree with what Poteat said, but he always heard something that made him think.

Working with Miss Geraldine Cate, Minister of Music, Poteat began to introduce to Pullen a different pattern of worship. Since the beginning of her work with Pullen, Miss Cate had chosen the best of church music for both choir and congregation. The order of service, however, though it was varied a bit from Sunday to Sunday, was much like that in other Baptist churches throughout the area. Shortly after Poteat's return, he and Cate developed a service that was more liturgical and that involved both choir and congregation much more than had been the practice. In the church bulletin for Sunday, January 9, 1949, the following note appeared:

> You have observed changes in our order of worship. Since the experience of congregational worship is enriched in such measure as the congregation shares in it, we are planning for maximum fuller participation by all who enter the sanctuary. This requires that all of us follow the order of worship carefully so that the service shall suffer as little interruption as possible due to inattention.

The new service incorporated litanies and prayers and responses drawn from the long history of the church, from hymnals and prayer books, from the devotional writings of great spirits of the past. From that time on the worship services at Pullen involved the congregation actively in some way in almost every part of the service—in praise and prayer and offering.

A number of important developments in the life of Pullen Memorial Church occurred in the period between December, 1948, and May, 1954. One was the construction of the long-anticipated church sanctuary. Almost from the time the church had entered its new Sunday school building, in 1923, church members had eagerly anticipated erecting a sanctuary. Over the years they had contributed to a building fund. The fund had never grown very large, and at times some of it had been used in remodeling the old plant. It was always in the budget, however, and always the church expected to complete the facility. The church had been on the verge of beginning construction when the war broke out in 1942, and had had to abandon the project temporarily. They had continued to plan, however, and by the end of 1948 there was more than $40,000 in the building fund; plans had been drawn by Carter Williams; and a contractor had been chosen. On May 7, 1949, the church approved final plans, and a groundbreaking ceremony was held on April 17. Construction was soon under way.

When construction on the $200,000 project was begun the building fund had grown to $50,000, and the members had pledged another $26,500. The church borrowed $50,000, the maximum loan available at the time. They appealed to the Mission Board of the Baptist State Convention for help in the amount of $75,000. To present the case to the Board, Poteat prepared a document in which he stressed the activity of the Board in assisting other churches in university settings, and in which he reminded the Board of the denomination's historic commitment to Pullen as a mission to students. He pointed out the fact that in the twenty-five years that Pullen had been at its present location the student body at State had increased more than five hundred percent; Meredith had grown and had moved to a location nearer Pullen than to any other Baptist church; and the State School for the Blind had grown significantly. The church building was quite inadequate to provide a satisfactory ministry to the student population, and the church itself was not sufficiently strong financially to provide the necessary facilities. He concluded:

> The State Convention commissioned us to do a piece of work and has stood by waiting for us to develop to the point where it could come to our help 'at a later date.' That time has come. We have grown, but nothing like so greatly as the task has grown. We desperately need the help of the Board to complete the building program. After that we shall not ony be in a position to do the Board's work here, but to help more outstandingly in the Board's work elsewhere.

Pullen Memorial Baptist Church
1950

As eloquent as the appeal was, the request was not granted. The church, however, managed to scrap together a total of $100,000. Having invested that much in the building, it was able to get a construction loan for the other $100,000 necessary to complete the project.

To help meet the financial obligation incurred by constructing the new building, the church reluctantly reduced its contributions to the Cooperative Program. For many years, in addition to the mission contributions of the Woman's Missionary Society and the special offerings for the Children's Home and the Baptist Hospital, the church had been contributing twenty percent of its income to the Cooperative Program. Meeting on June 25, 1950, the deacons agreed to recommend to the church "that we no longer contribute automatically all of the 20% of our annual benevolences to the Cooperative Program until such time as we are able financially to increase our contributions to the Cooperative Program."

The first worship service in the new sanctuary was held on Sunday morning, October 2, 1950. On the last Sunday of that month, October 29, in a service which the *Biblical Recorder* called "impressive and challenging," the sanctuary was formally dedicated. The *Recorder* (11/4/50) described the service:

> Dr. E. McNeill Poteat, pastor of Pullen Memorial Church, presided over the service and conducted the liturgy of dedication. This service was beautiful and impressive. The new sanctuary, with natural finish oak pews and gray-green walls, was filled to overflowing, and many people had to listen in over a public address system from two auxiliary auditoriums.
>
> Special recognition should be given to the appropriate and beautiful music. Miss Geraldine Cate directed the enlarged choir for the occasion and A. H. Arrington, Jr., played the new organ, a gift from Dr. and Mrs. Z. M. Caviness, which is to be dedicated November 12.
>
> For the first time, two antique silver urns given the church as memorials were used during the dedication services Sunday. One of the urns was purchased with funds contributed by the public for a memorial to John T. Pullen, for whom the church is named; the other was given by Mr. and Mrs. Roy Medlin in memory of Mrs. Medlin's mother, Mrs. Eula Hatcher. Both vases contained lovely flowers.

The preacher for the service was Dr. Harry Emerson Fosdick, pastor emeritus of Riverside Church in New York City. Fosdick based his sermon on Paul's question, "Despise ye the church of God?" (1 Cor. 11:22). He said that "Only the Church's message can save the world," and he focused on the present opportunity of the church and the necessity of Christians working through the church. Denying that scientific progress could save the world, he said, "The road to hell is paved with good 'inventions.'" Then he declared:

137

> We must make of the Church a fellowship in worship and service. The Church is a symphony and it takes an orchestra of many parts to interpret a symphony. Christianity is like that.
>
> Ah, you solitary piccolo—trying to render Beethoven's Ninth Symphony alone. It can't be done, but you can help in the orchestra. (N&O, 10/20/50)

That morning service of dedication was very much of a public affair. The fact that an important church was dedicating a new sanctuary in itself attracted much attention. The fact that the guest preacher was the most famous pulpiteer in America lifted it far beyond the ordinary. In anticipation of the crowds that were expected, members of the congregation were issued tickets to ensure them of places in the sanctuary. The general public, for the most part, had to be satisfied with the accommodations in the overflow auditoriums.

The evening service was a different matter. Appropriately, it was a celebration of the Lord's Supper, with the pastor presiding. The people who participated in it had long been intimately involved in the life and work of the church, were committed to its ministry, and would be trying to act in the way in which Fosdick had challenged them. Many others who shared just as fully in the life of the church could not be present, but the service nevertheless had the air of the family of God at worship.

The new pipe organ, a gift to the church by Dr. and Mrs. Z. M. Caviness, was dedicated on November 12, 1950. In addition to all of his other involvement in the life of the church, Dr. Caviness was often on the music committee and the provision of a fine organ for the church had been very much on his mind. On May 7, 1950, as the sanctuary was under construction, Dr. Poteat announced to the deacons "that a pipe organ had been given the church by Dr. Caviness. Installation will be completed by Oct. 20." A. H. Arrington, Jr., gave the dedicatory recital. In announcing the recital the *News and Observer* said:

> A. H. Arrington, Jr., organist at Pullen Memorial Baptist Chruch, will present an organ concert at dedication services for the church's new two-manual organ, which will be held tomorrow afternoon at 4 o'clock. An augmented choir of 70 voices, under the direction of Geraldine Cate, will sing compositions by Bach, Mozart, and Brahms and will conclude with a composition by Dr. Edwin McNeill Poteat, pastor of the church. Dr. Poteat's composition is entitled, "Jesus Thou Joy of Loving Heart." Arrington will play works by Martini, Bach, Pierne, Vierne and Karg Ebert, and two chorale preludes by Brahms. The organ is being given to Pullen Memorial Baptist Church by Dr. Z. M. Caviness and his son, William F. Caviness. It was built by the Wicks Organ Company.

When the new sanctuary was constructed, rose-colored cathedral glass was placed in the windows. From the beginning it was expected that some day stained glass windows would be installed. That was a matter which Poteat had very much on his mind, and it was a dream which Dr. and Mrs. Z. M. Caviness shared with him. In December, 1952, the first five of those stained glass windows were installed in the chancel, the gift of Dr. and Mrs. Caviness and their son, Dr. William F. Caviness. Poteat had played a major role in determining their design. Rejecting the artist's first proposal, he suggested instead:

> The figures of the Four Evangelists flanking the central figure of Christ the Eternal King, are a conventional pattern widely used. It occurs to us that the substitution of four other figures would provide the artists with something original and even more significant. We are asking that you ask Mayer to make four panels of the following figures: Moses, Elijah (or Isaiah), St. Peter and St. Paul. These are representative of The Law, The Prophets, the First Disciples, and the Epistles (the greatest interpretation of the Gospel.) This gives a much broader sense of history, and brings into focus, with Christ at the center, the entire Hebrew-Christian tradition.

Poteat's proposal was adopted and beautifully executed. On December 14 the deacons asked him to "write a suitable item for the church in regard to the windows for filing with the permanent records of the church." Poteat wrote:

> These windows, designed according to suggestions made after much study of pattern and symbolism, were executed by the Franz Mayer Company of Munich, Germany, one of the most famous of European glass manufacturers. They were the gift of Dr. and Mrs. Z. M. Caviness, and Dr. William Fields Caviness whose devotion to the church has been demonstrated in many ways over many years. The pipe-organ which was also their gift, is now complimented by the chancel windows. These provide resources of beauty in color and harmony that unite the musical and graphic arts in the experience of devotion in a way that will be deeply satisfying to countless persons who will come to this sanctuary to worship God. To say that we are grateful to our generous friends is to put into poor words something that is too rich for language. We shall feel our gratitude in many ways over the years as we are helped to realize increasingly what the beauty of holiness can mean to those who worship God in spirit and in truth.

In January, 1954, the two rose windows depicting the Twenty-third Psalm and the Beatitudes were installed. Those windows were the gifts of Mr. and Mrs. Wade C. Lewis, and again Poteat had a hand in the design. In December the Luke window was installed, the gift of Dr. William Caviness. Not until the early 1960's were the other windows installed. The Creation window in the chancel was given by Mr. and Mrs. John A. Edwards, and the Passion window was donated by "the congregation and friends of Pullen Memorial." Dr. George Paschal gave the Roger Williams windows, which are on the east side of the sanctuary. In memory of her husband, Mrs. Fred Wheeler gave the William Carey windows, which are on the west side. Along with the Azalene Medlin Memorial Library, they were all dedicated in a service on Sunday morning, April 12, 1964.

Once the sanctuary was completed the church gave attention to the remodeling of the old part of the building to make it more suitable for use in the educational program. Early in 1953 a committee was appointed to begin to formulate plans. At a joint meeting of the deacons and the Business Board on April 12, 1953, preliminary plans were presented and approved, and the committee was authorized to engage an architect to draw up preliminary sketches. Again Carter Williams was chosen as the architect, and he worked closely not only with the deacons and the Business Board but also with church school officials. The plan called for completing the ground floor and the first floor immediately, and completing the second floor at a later date. Within a year the church had let the contract and was seeking ways to pay for the work. By the end of the year the new facilities were in use.

The question of women deacons was finally settled in 1950. As noted, the first women deacons were elected, with some difference of opinion, in 1927. How long they served we do not know, but in 1930 there were no women on the board and none was elected for many years. In the fall of 1946 the deacons had considered the matter again, but had taken no action. On June 4, 1950, the issue came before them again. According to the minutes, "Motion made and passed to have nominating committee confer with the Woman's Missionary Society and determine if it is the desire of the Society to have women serve on the Board of Deacons." The minutes do not report the results of the consultation. No church minutes have been filed which indicate that any action was taken by the church. The list of nominees for the board of deacons presented at the regular meeting of the deacons on September 10, 1950, contains the names of ten men, but no women. Yet begining in October, 1950, tour women were members of the board: Miss Mary Yarbrough, Mrs. E. N. Peeler, Miss Carolyn Mercer, and Mrs. Roy Medlin. Each year thereafter, for several years, the church elected four men and one woman to serve on the board.

The support of missions was a continuing interest of Pullen Memorial Baptist Church. The church continued to see itself as a mission to the student population, and constantly made efforts to expand its work with the young people at North Carolina State, Meredith, and the State School for the Blind. The minutes of the deacons' meetings contain frequent references to that work. On December 2, 1941, for example, in his remarks to the deacons Poteat "stated that there were 103 students in the College Class."

In addition to seeing itself as a mission station, the church reflected a concern for missions beyond its walls—even when it found it necessary to reduce its contributions to denominational programs. Disappointed in their expectations of receiving help from the State Mission Board in constructing the new sanctuary, they had adopted the policy of withholding mission contributions budgeted for the Cooperative Program and applying them to the building fund. That was, of course, a sensitive issue, and many people were not happy with the plan, although they could offer no alternative. The motion passed by the deacons to implement the plan recommended continued support for the "special causes" such as the Children's Home and the Hospital. And it recommended withholding the funds from the Cooperative Program only "until such time as we are able to increase our contributions." (Deacons, 6/25/50) The treasurer's summary for the year 1951 reported an income of $45,213. The disbursements included $3,013 for "specials." Of the "specials" item, where the missions contributions were listed, only $712 went beyond the local church. Many church members were concerned about that fact. At the deacons' meeting on December 2, 1951, "Dr. Yarbrough raised the question about the small amount our church was paying to missions. There was much discussion on this point." No action was taken, but the concern continued. Although the income for 1952 was approximately the same as for 1951, the treasurer reported that the "balance on hand" as of January 1, 1953, was just under $5,000. In their meeting on December 14, 1952, the deacons had asked that "up to $1000 be paid into the cooperative program." The response of the Business Board was to recommend an increased contribution of $500, and the addition of "a fund to be available for assistance in the organization of new churches in the Raleigh area when needed, including the purchase of land for church sites, in the amount of $500." (Business Board minutes, 1/11/53) The records do not show the final disposition on the amount of the increase, but the treasurer's final report for the year 1952 contains the statement that "A payment of 2,000.00 was paid to the State Board for the Cooperative Mission Progam."

Another expression of the church's missionary interest was the annual School of Missions, begun in 1952, and continued for many years. Each Sunday evening in March the church gathered for study in classes and for hearing missionary addresses. Each year the studies focused on a major area of missionary concern: Africa, Indian Americans, Southeast Asia, India, Pakistan, and Ceylon. Each year the leaders were people in the forefront of missionary work. And each year a large number of Pullen people—young and old, male and female— were involved in the study. The *Biblical Recorder*'s announcement of the 1953 School provides a good picture of what was done each year:

A distinguished editor of Harper's Magazine, Eugene Exman, will highlight the special feature of Pullen Memorial (Raleigh) Church's second annual School of Missions this March. Each of the five Sunday evenings during this month will be devoted to a study of "Africa," the topic chosen by representatives of 30 (thirty) protestant denominational boards of missions for courses this year.

Each session will include 5:30 p.m. class periods for all ages from primary through adult groups, supper at 6:30, recreational features at 7:00, and the assembly period at 7:15. . . .

Mr. Exman, editor of Harper's department of religious books, who recently returned from a two-week visit with Dr. Albert Schweitzer in Lambarene, Africa, will be a featured speaker for the Albert Schweitzer evening planned for March 15. His address is scheduled for the 7:15 assembly period. Other assembly speakers are to be Mrs. Ellen Alston (March 22), executive secretary of the Negro WMU, who was sent by that association to Africa; and Mrs. John McGee (March 8) of Durham, Southern Baptist missionary home on furlough from that continent, whose talk will be illustrated by colored slides.

The opening assembly session (March 1) will feature the movie, "Challenge of Africa," and the final evening (March 29) will sum up the month's learning by each class group, through costumed skits and games. This session will be called "The Great Palaver," after the African term for any get-together. (BR, 2/28/53)

The church continued to share fully in the life of the denomination. It regularly sent messengers to the meetings of the Raleigh Baptist Association and to the Baptist State Convention. Poteat usually represented the church at the meetings of the Southern Baptist Convention. In February, 1950, the church shared in the responsibility for taking a religious census in the city of Raleigh. In October, 1950, it hosted the meeting of the Raleigh Baptist Association. At the deacons' meeting on September 7, 1952, "Dr. Poteat urged as many as possible to attend the meeting at the First Baptist Church on September 8th to hear a report of the 9-year program of the Baptist Church. He reported that the Com. had done a splendid job and had developed a statesmanlike report." On September 6, 1953, the deacons approved a contribution of $100 "to the new church at Carolina Pines to help them with their building project." At that meeting the pastor also encouraged attendance at a meeting "to be held at Tabernacle Church to discuss the Nine Year Advance Program."

There was, however, some uneasiness about what to do about the denomination's cooperative revival activities. In 1950 the church made a small contribution toward the cost of holding a Youth Revival in Raleigh. At the meeting of the deacons on January 8, 1951, Poteat "discussed briefly the South wide and State wide revival meeting. He mentioned that he was puzzled as to what we ought to do and asked for suggestions from the Board." The minutes do not report any suggestions, and there is no indication that Pullen did anything. Although Billy Graham's Crusade in Raleigh on November 16-18, 1951, was not a denominational project, it did have wide support from the Baptists. There was no official support from Pullen, however. At the deacons' meeting on November 4, "Dr. Poteat read a letter from Billy Graham headquarters asking for cooperation (1) by choir (2) in attendance at prayer meetings, the date and time to be announced later (3) in enlisting personal workers for the three services of the Evangelisic Crusade." After the reading of that letter, the deacons moved on to other matters.

As a church cooperating with the denomination, therefore, Pullen Memorial took a special interest in the Ferre incident. Nels F. S. Ferre, of the faculty of Andover Newton Divinity School, had been invited to address the fall, 1953, convention of the Baptist Student Union of North Carolina. A campaign to have that invitation withdrawn was mounted by some of the more conservative elements in the Baptist State Convention. James W. Ray, Student Secretary for the Baptist State Convention, refused to give in. A few days before the meeting was to be held, M. A. Huggins, Executive Secretary of the Baptist State Convention, overrode Ray and himself withdrew the invitation. At the Baptist State Convention, a special committee was appointed to study "the personnel, activities, and programs" of the State Baptist Student Union. In March, 1954, that committee recommended that Ray and two campus chaplains employed by his department be dismissed.

Pullen was concerned about these developments both because of its own sense of mission to students and because of the theological stance which the committee's recommendation represented. The minutes of the deacons' meeting on March 21 state:

> The chairman asked if the Board would like to take any action or express any opinion on the recent action of the special committee of the Baptist State Convention named to probe "liberalism" in the student union program—resulting in the recommendation for dismissal of Rev. James Ray, State Director of B.S.U., Rev. J. C. Herrin, Baptist chaplain at the University of North Carolina, and Max Wicker, chaplain at Duke University.

> After some discussion it was decided that because of the importance and significance of this matter, it would be advisable for individuals to write the General Board asking that action be deferred until further investigation could be made.

The records made no other direct reference to the incident. There may have been some connection, however, between Pullen's response to the incident and a request from Huggins, presented to the deacons on August 1, that either Huggins or a member of his staff be invited "to meet with the leaders of our church." It was agreed that Earl Bradley

143

should be invited to meet with the deacons, the W.M.U., and the church officers on September 8. Whether the meeting took place, and if so what was discussed, is not reported.

For many years Pullen Memorial Baptist Church had seen itself as cooperating not only with other Baptist churches but also with the wider Christian community. When the Raleigh Council of Churches was formed in 1945, Pullen Memorial was a charter member. From the beginning of the North Carolina Council of Churches in 1935, Pullen had made an annual contribution to its support. When, therefore, in 1949 the Council amended its by-laws to make possible the affiliation of local churches, Pullen promptly applied for membership.

From time to time in the early 1950's the church was confronted with a question about its membership policy. In 1933 the church had begun to accept "associate members" from churches of other denominations. In November, 1942, the deacons had debated but had taken no action on a proposal that "restrictions placed on Associate Members . . . be eliminated." In 1950 Poteat brought up the matter again. The minutes for December 10 report:

> Dr. Poteat stated that he had made 1100 calls this year. He was continually encountering people who like us and wonder if they should join if they are not members of the Baptist Church. He raised the question about first and second class members. He stated that 23 churches in Virginia had open membership. He pointed out that this was a topic about which much thought should be given.

Again no action was taken. Several years later Poteat spoke to the issue in one of his sermons. At the meeting of the deacons on January 4, 1954, "The chairman raised the question as to the status of the associate members in our church, based upon the statement by the pastor in his anniversary sermon. After much discussion it was suggested that this matter be included in the proposed constitution of our church."

Like many, perhaps most, other Baptist churches, Pullen Memorial had never had a constitution. For Pullen, as for many other churches, consideration of the need for a constitution was prompted by what happened in the North Rocky Mount Baptist Church case. For reasons that are not germane to this matter, on August 9, 1953, a majority of the members of that church had voted to withdraw from the Baptist State Convention and the Southern Baptist Convention. The minority who favored remaining within the denomination began holding services elsewhere, but sued to gain title to the church property. The judge ruled that even if a majority voted to secede, the property belonged to the minority who remained faithful to "the doctrines, customs, practices, and usages" of Missionary Baptist churches. In making that judgment, the judge relied upon arguments about Baptist history and doctrines, not upon legal documents that actually spelled out the organizational and property rights of that particular congregation. In the aftermath of that case, with the encouragement of the Baptist State Convention, many churches began the process of adopting constitutions. The State Convention even prepared a model which it offered for the use of interested churches.

The matter of a constitution was already being discussed at Pullen when the deacons decided (1/3/54) that the question of the status of associate members should be addressed in the "proposed constitution of our church." At the meeting of February 7, 1954, the chairman of the deacons appointed a committee "for drawing up the constitution for the church." The issue next came before the board on December 5, 1954, when "Mr Poole brought up the subject of the new constitution which was to be written. Dr. Mumford, ch. of the committee, reported that some work had been done on the constitution." It was to be some time, however, before the church took action on a proposed constitution.

Another matter to which the church addressed itself was that of racial segregation. For many years the church had followed the policy of welcoming into its services all who presented themselves. There is no record of when that policy was established or when the first blacks visited the church. But during Poteat's second ministry, at least, it was not at all unusual for blacks to be a part of the congregation. The May 17, 1954, decision of the Supreme Court which declared racial segregation in the public schools to be unconstitutional prompted Christian groups to examine their own practices. Meeting in June, only about three weeks after the Supreme Court decision, the Southern Baptist Convention approved a recommendation from its Christian Life Commission which endorsed the decision and urged the churches to help implement it. The crucial statement in that recommendation was: "That we recognize the fact that this Supreme Court decision is in harmony with the constitutional guarantee of equal freedom to all citizens, and with the Christian principles of equal justice and love for all men." Another paragraph in the statement urges:

> That we urge our people and all Christians to conduct themselves in this period of adjustment in the spirit of Christ; that we pray that God may guide us in our thinking and our attitudes to the end that we may help and not hinder the progress of justice and brotherly love; that we may exercise patience and good will in the disucssions that must take place, and give a good testimony to the meeting of the Christian faith and discipleship.

On August 1, 1954, Dr. Poteat "suggested that the Board of Deacons make a statement relative to the long-standing practice of our church in nonsegregated seating of worshippers." It was agreed that the matter would be discussed at the next meeting. At that next meeting, on September 12, Poteat proposed that "the Board of Deacons of Pullen Memorial Baptist Church recommends that the church affirm that in worship and service, it continues to welcome without distinction of class or race all who share with us our dedication to the Lordship of Christ." After some discussion, the deacons voted to approve the statement and present it to the church for its consideration.

Before the matter could be taken to the church it was discussed at another meeting of the deacons. At that meeting Poteat stated that before the issue was presented to the church "he would like to add the word 'fellowship' to the resolution." The deacons decided to postpone action on that request until the regular meeting in November. At the November 7, 1954, meeting the request was carefully discussed. The minutes report:

> After some discussion as to the best way to present the matter to the church, Dr. Beck made the motion that the Board of Deacons of Pullen Memorial Church submit to the membership of the church through its Missionary and Educational agencies the following topic for full consideration: "That we welcome in worship, service and membership, without distinction of race, all who share our dedication to the Lordship of Christ.

The motion was carried, and a committee was appointed to make plans for presenting the matter to the appropriate groups. At the December 5 meeting Turner Williams, chairman of the committee, reported the plans which the committee had formulated and stated that "the committee was preparing a bibliography of material on the subject to be used by those who would lead the discussions." He also suggested that the process might be completed in time for the matter to come before the board on the first Sunday in March, 1955. Another committee was appointed "to work out a procedure for carrying the matter to the organizations." Like the race problem itself, Pullen's policy on membership would not be settled in 1954.

When Poteat had returned to Pullen in late 1948, he had come with the expectation that the church would employ a Minister of Education. That expectation was not fulfilled until August, 1954, when Miss Carolyn Massey assumed that responsibility. Miss Massey was a graduate of Meredith College and of Union Theological Seminary in New York. Because the church had never had a full-time minister of education there was some uncertainty among the deacons about exactly what her work should be, and she found it necessary to chart her own course. At the deacons' meetings Poteat often spoke with considerable appreciation of the help which she gave him. And the comments of the deacons were always appreciative.

One of the most striking characteristics of the life of the church during the early 1950's was Poteat's commitment to what might be termed the pastoral ministry. For him, visitation—in homes and in the hospital—was a major function. At the November 6, 1949, meeting of the board of deacons, the last meeting to be held that year, he had "a few brief words . . . in regard to the number of visits made by him." At the December 10, 1950, meeting he reported 1100 calls during the year. At the meeting on December 2, 1951, the minutes report:

> He pointed out that this was an exciting period in the life of the Church. He stated that he had made 1400 calls or rather he had had 1400 good times because he likes to visit people. He pointed out that this statistic was not the important thing but the opportunity to talk with people.

After 1951 he did not keep records of his visits, but that activity continued to be a major part of his work as pastor.

At the end of 1954 Pullen Memorial Baptist Church was looking to the future with optimism and enthusiasm. Its members were happily following the leadership of a man who was at once a dynamic and challenging preacher and a loving and beloved pastor. They were worshipping in a lovely new sanctuary, made even more beautiful by a new organ and by the first seven of its magnificent stained glass windows. With the help of a new minister of education, they were carrying on a stimulating program of religious education in renovated quarters. They were sharing in the mission of the church in the world both in ways that characterized most Baptist churches and in ways that were unique to Pullen. They were examining their membership policies with an eye to a greater openness to Christians from other denominations. And they were responding to the challenge of a changing pattern of race relations by considering whether Pullen Memorial Baptist Church should declare itself ready to welcome into its fellowship "without distinction of race, all who share our dedication to the Lordship of Christ."

Chapter 7
A Prophetic Church
In An Era of Revolution
(1955-1972)

Not just in the United States, but throughout the world, the years 1955 to 1972 were a revolutionary era. There was a political unrest all over the world. Long-time leaders were ousted from their positions of power: Churchill, Peron, Khruschev. Others died natural deaths: Nehru, Ho Chi Minh, Nasser. Terrorist activities troubled many nations: Cyprus, Algeria, Northern Ireland. Rebellions broke out in Hungary, Poland, and Czechoslovakia. A four-year civil war in Cuba brought Castro to power. Four African countries became independent nations. A six-day war gave Israel control of territory that had belonged to Egypt and to Jordan. A wall was built to divide Berlin, and a political rift developed between Communist China and the Soviet Union. The United States became embroiled in action in Vietnam that began as "advising" and became a major war.

For Americans the period opened with a noble quest for peace. In 1955 the United States participated in the Summit Conference at Geneva. While that was going on the U.S. occupation of Germany was ended and Dwight D. Eisenhower, the military man become President, was working to establish peaceful relations between the nations.

Meanwhile, both in the East and in the West, nuclear research continued, deadlier new missiles were constructed, and more sophisticated planes and submarines were built. Time after time the nation was on the verge of war. An American U-2 plane was shot down over

Russia in 1960. In 1961 the United States ended diplomatic relationships with Cuba. In that same year the ill-fated anti-Castro invasion of Cuba at the Bay of Pigs was crushed. War very nearly broke out in 1962 over the Russian missiles based in Cuba.

In the mid-1960's the United States was at war in Vietnam. The conflict had begun in 1957, with Viet Cong guerrilla and terrorist activity against the government of South Vietnam. The Viet Cong leadership had been trained in North Vietnam, and before long they were receiving aid not only from North Vietnam but also from the Soviet Union and China. The government forces of South Vietnam were receiving military assistance and economic aid from the United States, and almost from the beginning American military advisers were there. In 1965 the first American combat units entered the country, and by 1967 nearly half a million men from the United States were there. It was a war such as America had never fought before. War was never officially declared. It was a civil war, so that lines could not be fixed. It was not always possible for the troops to know who was friend and who was enemy. It was nothing like conventional warfare.

The participation of the United States in the war became one of the most divisive issues the country had ever known. There were sharp differences on who was responsible for America's becoming involved, on whether American forces should remain there, on what tactics should be used, on how to get out. In 1968 talks were begun between the United States and North Vietnam in an effort to bring about a settlement. Troop withdrawals started shortly thereafter, but the last United States ground troops would not leave until 1972.

This period was also one of internal strife for the United States. The Supreme Court Decision of May 17, 1954, outlawing segregation in public schools, was followed by a general movement to bring about broad social changes. After his leadership of the Montgomery bus boycott in late 1956, Dr. Martin Luther King, Jr., became both the spokesman for black protest and the leader of black activism in the form of nonviolent resistance. As the mass protest movement mounted, the NAACP pressed its claims in the courts by challenging the legal status of a wide variety of discriminatory laws. At the same time Civil Rights legislation was being passed by Congress. Federal agencies were bringing pressure upon Southern states to guarantee equal treatment for all citizens. Violence broke out: Little Rock, Birmingham, Oxford, Harlem, Newark, Detroit, Los Angeles. There was a resurgence of Klan activity, and the appearance of activity by the Black Muslims and the organization of the Black Panthers. Three assassinations shocked not only the nation but the entire world: John F. Kennedy in 1963; Martin Luther King, Jr., in 1968; and Robert F. Kennedy in 1968. Mob violence was met by police force, some of it disciplined and some of it irrational.

149

In this era of change there was in the United States significant evidence of the desire for some kind of Christian unity. A number of denominational mergers took place, one of which brought together groups with different theological tradition and different ecclesiology. Under the leadership of Eugene Carson Blake, a number of churches entered into the Consultation on Church Union, and several others not officially involved in the Consultation sent official observers to the talks. The twenty-first ecumenical council of the Roman Catholic Church, popularly identified as "Vatican II," met from 1962 to 1965, and one result of that council was a greater spirit of openness to Protestant Christian groups.

The post-war revival movement crested in the late 1950's. Throughout the rest of this period it continued to be a factor in the religious scene, but its importance was decreasing. Theological ferment gave rise to new emphases and new schools of thought: "the theology of the secular," the "death of God" theology, "black theology," "liberation theology," "feminist theology." At the same time there was a resurgence of conservative evangelicalism, particularly evident in the neo-Pentecostalism and the growth of para-church religious groups such as the Full Gospel Businessmen's Fellowship. Many denominations found themselves unsure of what to do about the charismatic movement.

By the end of the 1960's most churches were having trouble holding the loyalty of their people. Some people decided that what the church was saying and doing was irrelevant to what was happening in the world, and found greater challenge in social movements. Others felt that the church was no longer satisfying their need for a personal spiritual experience and a personal security. The older methods of evangelism were no longer working, at least not to the extent that they had been, and the church had no new method to replace them. A decline of involvement in traditional religion set in, therefore. The rate of growth of church membership slowed in every major denomination, and for many of them by the end of the 1960's there was actually a decline.

For Raleigh this revolutionary era was, for the most part, one of progress and hope. The city was growing and the future seemed bright. The creation of the Research Triangle Park, plans for which were announced by Governor Luther Hodges in 1958, did more than any other single factor to change the city. Beginning with Chemstrand in 1959, new industries and new research facilities moved into the area with such speed that the population increased by nearly a third in the decade between 1960 and 1970. Not all of that growth, of course, was the result of new industry, but a great deal of it was. The people who came with the new industries were, for the most part, highly skilled and highly educated people. They came from all parts of the country, and Raleigh became more cosmopolitan, more mixed religiously, and more of a cultural center. Even though as yet it could hardly be ranked as a big city, it lost both the advantages and the disadvantages of the small town. The new situation created a challenge for the churches, and the churches had not fully learned how to meet the challenge.

To what extent the blacks of Raleigh saw the era as one of "progress and hope" is an open question. Before the 1960's there was little open conflict between the blacks and whites of Raleigh; whether that means that relations were good is another question. As in other places in the South, the 1954 decision of the Supreme Court was met with efforts by the majority of whites to find some way to avoid implementing the desegregation order. In the late 1950's and early 1960's black activist groups, such as the Raleigh Citizens Association and the local chapter of the NAACP, tried to increase black involvement in the political process and to upgrade employment opportunities for blacks. Martin Luther King was almost universally admired by blacks, his objectives seen as proper, and his methods approved. It could hardly be said that blacks were satisfied with things as they were and that they thought that there was real hope for them in the new prosperity of Raleigh.

When the sit-in movement started in Greensboro, black students in Raleigh quickly joined, targeting the S & W Cafeteria, the Sir Walter, the Ambassador Theater, Gino's Restaurant, and the Statehouse dining room. An outbreak of violence was feared, and a number of arrests were made. There were marches and demonstrations. Black leaders and white made great efforts to resolve the problems by negotiation. In the black community and in the white, the situation was explosive. But violence did not flare up; the city began to move toward integration of public facilities; and the business community did the same. Within a year, nearly all downtown businesses were serving people without regard to race. In all fairness, it must be admitted that in many instances integration was only a token affair. That certainly was the case with the schools. Yet it was progress, and it had been accomplished without the violence that both blacks and whites knew would be disastrous.

What happened in the churches is one chapter of the developments in the society at large. Beginning in 1964 there were "kneel-ins," in which black students, notably from Shaw University, sought admission to white churches. The reaction in the white churches varied. In most, the students were admitted without difficulty and treated with courtesy, if not warmly welcomed. They were turned away from some, however. Many white churches held discussions on what to do if blacks did put in their appearance, and about what to do if blacks should ask for membership. It was that latter issue to which McNeill Poteat had asked Pullen Memorial Baptist Church to address itself in 1954, ten years before the sit-ins.

At every meeting of the Board of Deacons between January and June, 1955, attention was given to the question of whether the church should be asked to adopt a policy of accepting blacks into its membership. The Board devised a plan for having the issue discussed in the missionary and educational agencies of the church. They prepared an "Outline for Discussion" for the use of the carefully-selected discussion leaders, and they provided literature which the leaders could use to prepare themselves for the discussion. They requested from each group—each Sunday school class, each circle of the W.M.S., each Training Union department—a "brief report summarizing pertinent ideas and general attitude." They also asked that a formal vote not be taken because they believed that any voting should be done by the church in conference.

As carefully as the plan had been worked out, there were problems of implementation. The committee reported to the deacons on June 5, 1955:

> There was some objection by those who did not want to go on record, even anonymously; so the Board of Deacons passed the motion that no group was under obligation to submit a formal statement. After this motion was made public, the general reaction was that the discussion had been dropped and that no report was desired. As a consequence of the misunderstanding, only four reports were received, two from college B.T.U. classes and two from circles of the W.M.U. In addition, a poll made by the Poteat Bible Class was made available to the committee. . . . Our summary is based on these reports and on conversations with members and leaders of various groups which did not submit written reports.

The committee decided that the issue should not be taken to the church for action. They said:

> We believe that if the matter of membership for Negroes could be considered on ethical grounds alone, the majority of the members would vote for the resolution. They will not, on the other hand, favor the resolution in the face of the extent of the apparent opposition in the church. Almost all opinions, which were expressed in writing or verbally, were to the effect that the resolution should not be submitted to a vote until some time in the future, with the hope that the membership will be better prepared for this step.

The minutes note that "After a brief discussion, a motion was made, seconded, and passed without a dissenting vote that the report be accepted and that the committee continue a study of the matter."

There is no indication that the study was continued, however. In the months that followed several members wrote letters indicating their belief that the church should open its membership to Negroes. In the deacons' meeting on December 4, 1955, "Gordon Poole raised the question as to what racial pattern the church would follow with reference for example, a colored person presented himself for membership. The matter was discussed but no decision was reached."

Miss Carolyn Massey, Minister of Education, resigned at the end of June, 1955. The church lost no time in finding a replacement, and William (Bill) M. Everhart began his work on August 1, 1955. Everhart was a graduate of Wake Forest College and of Crozier Theological Seminary. He had taught for a year and a half in the public schools, and had been interim pastor of a church near Chester, Pennsylvania, while he was a student at Crozier. Poteat had great confidence in him and wanted the church to "make full use of Mr. Everhart's talents and many capabilities." (Deacons Minutes, 12/4/55)

Bill Everhart
Minister of Education 1955-1957

Just before Christmas, 1955, McNeill Poteat died. His death was not totally unexpected, for he had been in poor health when he came to the church. He had carried a heavy schedule of activities at the church and in the wider community. His last address to a college community had been the baccalaureate address at Wingate College on May 29. His last article to be published before his death, appearing in the *Biblical Recorder* for June 25, had dealt with "Separation of Church and

State." During the fall of 1955 he had had some difficulty, having to miss some services, and the deacons were quite solicitous of his health. At the instruction of the Board of Deacons, the secretary, on October 9, wrote to Poteat expressing "gratitude for your continuing improvement." The letter stated, "We have missed you greatly but are anxious that you curtail your church activities as long as the doctors recommend." The deacons even suggested that he have assistance in conducting the morning services, and that he not speak to the members of the congregation at the close of services. At their December 4 meeting the Board heard their chairman report on a conference with Poteat:

> The pastor was insistent that the church make full use of Mr. Everhart's talents and many capabilities. The chairman stated Dr. Poteat was much in favor of the church having an assistant to the pastor. In the event he, Dr. Poteat, had to retire from the active ministry of the church, there would be immediately available a minister to carry on the pastoral duties. The matter was discussed but no decision was reached.

Dr. Poteat died on December 16, 1955. The next day the Raleigh *News and Observer* stated:

> Dr. Edwin McNeill Poteat, 63, pastor of Pullen Memorial Baptist Church and one of the South's best-known clergymen, died unexpectedly last night at 9:15 o'clock from a coronary occlusion.
>
> Dr. Poteat had just arrived at Pullen Church to perform a marriage ceremony when he was stricken. He was rushed to Rex Hospital by ambulance.

The article then reviewed Poteat's career, stressing the wide variety of positions which he had held. Then it gave additional information with, it must be recognized, a bit of editorializing:

> Dr. Poteat's influence spread beyond the confines of his church. During his first term at Pullen Memorial he was appointed by Governor O. Max Gardner to the State Board of Charities and Public Welfare. Governor J.C.B. Ehringhaus appointed him to the Commission of Five to study the State hospitals with a view to their improvement.
>
> He associated himself with many progressive political and social movements. For some of these actions, he received criticism as well as praise. A leader in the fight to maintain the separation of the church and state, he often was roundly criticized by groups which he thought were encroaching on that constitutional provision.
>
> Dr. Poteat's personality and wide interests resulted in a heavy speaking schedule. His talks were not confined to religious subjects. He was asked to speak on literature, music, science and other subjects, and he was able to fill the bill.
>
> The American Association for the Advancement of Science honored him in 1946 by inviting him to address its convention. It was the first time a clergyman had ever been asked to talk to that group.
>
> His speeches were delivered with the skill of an actor and in the language of an accomplished writer. They were characterized by a change of pace that ranged from philosophy to pathos and wit.

Before, during and after college he was interested in athletics both as a participant and as a spectator. While serving in China he was the star pitcher on the All-American baseball team. He recalled in later years that one of his greatest thrills was in coming from behind to defeat Walter Lippmann, the political writer, in a hotly-contested tennis match. He even served as a trainer in 1916 for a challenger for the world's wrestling championship. . . .

Dr. Poteat's knowledge of music was extensive. The possessor of a fine tenor voice, he was also an accomplished organist and he wrote both the words and music for several hymns. . . .

His literary output was marked by the same variety that characterized his speeches and his music. He had articles, stories and poems published in such well-known magazines as Harper's the Saturday Review of Literature, the Christian Century and others.

Within his church, he served on many important commissions and committees. Of particular interest to him was the application of Christianity to the everyday problems of the South and the world. He felt that Christianity must be a potent force for the economic and moral betterment of the common man if it were to serve to its fullest and to spread its influence.

An editorial in the Raleigh *News and Observer* on Monday, December 19, captured something of the spirit of Poteat:

Death came as no stranger to Edwin McNeill Poteat. But it will be hard for those who knew him in Raleigh in the last years of his life to reconcile his richly shared vitality with his death when he was barely 63. He seemed far too young to die. He had so very much more to give. Even now, in the face of the fact that he is dead, it is hard to associate with death the one who in his goodness and his wit, his courage and his charm was as gay a saint as has ever walked our streets.

It may still be that the reason that we loved him so much, without knowing it till now, was that he debonairely served both his Lord and his fellows while he knew always that Death walked at his side. . . . The frailty of his health was, of course, realized by his friends. But he made his church here such a real corner of the kingdom—he carried still his convictions and his faith with such compelling voice to every part of this country—that he seemed almost the embodiment of the strength of the spirit.

He never departed from stern, simple Baptist doctrine but he knew that the bones of faith can be dressed in beauty. He required no sanctimony and as a man who could write great sermons and important books he never feared any damage to his dignity when he wrote comic verse, too. There was never any lapse in his willingness to fight, however, for such things as the separation of church and state and the oneness of God's concern for all men. About such things he was always a very serious man, but no seriousness ever hardened his heart, stilled his laughter or dulled his wit. There was gaiety in his heart to the moment it stopped beating.

No man ever retired from a great national career to greater service. And if in these last years when Raleigh had been blessed with his presence he walked close to death he also walked close to people who needed his courage, his faith, his kindness and his humor, too. His death seemed almost designed in poetry for the close of such a life. He was on a gay errand. He was on his way to such a joyous occasion as a wedding and he stopped as he went to pick up a Christmas wreath. He had already written a Christmas sermon with the sound of Christmas bells in it. The wedding awaited him. The wreath was beside him. And death met him as he stopped at the door of his church. The meeting was not unexpected. In many ways they were old friends.

Within days after Poteat's death the church established a special fund to be used to honor him. In conference on May 20, 1956, the congregation voted to use the fund to complete the chapel as a memorial. Work was begun in December, with architect Turner Williams as consultant. Contributions came in such a rate that the chapel and its furnishings had been paid for when the work was completed. The dedication service was held on Sunday, February 17, 1956, with Dean Oren H. Baker of Colgate Rochester Divinity School as the speaker. Other participants were McNeill Poteat's son, William H. Poteat, professor of philosophy at the University of North Carolina; William R. Strassner, president of Shaw University; Carlyle Campbell, president of Meredith College; and W. W. Finlator, pastor of Pullen Memorial Church. The words of the plaque placed at the entrance to the chapel, taken from Poteat's own poetry, capture the spirit of the person to whom the chapel was dedicated:

Come In
with love for God and man...nor fear
to wait as stranger in this quiet place...
    for God himself
will presently appear and smile a welcome
    from a friendly face
and offer you, with others waiting here
    the Bread of Fellowship...
    the Cup of Grace.

Within days after Poteat's death an eleven-member pulpit committee was appointed, with John A. Yarbrough, chairman of the Department of Biology at Meredith College, as chairman. As might be expected, the committee sought suggestions from the church about the kind of person who should be called, and it received nominations from many people both in the church and outside of it. On that basis they prepared the following document entitled "A Statement of Principles and Goals," which they used as a guide in their search and copies of which were given to the persons with whom they discussed the possibility of their coming to Pullen:

These statements do not necessarily represent official church action. They are approved, however, by the present pulpit committee of ten individuals and reflect an earnest effort to capture the underlying qualities of our church and to state the most important goals for our future growth.

1. A free pulpit. As in the past, we want our pastor to be free to interpret the Christian message for ourselves and the world as he conceives it.

2. A dignified service. Our fellowship has responded very favorably to an order of service that emphasizes quiet worship, participation by the worshippers, and a balanced use of liturgy consistent with our faith as Baptists. We have made considerable progress in developing our music for the worship services and are anxious to keep this as an important element in such services.

3. A challenging message. In keeping with statement #1 above, our fellowship will almost demand sermons which are thoughtfully planned and which are distinctly related to the current problems facing Christian bodies over the world today. While we wish to remain Baptist in the truest sense and tradition we also wish to raise our voice in support of the church in a wider sense, the church universal.

4. An organized and participating membership. It is at this point that we feel the need of further strengthening. We are not lacking now in organizations and in plans for educational activities but we want to improve upon the participation in these existing programs. Changes in this program and its extension into new areas may be needed. We particularly feel the need of well-planned activities for our own children and the young adults of our membership.

5. Our service to college students. Our strategic location provides a fine opportunity for ministering to State College and Meredith College students and to pupils at the State School for the Blind. In this service we recognize a need for improvement. Our College Sunday School and B.T.U. organizations should be strengthened. Yet we want this work to be a phase of our larger church ministration, not our single or even our primary goal.

6. Church size and growth. We do not anticipate our growth into a large city church. Such a goal is not possible in our existing plant, nor is it consistent with our wish to offer a distinctive type of fellowship in the community. Our membership could and should probably expand to about 900 or 1,000, but probably not larger. On the other hand, we feel that this church under challenging leadership can project its voice and influence throughout our state and even the nation.

7. Basic church mission. We have not mentioned in these statements those things which characterize any true missionary Baptist church, e.g., testimony of the gospel message in the community, enlistment of new people into the church and its organizations, and interest in missions at home and abroad. We hope that you may correctly assume that these are abiding goals in our church.

8. Summary. In summary we would say that it is the hope of those of us now working in Pullen Church that this fellowship continue in its tradition of offering a distinctive emphasis in church life along the

lines indicated above. We wish to remain loyal to our Baptistic relationships, to support its state and Southwide programs and cooperate in its missionary enterprises. Yet we desire to bear our own testimony in our own way in this community and to avoid an unthinking following of a mass program. We will always need a minister of such stature that we cannot afford to pay him what he is actually worth to the cause. This challenge which is ours at Pullen must also be his who will serve us as minister.

As is usual with pulpit committees, this one gave out no information about the persons whom they were considering. And as is usual, there was some concern in the church about the lack of information. When that was voiced in the deacons' meeting, Yarbrough explained "that no information of any value to members could be given at this time." (Deacons, 6/3/56)

In July, 1956, the committee recommended William Wallace Finlator, pastor of the First Baptist Church of Elizabeth City, and on Sunday, July 8, the church unanimously voted to call him. Finlator was born in Louisburg, but his family had moved to Raleigh when he was a boy. He had grown up in the Tabernacle Baptist Church, and had been educated in the public schools of Raleigh. He was a graduate of Wake Forest College and of Southern Baptist Theological Seminary. He had served a field of three churches—Pittsboro, Liberty, and Bonlee—from 1937 until 1941. In 1941 he went to Weldon, where he remained until he was called to First Baptist in Elizabeth City in 1946. The issue of the *Biblical Recorder* which reported the celebration of Finlator's tenth anniversary at Elizabeth City also carried an announcement of his call to Pullen. (7/14/56)

Finlator was well-known, at least in Baptist circles, when Pullen called him. For twenty years before he came to Raleigh he had contributed a large number of articles to the *Biblical Recorder*, many of which dealt with issues that were of life-long concern to him. His first article in the *Recorder*, published on October 4, 1939, was entitled "Beatitudes and Battlefields." Two articles published in 1940 were entitled "The Importance of Knowing How to Hate" and "Safeguarding our Baptist Democracy." In 1940, 1941, and 1942 he was the author of a weekly series of articles, some whimsical and some satiric, published over the pseudonym "Festus Erastus." During World War II, while he was pastor in Weldon, he had several articles on the issue of war. In that same period he wrote on race, on religion and the schools, and on denominational concerns. During his ten years at Elizabeth City he continued to send in articles: "The 'Pink' People Called Methodists," "This I Do Believe," "The Book Nobody Plugs," "How to Keep the Smear from Sticking." "Naked and Ye Clothed Me," and so on. He wrote in support of an anti-gambling bill, in opposition to

W. W. Finlator
Minister 1956-1982

universal military training, against censorship, against the removal of Nels Ferre from the State B.S.U. program. For the Council on Christian Higher Education he wrote a series of articles on "Town and Gown." And to top that all off, he dashed off a number of "Letters to the Editor."

Finlator was a denominationally-minded minister. Many of his letters and articles show that while he was sometimes critical of the denomination, he was critical from within. Respected as a thoughtful and forthright individual, he was used not only by the Council on Christian Higher Education but also on the Committee on Social Service and Civic Righteousness. Occasionally he was invited by other ministers to preach in revivals and was asked to speak in colleges across the state. At the time that Pullen called him he was a member of the Council on Christian Higher Education, a trustee of Meredith College, and a member of the General Board of the Baptist State Convention.

When Finlator began his work at Pullen on August 15, 1956, the church had a major item of unfinished business on its agenda. That was the adoption of a constitution. A committee of deacons to work on a proposed constitution had been appointed on February 7, 1954. The work moved slowly, and from time to time the deacons asked about progress. On October 10, 1957, copies of a proposed constitution were mailed to the congregation. Members were invited to respond in writing with suggestions and criticisms, and many did so. All responses were carefully considered, and that process took additional months. The church took final action to adopt the constitution on April 20, 1958.

Although the committee had studied carefully both the model "Constitution and By-Laws" circulated by the Baptist State Convention and constitutions which had been adopted by a number of local churches, the new constitution was distinctly Pullen's. It made it clear that Pullen Memorial Church stood firmly in the Baptist tradition and fellowship. At the same time it enunciated three distinctive Pullen emphases and practices. The opening paragraph of "Article IV — Membership" states two of them:

> Any person who shares with us a common dedication to the Lordship of Jesus Christ and who is committed to those percepts set forth in the two preceding articles is eligible for membership. Such person shall be a member of this church when received either (1) by baptism upon profession of faith; or (2) by a letter of transfer from another church in the evangelical tradition; or (3) by a statement of former church membership acceptable to the church in conference.

The first of these distinctive emphases is the fact that the church is open to people of all races. During Poteat's last year the church had debated the question of whether to admit blacks into membership, but

160

had failed to decide the issue. In approving the first sentence of this article, the church decided that race would not be a factor in the acceptance of new members. The second distinctive emphasis is that people from other denominations may be accepted into full membership in Pullen Memorial Baptist Church. For many years the church had had as associate members persons who came from other denominations and who had not been baptized by immersion. Item (2) in this paragraph determines that anyone who comes from "another church in the evangelical tradition" may be accepted into full membership. The third distinctive emphasis was specified in Article VI on "Affiliations." Affirming Pullen's relationship to denominational organizations, it added that "This church may also be associated with more inclusive organizations such as the North Carolina Council of Churches, the National Council of Churches of Christ in America, and the World Council of Churches."

The Constitution was revised slightly in 1965. The most significant change at that time was the addition of two standing committees. The first was the Area Ministry Committee, whose responsibility is to keep the church acquainted with its members and prospective members. The other was the Information Committee, responsible for the annual publication of a church direcory and for other public information activities on behalf of the church.

The Constitution was revised again in 1971, and several significant changes were made. The first provided for the acceptance of new members "by letter of transfer from another Christian Communion" rather than "from another church in the evangelical tradition" (Article IV, Membership). The second added "the American Baptist Convention" to the list of affiliations (Article VI). The third added the requirement that two weeks notice be given in writing for a church conference in which major matters are to be acted upon (Article IX). The fourth provided for the possibility of the church having an Associate Minister (Article I).

In the 1971 revision of the Constitution two major standing committees were established: the Committee on Community Concerns and the Worship Committee (Article IV, Sections E and Q). The earliest call for a "Community Concerns Committee" may have been the undated document found in the files of the Committee which calls for the creation of a "Committee on Social Concern." The idea first came before the deacons on September 13, 1964. According to the minutes:

> Mr. Highfill raised the possibility of having the Minister appoint a special Church Committee to deal in the area of the social concern of the community. Mr. Finlator discussed the idea briefly and indicated that if the Board favored the idea he would like to have them authorize him to appoint such a committee.

The deacons approved the suggestion and at the next meeting Highfill was appointed chairman of a committee "to work with the pastor on a statement outlining the area of responsibility of a proposed committee to deal in matters of social concern." They presented their report on December 6, 1964, and the appointment of a committee was approved. It was noted that the by-laws give the minister the authority to appoint such committees as are deemed wise. Finlator "stated that he visualized the committee as a study group which would keep the church informed on issues of concern."

The committee was appointed in January, 1965. On June 6 the committee issued a report but there is no indication as to the group to which it was addressed. The opening paragraph states that the committee "was established to provide the members of Pullen Memorial Baptist Church with a forum to reflect their community concerns at every level." According to the report, the committee met several times, collected information on a wide variety of subjects, heard speakers on a number of topics, and wrote letters urging support of various programs. The report then spoke briefly to two concerns: President Johnson's efforts to help students find "meaningful work or training opportunities this summer," and the resurgence of the Ku Klux Klan in North Carolina. It concluded: "Suggestions from members of Pullen Memorial of subjects that should be of concern to this Committee and how it can serve most effectively will be welcomed."

In March, 1967, the committee addressed a report to the congregation in which it spoke of issues which the members had discussed. In July and August, 1968, the committee sponsored at Pullen a "Dialogue on the Urban Problems of Raleigh and their Solution." From time to time the committee made statements to the church, and occasionally made statements to the community at large. At times it communicated with city, county, and state officials on social and political matters.

For several years the committee functioned in this manner. A significant change in their functioning, however, was instituted in 1972. The budget which the church adopted that year contained an allocation of $5750 for the committee, to be expended for day care programs, support for housing, a summer tutorial program, educational programs on community problems, the Raleigh drug problem, the ecumenical work of the Raleigh Experimental Ministry, and a token amount to be paid to the City of Raleigh as an expression of appreciation for its services. For the first time the committee was allocated funds with which to do some of its work.

About the same time the Community Concerns Committee took on another major project and asked for the church's help. The chairman of that committee addressed a letter of the deacons dated November 2, 1971, in which he stated:

Some young people (Cookie Hall, Dan Pruitt, etc.) have a dream of a coffee house to fill the void of boredom that leads some people to drugs. They came to Mel Williams and then to the Community Concerns Committee requesting only a place in which to set up shop. . . . We are impressed with their enthusiasm, energy, sense of responsibility, and goals. We have agreed to serve as the sponsoring committee for them and on their behalf make the request that you, the Board of Deacons, grant their request for a place in which to set up a coffee house.

The request was considered at length in the deacons' meeting on November 7, 1971. There was an obvious wish to be helpful and at the same time a certain wariness because of potential problems. The practical concerns of maintenance and of the possibility of the institution becoming a problem in the community were debated. Then, with five dissenting votes, the deacons approved the request. The coffee house was opened almost immediately and operated until the end of the school year.

The other standing committee created by the constitutional revision in 1971 was the Worship Committee. As an *ad hoc* committee it had come into being rather spontaneously when a number of people expressed a desire to be involved in some non-traditional patterns of worship. Even after the committee was given constitutional status it maintained that approach. Introducing a *Pullen Views* (December, 1974) article on the committee, Suzanne Newton said, "Since its constitutional beginnings four years ago, the worship committee has become Pullen's Committee-of-What's-Happening-Next." According to the constitution, the function of the committee is:

To work continually in evaluating, deepening, and enriching the overall worship life of the church. The committee shall counsel with the ministers and the Director of Music regarding worship, and shall work in planning special worship experiences such as the 9:00 a.m. summer family services, Advent and Lenten services, or 'suggested services' which enrich the worship life of the congregation.

In that same *Pullen Views* article, Newton said:

Seeking out the gifts of Pullen's members is one of the committee's major responsibilities. In recent years (with the committee's delighted affirmation) church members of all ages have composed songs, written poetry and litanies, choreographed dances, made banners, and contributed various original works of art to enhance the worship experiences of the congregation. Beyond that, however, the committee also looks for opportunities for people to participate directly in worship services—as liturgists, as music makers, or as bearers-of-witness.

In its planning the worship committee constantly returns to two questions: what is worship, and how do we worship. During the coming year, in the process of exploring these "mysteries," the committee hopes to find ways to offer the congregation some instruction in worship, perhaps by bringing in knowledgeable people for workshops and discussions.

Finally, the worship committee sees one of its functions as being a channel of communication between the ministers and the congregation. It can serve as a sounding board—as a body to receive and make use of critical feedback that will help all those concerned with worship planning to get in touch with the needs of individuals within the congregation. Pullen people are invited to speak with worship committee members about any matters of worship.

When Carolyn Massey had resigned as Minister of Education in 1955 she had recommended that the church establish a Board of Education. Her recommendation was taken seriously, though its consideration was delayed by the death of Poteat. Early in 1956, however, a Board was formed. At the June 3, 1956, meeting of the deacons, "Scarborough reported that the Board of Christian Education had been organized and two meetings held. . . . The meetings were concerned with getting acquainted with educational problems of the chruch, particularly the need for personnel in several positions." There were some problems of functioning, however, and the deacons worked with the Board in an effort to determine its proper role. Bill Everhart, who had succeeded Massey as Minister of Education, gave valuable assistance to the deacons and the Board of Education as they were working out the plans. Everhart, however, resigned in September, 1957, to accept a call to become pastor of the Fremont church.

In his letter of resignation Everhart spoke with much appreciation for the people with whom he had been working and with confidence in the future of the church. He observed: "I sincerely believe . . . that the Pullen Memorial Baptist Church is entering a period of even 'greater expectations' than realized in her notable past. In the preaching and pastoral ministries of William Wallace Finlator one sees what I believe to be one of the most mutually beneficial associations (Minister-Church) among Baptists in the state." He then made two recommendations. First, he recommended that "without delay, an *ad hoc* committee be appointed to study the enrollment trends within the church school and the space arrangement and facilities to insure an optimum use of space, personnel and facilities in the coming years." And second, he said that before employing his successor "It would be wise to develop a job description, defining the task and area of responsibility and authority for the position." The church did not immediately implement either of these recommendations, but several years later both ideas came up again.

On April 13, 1958, while the church was working on its proposed Constitution, the deacons appointed an interim Board of Education. It was chaired by C. C. Scarborough, Professor of Education at North Carolina State. That board presented its first report, quite well organized, to the Board of Deacons on September 7, 1958. It was authorized to proceed "along the lines of the authority to be conferred by the new Constitution upon its adoption."

In the By-Laws of the Constitution adopted on April 20, 1958, the structure and functions of the Board of Education were carefully specified. Article I states the duties of the Church Staff. The second staff person listed is the "Director of Education," who works "under the direction of the Minister and with the Board of Education." The statement on the membership of the Board of Education specifies that "The Director of Education of the church shall serve as secretary of the Board of Education." At the time of the adoption of the Constitution, the church was without a Director of Education, and continued without one until Alton Y. Buzbee began work on March 1, 1959.

Buzbee came to Pullen from a similar position at the First Baptist Church of Clarksville, Tennessee, where he had served for two years. Prior to that time he had been for two and a half years Minister of Education at Waynesboro Baptist Church in Waynesboro, Virginia. He was a native of Alabama and had attended Howard College and the University of Alabama. He had received his theological training at the Southern Baptist Theological Seminary in Louisville, Kentucky. It was hoped that his leadership would bring new life to an educational program which was generally regarded as lacking in depth and vitality. As chairman of the Board of Deacons, Carter Williams wrote in his report on the church year 1959-1960:

> Several years ago we embarked on a program that has as its key a thorough preparation of the teaching personnel plus family cooperation. The literature was some of the best available. We are still having difficulty in really making this program develop its potential. A sufficient number of dedicated and capable teachers is a surprisingly constant need in a church blessed with such qualified members. Definition of responsibility, clean-cut decisions, and smooth functioning of our Board of Education is still a desirable goal in providing a coordinated program after many long hours of earnest efforts. Employment of our Educational Director, capable and devoted though he is, cannot be the complete answer to providing in all departments vigorous and inspiring programs which are the life-blood of our church.

On August 12, 1961, the deacons were informed that Buzbee had resigned to accept a position with a publishing firm. Neither the creation of the Board of Education nor the employment of a Director of Education had brought the hoped-for revitalization.

Following Buzbee's resignation the Board of Education began to discuss two matters of concern. The first was the general dissatisfaction with the Sunday school literature, and steps were taken to investigate alternatives. The other was the provision of a specific job description for the Minister of Education and finding someone to fit that description. In light of these concerns, and of others that were no less important but were less crucial at the moment, the church employed Dr. Denton Coker, of Southeastern Baptist Theological Seminary, to serve as a consultant for six months. Coker began his work in January, 1962, at a time when the church was giving attention to other urgent matters as well. His work gave a new sense of direction to the educational program.

The deacons of Pullen Memorial Church began in 1959 to consider affiliation with the American Baptist Convention. W. W. Finlator first brought the possibility to the attention of the deacons on December 7, 1958, when he asked them to "give the matter some thought and consideration." Several months later he reported that he had been in touch with the Secretary of the American Baptist Convention. Nothing was done for the next two years. But on May 7, 1961,

> Bill Finlator invited the Decaons to participate in a discussion to be led by a representative of the American Baptist Convention at Pullen Church on Monday evening, May 8. Representatives of the First Baptist Church of Raleigh, the Watts Street Baptist Church of Durham, and the O. T. Binkley Baptist Church of Chapel Hill will be present. The possibility of a closer association between the two Baptist Conventions will be explored.

The purpose of that meeting was not to discuss dual alignment but to consider the possibility of "a closer association between the two Baptist Conventions." On December 3, 1961, however, Finlator reported to the deacons on a conversation with a representative of the American Baptist Convention in which dual alignment was discussed. The minutes on the discussion that followed report:

> A small contribution by Pullen to the American Baptist conventions. This might grow as we become active in the ABC. This would enable us to belong to the World Council of Churches. This would imply that we would leave the Southern Baptist Convention. Meyers [sic] Park Baptist Church, Charlotte, has aligned with the ABC.

Then a motion was passed that "we express our interest, talk among our church members and those of other churches. The committee to report in two or three months." Curtis Fitzgerald was appointed chairman of the committee. There is no record of what the committee did, and Fitzgerald was away from his post at North Carolina State for the school year 1962-63.

The matter came up again in the spring of 1964. A letter dated June 30, 1964, addressed by Mrs. Margaret Scarborough to E. L. Rankin, Jr., chairman of the Board of Deacons, refers to a session, apparently an informal one, which Rankin could not attend. The letter states:

> The concénsus of opinion of this group—W. W. Finlator, Mrs. Woodbury, David Pittman, Leroy Richardson and myself—was that we would like to see a committee appointed to study the possibilities—advantages and disadvantages—of a dual alignment of our church with American Baptist as well as Southern Baptist Convention.

On July 5, 1964, Mrs. Scarborough presented the following request to the deacons:

> I ask the board to consider recommending the chairman appoint a group of interested and informed members to study the possibility of associating our church with the American Baptist Convention. This would make a dual alignment with both the Southern Baptist Convention and the American Baptist Convention. This group would bring us facts to consider before making recommendations to the membership.

After a wide-ranging discussion, the deacons authorized the appointment of the committee.

The committee began work immediately. On September 13, 1964, it reported informally that it had met three times to discuss the matter, that it was not yet ready to make any recommendation, but that it was leaning toward a strong recommendation of dual alignment. On November 1, 1964, the committee presented in writing a lengthy report, concluding with the recommendation of four steps:

(1) To apprise the church of the interest in the possibility of affiliation with the American Baptist Convention;
(2) To provide for the church ample opportunity for the study and discussion of such affiliation;
(3) To invite an official representative of the American Baptist Convention to meet with appropriate officials and Boards of this church and with the congregation;
(4) To bring before the church in business session a recommendation on the question of the affiliation of Pullen Memorial Baptist Church with the American Baptist Convention and to provide the opportunity for the congregation to vote on the recommendation.

There was considerable discussion, with significant difference of opinion. It was finally agreed, without motion, that the committee be asked to continue its work and make plans to present the matter to the church.

Apparently the committee did no further work. Not until a year later did anyone ask in the deacons' meeting about what was happening. Two months after that the chairman submitted his resignation "for compelling personal reasons." He affirmed a continuing interest in the proposal, and he indicated that he believed that there was a strong interest in the church. Notice of his resignation did not make its way into the deacons' meetings, however. On May 1, 1966, one of the deacons asked about the status of the committee, and at that time it was announced that the chairman had resigned and a new chairman should be named. On July 3, 1966, the chairman of the Board of Deacons announced "that he was appointing Bernard Cochran new Chairman of the Committee on Wider Affiliation and is asking him to proceed to bring this matter before the congregation."

Cochran made his first report as chairman of the committee on January 1, 1967. He announced that the committee had planned for

167

discussion at a "family night supper" under the leadership of Dr. Sam Hill, of the University of North Carolina at Chapel Hill and a member of the Binkley Memorial Church. Cochran stated that "The Committee will make some recommendations to the church in March, 1967." The deacons received the report on April 2, 1967. The minutes state:

> After full discussion it was moved and seconded that the Board of Deacons accept the unanimous recommendation of the Committee on Wider Affiliations which is as follows: 'The Committee on Wider Affiliation, by unanimous vote, recommends the extension of the affiliation of Pullen Memorial Church to include membership in the American Baptist Convention by applying for membership.' The Board of Deacons voted unanimously in favor of the motion.

At a church conference held on Sunday, April 30, 1967, the church voted to affiliate with the American Baptist Convention. The deacons elected Carlton Blalock as "our official representative at the American Baptist Convention's annual session on May 17, 1967."

Another type of wider affiliation was considered by the deacons in 1971 and 1972. On August 1, 1971, Finlator informed the deacons that one of the Pullen members had asked "that Pullen align itself with the Wake Baptist Association (Black) as well as with the Raleigh Baptist Association (White)." Finlator had discussed the matter with O. L. Sherrill, executive secretary of the black Baptist State Convention, and with Charles Ward, pastor of the black First Baptist Church, and "they expressed an interest." It was agreed to send visitors to the meeting of the Wake Association. Ten members, including the pastor and Bernard H. Cochran, who had been chairman of the Committee on Wider Affiliation, attended. The matter was discussed in depth on September 12, after the meeting of the Association, and a committee to consider the matter was appointed. Hal Littleton served as chairman. The committee reported "progress" on November 7, but after that the matter was dropped. There is no further reference to it in the minutes of the deacons.

One matter which demanded a great deal of attention from the deacons during most of 1960 was finally resolved by a decision to make no change. On May 6, following the suggestion of one of the deacons, a committee was appointed "to study the mechanics of accepting church members during the morning worship service." The committee began work immediately, but on June 5 reported that they had "as yet been unable to agree on an alternate plan for receiving members into the church." They were instructed to continue their work. In September they "had no final report," and the deacons voted to continue the committee. On February 5, 1961, they reported that they still had reached no conclusion and recommended that the committee membership be doubled. Instead, the deacons voted to discontinue consideration of the matter.

Another activity to which the deacons gave a great deal of attention in 1962 was the sponsorship of a refugee family from Cuba. The action was sparked by Mrs. Bea Anderson, who brought to the deacons a request from the American Baptist Missionary Board for help for a Dutch Indonesian family. The deacons agreed to appoint a committee to explore the possibility. There is no hint of what was done about that family, but at the meeting on May 7, Mrs. Anderson reported a request from the same Board for help for a Cuban refugee family. The deacons passed a motion that "The Board of Deacons endorse the specific family, that the W.M.S. appoint specific circles to furnish specific items and that the general congregation 'pound' the family. Note: money can and may be as acceptable as food in the 'pounding.'" On October 9 the deacons heard from the committee that the family still needed help in paying rent, and voted to give help through October. The chairman of the Board of Deacons, in his report submitted on September 30, 1962, stated that "Our church sponsored a Cuban refugee family by arranging for a position through one of its members, making certain financial arrangements for them and through food, clothing and furniture, in getting them settled in our community." On November 4 the deacons endorsed an item in the budget for the new year to provide assistance for six months, and in addition passed a motion "That there be appointed a 3 member special church committee to consult with, assist, supervise and determine for Cuban family and report, to work closely with Mrs. Anderson." The family continued to need—and to receive—help through 1963, although there was the constant effort to get them to become entirely self-sufficient. Apparently that objective was achieved by the end of the year, for there are no further references to the situation.

In the fall of 1960 the Board of Education began to give serious attention to a critical evaluation of the educational program of the church. The Sunday school curriculum which was in use required for its success a high degree of family involvement and parental support. It had not had the necessary cooperation and the board was concerned about dealing with the problem. In their meeting on October 16, 1960, they decided that "special effort should be made to make everyone, particularly parents, fully aware of the Sunday School Curriculum and necessity of their participation in the program." In addition they discussed the need for a careful and objective evaluation of the educational program.

After Alton Buzbee's resignation in August, 1961, the church decided to examine the educational program carefully before it moved toward the employment of a successor. In his report on church activities during his year as chairman of the Board of Deacons, C. E.

Bishop listed what he saw to be the needs of the church in its educational activities:

1. Reappraisal of our educational activities in relation to the goals of our program as stated in the purpose of the church.
2. Better coordination of the total educational programs.
3. Revitalization of the educational activities for adults.
4. Closer coordination of the educational programs with the Board of Deacons and with the church at large.
5. Review and redefinition of the responsibilities of the Director of Education and the employment of a competent director as soon as is feasible.

In line with Bishop's ideas, and on the recommendation of the Board of Education, Dr. Denton Coker, professor of Religious Education at Southeastern Baptist Theological Seminary in Wake Forest, was employed in January, 1962, to serve for six months as a consultant. He was given the responsibility of studying the religious education program and making recommendations. He worked closely both with the Board of Education. A report entitled "A Study of the Program of Christian Education of the Pullen Memorial Baptist Church Containing Suggestions for Improvement" was submitted at the end of his six-months study. It was a thorough analysis with recommendations concerning the objectives of the program, the work of the Board of Christian Education, and each department of the Sunday school. It represented not merely Coker's thinking but also the ideas of the Board of Education. It concluded with a "Summary of Emergencies that Need to be Met by Fall of 1962":

I. A Minister of Religious Education.
II. New quarters for the nursery departments.
III. New equipment and the redecoration of the Nursery, Junior, Junior High, and Senior High departments.
IV. A leadership committee.
V. A teacher orientation and training program.

The church began its implementation of Coker's recommendations by employing David Pittman as Minister of Education. Pittman was a native of Marion, North Carolina, and a graduate of Furman University and Southeastern Baptist Theological Seminary. For two years he had been pastor of the Saxapahaw Baptist Church, and at the time of his call to Pullen he was nearing completion of his work on his doctorate in Christian Education at Hartford Theological Seminary. He was also serving as Minister of Education in the First Baptist Church of Dearborn, Michigan. All three of his predecessors had had theological training. Pittman, however, was the first person in that position to have had a specific interest in and preparation for work in Christian education. In conference on September 22, 1962, the church voted to call him, and he began his work at the first of the year in 1963.

David Pittman
Minister of Education 1963-1969

Pittman's strength lay in organizing and administering the program, and in enlisting and training workers rather than in trying to do the work himself. In a letter dated February 5, 1963, he outlined the approach to his work which he intended to take:

Individual conferences provide an opportunity for persons to discuss with me matters that can be dealt with more effectively on a personal rather than a group basis. Studying curricular materials, developing units of study and individual sessions, planning for parent-teacher cooperation, selecting and planning for the use of audio-visual materials, and developing suitable educational activities for church school groups are some of the ways in which I have found personal conferences to be helpful.

Church Education courses designed to meet specific areas of need may be offered. These would be on a two, four or eight months basis at times convenient to the largest number of interested persons. Basic Leadership Course in Christian Education, Educational Ministry to Children, and The Gospel and Contemporary Social Problems are examples of courses that could be offered.

Workshops of two to four sessions each may be conducted for the purpose of helping teachers handle the basic teaching skills.

Apprentice or assistant service may be arranged for persons interested in becoming a teacher in the church school. This would be under the supervision of a trained teacher and the minister of education. In addition to the work on Sunday morning, periodic conferences would be included.

Although not all of his ideas were implemented, Pittman did take the approach which he described, and he was eminently successful in enlisting and training workers. The minutes of the Board of Education are full of reports of successful programs in the church school and in other activities such as Youth Retreats, Vacation Bible Schools, Adult Programs, and the like. Interestingly enough, Pittman had been given no more specific job description than had his predecessors.

On May 15, 1966, Pittman reported to the Board of Education on his comprehensive analysis of the curriculum currently in use in the Pullen church school and recommended a change. He noted that in 1954 Pullen had adopted the Faith and Life Curriculum of the United Presbyterian Church, first produced in 1948. He observed that when Pullen began using that curriculum "the choice was no doubt a wise one especially in view of the fact that the curriculum was perhaps the best produced by any Protestant group." He found it "strongly based on reformed theology," however, and noted "a definite rigidity in terms of dealing with theological content." Furthermore, he found that it did not "reflect the free tradition of which Baptists are, at least historically, a part." The period of the 1960's, it might be noted, was one in which most of the major denominations were revising their curricula, and Pittman was acquainted with the developments that were taking place. He had introduced the curriculum of the United Church into use in the nursery and kindergarten departments in 1962, and into the senior high class and one adult class in 1965. The Board adopted his four recommendations:

(1) Use the United Church Curriculum experimentally through grades 12, and above as groups so desire.
(2) Let the Board carefully study the book, *Educational Mission of the Church* by Shinn which gives the philosophy behind the curriculum, and to study the total curriculum.
(3) Have periodic evaluative sessions with teachers and Board members.
(4) Decide in the Spring of 1967 about the future use of the curriculum for Pullen, recognizing that any effective curriculum must be modified and supplemented for individual church use.

Pittman remained with the church until the spring of 1969, when he resigned to accept a position as minister of education for the Community Church in New York City.

In the early 1960's there was constant concern about the inadequacy of the physical plant. The ground floor and the first floor of the old building had been remodeled in 1954 to provide space for the Sunday school program. At that time it was understood that as soon as feasible the top floor would be finished. Although the issue came up from time to time, there was no concerted drive to keep the project in mind.

In April, 1960, the church conducted a campaign to raise funds to do seven things: (1) pay for the recently-acquired home and lot adjoining the church property; (2) pave the parking lot; (3) remodel the second floor of the educational building; (4) renovate the vestibule and carpet the aisles in the sanctuary; (5) install the remaining stained glass windows; (6) air condition the church sanctuary; and (7) reduce the debt on the church. It was anticipated that the total cost would be $60,000, and it was not expected that the entire amount would be raised. Only about $15,000 was pledged. That was not enough to do the work on the second floor. It was enough, however, to pay for the newly acquired property, to pave the parking lot, and to do some necessary repairing of the building.

At the end of his term as chairman of the Board of Deacons, in October, 1970, Carter Williams had said, "Lack of available space is now blocking our progress and growth." On August 12, 1961, at the suggestion of Bill Finlator, the chairman of the Board of Deacons appointed a committee to "study the total Sunday School building needs." On January 7, 1962, the committee reported that "the facilities now in use" are "in dire need of renovation" and the equipment "should be discarded." They recommended that the Business Board be authorized to borrow up to $10,000 to take care of the emergency. That recommendation was approved. At the next meeting, however, the deacons had second thoughts and decided that before any attempt to borrow was made the church needed to take a good look at its financial situation. It was during this period that Denton Coker was serving as educational consultant. It seemed the better part of wisdom to wait until he had finished his work before undertaking any major renovation of the educational facility.

The problems persisted, however. David Pittman, the Minister of Education, was trying to make the church school program more significant, but he was working under the limitations of inadequate facilities and of the church's uncertainty as to whether it seriously intended to implement the recommendations of the Coker report. The situation was further complicated by the fact that the church was not meeting its budget.

At the meeting of the Board of Deacons on November 7, 1965, Walter Fuller, chairman, stated that

> during the budget hearings it became evident that a need existed to coordinate overall plans for physical plant expansion. He suggested that the purpose of such a committee should be to look into long range needs of this church and make recommendations for the future development of the physical plant.

The deacons approved a motion that they recommend to the church the appointment of a Long Range Planning Committee, and the church approved the recommendation in conference on November 21, 1965. The members of the committee were to be the chairmen of the Board of Deacons, Building and Grounds, Trustees, and Education;

the Pastor; the Minister of Education; and four members elected by the church. George Paschal served as chairman, and the other members were J. J. Brandt, C. E. Bishop, B. F. Bullard, Mary Ruth Crook, Arthur Woodbury, R. L. Lovern, J. W. Reid, David Pittman, R. J. Volk, W. W. Finlator, John Blackmon, and Mrs. Basil Sherrill.

The committee was requested to "endeavor to submit a report by July 1, 1966." It soon became apparent that much more time would be required. They had to make a careful study of the building; they had to have complete information on the educational program; and they had to think in terms of plans for the future. They submitted to the deacons a "progress report" on December 4, 1966. The draft of their "final report," dated March 3, 1968, evoked an immediate response from the Board of Education. That Board found in the report a number of statements that "do not reflect the current philosophy of the Board of Education" and proposed some changes which would "bring the report into harmony with the long range educational goals formulated by the Board of Education during the past five years." The committee agreed to give further consideration to their report. At their meeting on September 18, 1968, although they were in complete agreement on what was needed, they could not agree on priorities. By a divided vote, six to three, they decided on two recommendations to the deacons:

1. That they investigate the purchase of adjoining property (and purchase if feasible); and at the same time, proceed with plans to renovate the existing building, including the annex for Pre-schoolers; and make the construction of a new Pre-school (Day Care) addition a second priority to come later.
2. That the Board of Education be consulted in any building or renovation of the Church's physical plant, now or in the future.

The committee's report, dated October 7, 1968, was discussed by the deacons on January 5, 1969. There had already been considerable informal discussion among the church members. The deacons learned that the cost of the adjoining property would be approximately $60,000, and decided that it was not feasible "at this time to purchase this property." Carter Williams had been consulted on the proposed renovations, and he estimated that the cost would be approximately $120,000. There was considerable question in the congregation as to the wisdom of undertaking that major project. After discussion, the deacons decided "that the matter of renovations be referred to a committee consisting of the chairmen of the business board, board of deacons, and board of education for recommendations to the Deacons."

On January 30, 1969, a meeting attended by "certain leaders of our church" was held in the home of the chairman of the Board of Deacons. Presumably those leaders were the ones appointed to the committee on January 5. They recommended that the order of priorities be:

1. Air conditioning the sanctuary and the chapel with ducts installed for future cooling of the space over the chapel.
2. Renovation of the top floor.
3. Renovation of the annex building.
4. Renovation of the ground floor (basement).
5. Renovation of the main floor.

The minutes add:

> The group also recommended that a committee be appointed to consider financing these renovations. After extended discussion by the deacons, a motion was made that the list of priorities be adopted combining numbers one, two and three as number one with numbers four and fiv to follow and that a committee be appointed to investigate financing and to educate the church membership as to the needs outlined in the list of priorities. The motion passed.

At a church' conference held on Sunday morning, March 9, 1969, the congregation voted on recommendations which came from the Board of Deacons. In the conference the recommendations were revised a bit, and were approved as follows (*Pullenews*, April, 1969):

> First priority (three items included): air conditioning the sanctuary, renovating the third floor, and renovating the annex.
> Second priority: Renovating the basement.
> Third priority: Renovating the main floor.

A fourth priority was adopted at the request of the Board of Education: "that a new building be built on the land presently owned by the church, for the purpose of a Day Care and Educational facility." And finally it was stipulated that at each stage of the proceedings the Board of Deacons "must come back to the congregation for presentation of plans."

On May 4, 1969, the chairman of the Board of Deacons announced the names of the members of the finance and building committees, and the committees began their work at once. Carter Williams was again chosen as architect. The issue of "priorities" remained in the air, however. "Details on Each Priority" were published in *Pullenews* for October, 1969. At the deacons' meeting on November 2 an effort was made to revise them. A set of notes (not minutes) on conversation at an unspecified meeting of the deacons in the spring of 1970 reveals significant differences both about the priorities and about the way to finance the project.

Meanwhile, David Pittman resigned in the spring of 1969 and the Board of Education immediately began the search for a successor. They prepared a document entitled "Proposed Job Analysis for Minister of Education." After a statement on the "Philosophy of Education at Pullen," they listed the following qualifications which should be met:

1. Creativity and capacity for imaginative innovation.
2. Initiative and ability to plan and work independently.
3. Professional competence, as shown by graduate degree from theological school with specialization in religious education and by experience in this field.
4. Ability to work with all age levels, especially youth.
5. Commitment to ecumenical thought and practice.
6. Organizational skill including aptitude for dealing with the inevitable petty mechanics organization entails.
7. Leadership of the sort that guides rather than drives.
8. Awareness of developments in religious education and related areas.
9. Emotional and spiritual maturity sufficient to love human beings in spite of their failings.

Their description of the "Duties of the Minister of Education" was quite precise:

> Responsibility—shared with the Board of Education—for total educational work at Pullen including church school and extended hour, curriculum development, leadership for the program, youth council and retreats, family worship services (summer), coordination of the church calendar, and any other areas mentioned in attached documents.
>
> Responsibility for church participation in ecumenical and community enterprises including the day camp (summer), Raleigh School of Religion, Baptist Student Union Advisory Committee, and any other areas mentioned in attached documents as well as those that may develop in the future.

At their meeting on June 1, 1969, the deacons received from the Board of Education the nomination of T. Melvin Williams to serve as Minister of Education. Williams had grown up in Aberdeen, NC, and was a graduate of Wake Forest University. For a year after graduation from Wake Forest he had served as minister of education and minister of music at Oak Lawn Baptist Church in Winston-Salem, where he had been minister of music during his senior year in college. He then went to Yale Divinity School, where he earned a Bachelor of Divinity degree. For the use of the Board of Education in making its decision about him, Williams had prepared the following "Theological Statement":

> I consider myself basically orthodox in my theological beliefs. I believe that God revealed himself through his actions with the people of Israel, that his fullest revelation has come in Jesus Christ, and that he continues to reveal himself in the struggles of men today. The life, death and resurrection of Christ has removed my sin and through God's grace, forgiven all men. This event has freed me from my sin and thus enables me to live with newness and a measure of joy. For this gift, I live in continual gratitude. I believe that the church, the Christian community, is still centrally important. The worship and fellowship of Christians can be one of the most sustaining realities undergirding

God's work in the world today. I am convinced, however, that too often the church has failed to live out its calling in the world. With worship as the sustaining strength, I believe that Christians are to seek to serve their brothers in the world regardless of class, race, or belief. My attempt to live out the Christian life is not done within the cloistered walls of the church alone; I seek to live it primarily as I struggle with the problems I face about me, both individually and in society. Being daily involved in the struggles of work, family, community and nation, I must rely on the faith and aid of my brother to sustain me. Thus it is God's grace within the community of Christians that continually frees me and enables me to live—and to love and care for those persons and problems with which I am involved.

T. Melvin Williams
Associate Minister 1969-1979

Like all of his predecessors except Pittman, Williams was trained in theology rather than in Christian education. He was more interested in, and better equipped for, forming and working with special purpose groups than working with the traditional religious educational program. He was more interested in counseling than in the recruiting and training of leaders. His emphasis and his style, in other words, were quite different from those of David Pittman. It was for this reason that when the constitution was revised in 1971 it made provision for *either* a "Minister of Education" *or* an "Associate Minister."

177

Williams must have been bewildered at the confusion over the Long Range Plan when he began his work at Pullen. For some time it was much discussed but little progress was made on its implementation. After the completion of the air conditioning of the sanctuary, in the fall of 1969, the church struggled to pay for it. When the Long Range Plan was brought up in the deacons' meeting on February 7, 1971, two years after the congregation had approved the "priorities," the church still owed $15,000 on that one project. But the chairman brought up the question of whether it were not time to renew efforts.

> Mr. Mackie then began a discussion concerning the feasibility of taking significant steps to implement our building program. He introduced George Capel, Chairman of Building Committee who reviewed the status of the priorities which were agreed on two years ago. He noted that only the air-conditioning had been installed, and nothing had been done since October, 1969.

In the discussion that followed some people, including the pastor, expressed the desire to begin an all-out campaign to complete the entire project. Others expressed caution. There was disagreement as to whether the deacons should take a recommendation to the church or simply present the question for discussion and action. It was finally decided to delay action until there could be further discussion with the Business Board. After that discussion, in their meeting on February 28, 1971, the deacons agreed upon a recommendation to carry to the church. The following letter was addressed by the deacons to the congregation on March 4, 1971:

> TO THE CONGREGATION:
> At the meeting to discuss the implementation of the Church Building Program, the Board of Deacons unanimously adopted the following recommendation which wil be voted upon by the Church in conference on Sunday, March 28.

> > The Board of Deacons of Pullen Memorial Baptist Church recommend that the church begin immediately a fund-raising campaign to be carried on over a period of the next three months with a goal of $150,000 pledged to be paid over a period of three years.

> > When the goal is reached, all phases of the building program as outlined by the Building Committee will be undertaken with the total amount borrowed; $150,000 of the amount borrowed will be paid off over a period of three years, and the balance paid off over a period of fifteen years.

> > If this goal is not reached, then the church will reassess the building program.

> An outline of the Building Program as approved by the church in April, 1969, is attached.

At the March 28 church conference the recommendation was fully and freely discussed, and there were strong feelings both in favor of and in opposition to the recommendations. Some people spoke of the present condition of the building and of the need for space as "critical." Others spoke in equally urgent terms against spending so much money on ourselves in a world where the need of others is so desperate. Still others were concerned that the church was not strong enough financially to undertake such a project. When the vote was taken, sixty-two were cast in favor of the action and forty-one against. After the vote, the church directed the chairman of the Board of Deacons to name a committee to direct the fund-raising campaign. That committee was quickly appointed, with Basil Sherrill as chairman.

The minutes of the next meeting of the deacons reflect their sensitivity to the strong feeling of unrest in the church. The deacons were aware of the need for better communication between the church boards and committees on the one hand and the congregation as a whole on the other.

In April, 1971, the editor of *Pullenews* acknowledged the continuing differences and tied them in with an uncertainty as to Pullen's self-identity and sense of mission. He then expressed the hope that "Pullenites will feel free to use the PulleNews as a vehicle of expressing opinions and views." There were responses to the invitation and one in particular expressed what many who opposed the project felt. It stated:

> There are many of us who, in good conscience, cannot support the building program as it now stands. We feel that the plan should have been reassessed following the wonderful church conference in the spring which probably brought us closer to true community than we have ever been. It is unfortunate, I believe, that reassessment of the proposed plan should have been made contingent on *not* raising the initial $150,000. This puts many of us in the position of not contributing to this drive in order to try to effect a reassessment. This is not to say that we reject the objectives of adequacy, utility and beauty at Pullen; we would like these to be achieved with minimum outlay of expenditure with the really big drive concentrating on hunger or housing or program personnel or whatever seems to be the greatest human need. (*Pullenews*, July, 1971)

The minutes of the deacons' meeting for August 1, 1971, summarize their long discussion by stating:

> The gist of the discussion was that the pastor sought the full and whole-hearted cooperation of the entire board in this tremendous enterprise, and that the board concurred with him in expecting the best of the congregation in spite of opposition of a few conservative or, for personal reasons, non-participating members.

To assist in the fund-raising drive, the committee charged with the responsibility of directing the campaign engaged the services of Ketchum and Company, a professional fund-raising organization. This was the first time Pullen had ever used the services of such an agency, but recent efforts without such help had been notoriously unsuccessful. Ketchum's fee was paid by an anonymous donor, with the understanding that all other expenses of the campaign would be borne by the church. Some members of the congregation were skeptical about the use of the agency even though at least two other Raleigh churches had had good experiences with it.

In spite of the problems, the "Future of Pullen" campaign was a success. On October 3, 1971, the deacons heard a report that a total of $177,000 had been pledged, and that not all of the anticipated pledges had yet been made. In a letter of thanks to the anonymous donor who paid Ketchum's fee the chairman of the Board of Deacons stated:

> It is my belief that the church would not have approved the use of Ketchum & Company if the cost were to be deducted from the campaign pledges. The success of the campaign has been no small miracle and it has generated a spirit of united dedication which I hope will continue for many years to come.

Carter Williams began working on the plans immediately. Clancey and Theys were chosen as the general contractors, and the Bolton Corporation was chosen for the electrical work, plumbing, heating, and air conditioning. Construction was begun in June. As the work progressed, some serious problems with the old building surfaced. In addition, it became necessary to provide facilities for pre-school children in the main building. In a letter dated July 25, 1972, the deacons notified the congregation of the problems and stated two alternatives:

> *Alternative I.* Renovate only the interior portion of the old part of Pullen as required to improve our Church School facilities at an additional cost of $37,000 which will include the cost of financing and an allowance for furnishings.
>
> *Alternative II:* In addition to the interior renovations, provide the exit stairway and elevator at an additional total cost of $106,000 above the amount pledged in the Future of Pullen campaign to cover the costs of construction, interest charges and furnishings.

The letter added: "The architects, the Building Committee, the Business Board, and the Board of Deacons recommend the second alternative." Meetings were announced for Sunday, July 30, and Sunday, August 6, for discussion of the alternatives. A church conference was called for Sunday, August 13, at which a final vote was to be taken. At that conference the church voted in favor of the second alternative, and thus authorized a greater expenditure in order to complete the first three phases of the long-range building plans.

During all these years, when the church was undergoing so many changes in its own life, the nation was in turmoil and was undergoing many revolutionary changes. Not only were social relationships being altered, but also basic convictions were being challenged. No longer could anything be taken for granted. In that tumultuous situation Bill Finlator was constantly making the news. The *News and Observer* often reported on his sermons, and he wrote many "Letters to the Editor" to indicate what he thought was a Christian and/or a democratic approach to the problems. From 1957 through 1972 there were no less than eighty-one letters from him or articles by him or reports on him published in the Raleigh *News and Observer*. He spoke in support of minimum wage legislation, in opposition to capital punishment, in praise of the conduct of black students in the sit-ins, in opposition to the John Birch Society, in support of civil rights, in opposition to prayer in the public schools, in support of legislation for gun control. He discussed the war in Vietnam, the liquor laws, church-state relationships, the Christian academies, the Black Panthers. Often he spoke as the official representative of the American Civil Liberties Union. When he wrote, he always identified himself simply as "W. W. Finlator." When the newspaper wrote about him, however, it always identified him as "Pastor of Pullen Memorial Baptist Church."

In his Sunday sermons Finlator often spoke to those same issues. Indeed, many of the articles about him were reports on his sermons. When he spoke on highly controversial matters, he usually read his statements, and he often supplied the newspaper with a copy. Clearly not all of the members of Pullen Memorial Baptist Church agreed with him on all of his controversial positions, and indeed on some of them he had little support. Some of his sermons angered some members. Yet Pullen was committed to the freedom of the pulpit. In its "Statement of Principles and Goals," the pulpit committee which had recommended him to the church had stated that the church wanted "A Free Pulpit," and that they wanted from their pastor "A challenging message." Finlator took seriously that affirmation of the committee—and of the church. He assumed that it was his responsibility to bring the gospel to bear upon social and moral issues, and he realized that his judgments and pronouncements would be challenged both in the church and in the community at large.

The year 1960 might be taken as a typical one in this respect. On February 1, 1960, students at North Carolina A. and T. College in Greensboro had begun the "sit-in" movement to protest the treatment of blacks at the Woolworth lunch counter. That movement spread rapidly throughout the South, and within days black students in Raleigh were using that tactic at the downtown stores. On February 13, 1960, the Raleigh *News and Observer* announced:

181

A local Baptist minister spoke up Friday in behalf of Negro college students who're conducting protests at chain store lunchroom counters across the State.

The Rev. W. W. Finlator, pastor of Pullen Memorial Baptist Church, said, "The demeanor of self-discipline of the students has been exemplary."

The Rev. Mr. Finlator issued a statement which said in part:

"The only unusual thing in their action is that they're behaving like American citizens. The students are doing in our day what we honored our forefathers for doing in their day, and that is, struggling for liberty. There is one exception: the students are doing it by absolutely peaceful means. . . .

"They have shown a self-controlled, patient and even good-humored spirit under circumstances of duress and some harrassment, which is all the more admirable when you realize they know they have a cause and they're dead serious about it. . . .

"Our law enforcement officers and, for the most part, our entire citizenry have responded with similar restraint and self-control and for this we can be more thankful."

On March 2 Finlator was one of a group of fifty-nine Raleigh ministers who "spoke out Wednesday against racial discrimination in a public statement prompted by growing Negro picketing of segregated lunch counters." (N&O, 3/3/60) On March 27 the *News and Observer* published his article, one of a series requested by the newspaper, appraising the State of North Carolina. He devoted half his article to the strengths of the State, and the other half to the weaknesses—and the weaknesses he saw had to do with race and labor. On Monday, June 13, the paper published a lengthy report of Finlator's sermon on the day before in which he "spoke out strongly" against the gubernatorial candidacy of I. Beverly Lake. On October 1 of that year, Carter Williams, retiring chairman of Pullen's Board of Deacons, submitted to the deacons a report of the year at Pullen in which he said, in a section entitled "Accomplishments this year":

The minister has spoken out courageously and unrestricted on various issues of Christian living in today's world. This policy has at times been provocative of criticism as well as support. These are not times of easy decisions. Leadership must always be sensitive to objectives and capabilities but free in decision. It is hoped that Christian concern and mutual affection will continue to overcome differing viewpoints on controversial matters. The pulpit is undoubtedly the heart of a church and from it must come the inspiration, the stimulation, and the cohesive power that validates all the other programs and activities of the church.

In that same report Williams took cognizance of the fact that not everyone would respond to the kind of preaching that Finlator was doing. He stated:

The response to our consistently liberal and prophetic type of ministry has not and probably never will be a rapidly growing membership. The character of pioneering, liberal thought, accent on individual freedom with responsibility, and innnovation in worship is not of great popular appeal even in a denomination ostensibly founded on these principles.

People did come to Pullen because of its worship and because of the stimulating sermons. But other people chose not to come for the same reason. It is not surprising, therefore, that some long-time members grew increasingly restive, and a few of them painfully came to the conclusion that they could not remain at the church.

The next year C. E. Bishop, who succeeded Williams as chairman of the Board of Deacons, made the same kind of report. He wrote:

The membership of the Pullen Memorial Baptist Church is dedicated to a liberal and prophetic type of ministry—a ministry concerned not only with man's relation to God but also with man's relation to his fellow man. The church has a tradition of deep social responsibility and is regarded as serving the community in a position of leadership on matters pertaining to social morality.

In speaking of "ministry" Bishop had in mind the entire congregation, not the pastor alone. But in speaking of what was "Accomplished during the year" he said, "The Minister continued to speak courageously with freedom and responsibility on matters pertaining to major social issues in today's world."

Finlator did not expect, and he certainly did not receive, universal endorsement from his congregation for the stands which he took. He received a great deal of criticism from within the congregation as well as from the outside. Although in its constitution Pullen had declared itself open to Christians without regard to race, there was no agreement on specific issues involved in "the race problem." Not everyone was happy with Finlator's conclusions about the implications of the doctrine of the separation of church and state. Not all were opposed as he was to capital punishment. Not all favored gun-control legislation.

The reaction of one long-time, active member of the congregation to one of Finlator's sermons will illustrate the point. The sermon was entitled "In Sober Truth." Preached on December 11, 1966, it was a comment on proposals being considered by the State Legislature for revising the liquor laws. Fully recognizing the problems associated with the "increase in the sale and consumption of alcohol, particularly among young people," Finlator spoke of the "obvious" need for updating our laws so as to deal effectively with the problem. Citing Jesus' teaching that laws were made for man and not man for the laws, he said, "Our present laws on alcoholic beverages do not fall in this category. Our legislators have a solemn obligation to update them."

Then, in his concluding paragraph, he spoke of many other laws which also needed updating:

> And such is the law in North Carolina demanding the supreme penalty of capital punishment for certain crimes. Though the conscience of the people is against it and juries are reluctant to arrive at it and judges shrink from pronouncing it and penologists call for abandonment of it, the law is still on the books. And such too are all those harsh and inhuman laws dealing with drug addiction and sex deviation and alcoholism, treating as criminals people whom modern medicine and the insights of psychiatry and the wisdom of sociology and anthropolgy have shown us to be people in need of medical care and compassion and understanding rather than criminals to be jailed and humiliated and blackmailed and deprived of civil justice and dignity. And such too are the laws that decree that American citizens cannot marry certain other American citizens. Yes, by all means let the General Assembly address itself to outmoded and unworkable legislation with regard to the consumption of alcoholic beverages, and from this assignment learn to give a new look at all old laws that have lost their usefulness and can no longer stand the light of man's conscience today, nor be enforced without suppression and humiliation, nor command the respect and honor to which all law is entitled. Let them and let us face these realities in sober truth.

For that long-time member that sermon was the straw that broke the camel's back. After hearing it he wrote to the Chairman of the Board of Deacons "conditionally" tendering his resignation. After reading a copy of the sermon, he made that resignation final and made four observations:

> First. Those of our membership, be they few or many, and others elsewhere who are interested in increasing the manufacture, sale or consumption of alcahol [*sic*] as a beverage, in my humble opinion, have a very effective defender presently occupying our pulpit. I am unalterably opposed to the manufacture, sale or consumption of alcahol [*sic*] as a beverage, and I especially deplore its brazen acceptance and defense by the minister of our church.
>
> Second. If intermarriages of the colored and white races are objectionable to the membership of our Church or any substantial part thereof, they seem to have little sympathy or understanding by the present occupant of our pulpit. While I have no son or daughter that might be the victim of such an arrangement, I wish at this time to express my opposition to the removal of the legal restriction to such marriages, and deplore a statement from our pulpit which to me seems to encourage such marriages.
>
> Third. Our minister's apparent attitude and frequent utterances on moral matters "New Morality" and sex are distasteful to me, and in my opinion, dangerous to our young people. Again, while I have no one to be influenced or misguided by such an attitude and utterances, it is my conviction that some concern should be shown such serious matters.

Fourth. The sermon on December 11, 1966, was only the proverbial straw and climax. For some time I have been in disagreement with our minister's attitudes, utterances and leadership of our church. It now seems clear that any hope for an acceptable change is futile.

Not only did this deacon resign from the Board, but shortly thereafter he moved his membership to another church.

When that letter of resignation was submitted to the Board, there followed a general discussion of the resignation "and related matters." At the conclusion of that discussion a motion was passed asking the chairman to "appoint a committee of deacons to meet informally with the pastor and to relate to him the ideas and suggestions which had been presented." That committee was appointed and met with Finlator on February 27, 1967. In a report dated March 20, 1967, the chairman said that the pastor was informed of "the resignation of a Deacon and statements by some other members that they were considering moving their membership." A summary of the "thoughts and comments" expressed in the deacons' meeting were read to the pastor, without any names being revealed. "Each committee member then attempted to express his own interpretation of the dissatisfaction among these members, and of possible ways in which the church might improve its ministry to all its members with their varying needs." Finlator expressed similar concern, and the meeting concluded with the committee feeling "that the discussion was helpful and that the evidence of mutual understanding and desire for the good of the church indicate a spirit of working together toward solutions of church problems."

It could not be expected that a minister could consistently preach on controversial issues without arousing significant opposition, particularly when he comes out so frequently on the unpopular side. One issue on which Finlator encountered serious resistance from his congregation was American involvement in Vietnam. It is impossible to say when he first began to question that involvement. It is clear, however, that he was one of the first persons to call for our withdrawal from Vietnam. Under the headline, "Rev. Finlator Urges Withdrawal of U.S.," the Raleigh *News and Observer* for Monday, March 1, 1965, stated:

A Raleigh Baptist minister told his congregation Sunday to urge President Johnson to withdraw American military forces from South Viet Nam.

The Rev. W. W. Finlator asked his congregation at Pullen Memorial Baptist Church in Raleigh to petition Johnson to accept the offer of Secretary General U. Thant of the United Nations to mediate such a withdrawal, "with honor and with dispatch."

185

"From the scant news that trickles through the official censorship that has kept us uninformed we learn that the weapons used against us are our own, that the enemy we confront is neither Russians nor Chinese but Vietnamese, that the only foreign soldiers in the land are Americans who go by the name of 'advisers.'

"We find no stable government to work with, or as we say, to defend," he continued. "The government that invited us to assist is no more. We seem to contribute at will to the setting up and toppling of successive governments and apparently none has the backing of the people who regard them as expressions of neo-colonialism."

As the war escalates, the Rev. Mr. Finlator said, nations of the world, friendly and otherwise, "recoil in shock and dismay." He expressed the fear that soon nuclear restraint may no longer be possible.

After that, Finlator frequently spoke to that issue both in the pulpit and in addresses in other settings. In addition, he wrote letters to the editor, both to the *News and Observer* and the *Biblical Recorder*. A year after that first statement, he was chairman of a group of fourteen Raleigh clergymen who "urged President Johnson to end all bombing and aggressive warfare in Viet Nam." (N&O, 3/31/66) On January 21, 1967, the *Biblical Recorder* carried a letter from him announcing a "Mobilization" in Washington on January 31 and February 1.

Quotations from a sermon entitled "An American Tragedy," preached on January 22, 1967, will demonstrate the kind of thing that Finlator frequently said to his congregation about Vietnam. In the introduction he said:

In speaking today of the tragedy of our involvement in Vietnam I shall not talk, as on former occasions, about an unjust and immoral war, or dwell on the bankruptcy of American foreign policy so dramatized in Vietnam, or deplore the bombing of civilians, or describe the horror of napalm bombs or the shame of the nauseating gas (sometimes referred to as 'humane gas,' something no other nation has resorted to in modern times), or the defoliation of the forests or the poisoning of the rice fields. Instead I shall talk about what the war is doing to us as a nation and as a people. As horrible as the war is to the brave Vietnamese who for 20 long years have been fighting for their freedom and integrity, we shall consider it this morning as an *American* tragedy.

He concluded this sermon:

What to do about it all? This is not the burden of my sermon today. You already know how I feel. We went in unilaterally and we can come out unilaterally. Our interest there was self-created. We can un-create it. We could cease the bombing this very moment and withdraw our troops to enclaves, calling on the International Control Commission which was specifically set up for this purpose to begin taking over. We could announce a phase withdrawal and the dismantling of all our bases. We could call for a new convening of the Geneva Powers. We could declare our willingness to stand by and honor any government the people of Vietnam, North and South and Central, establish under internationally supervised elections. We could undertake reparations for the incredible damage done this people and this country. We could channel these reparations and much more, and would to God we would start right now. But brethren, as St. Paul put it, my heart's desire and prayer to God for America is that *they* might be saved! Saved from a tragedy of our own making. Saved from a loss of faith, a breaching of contract, a crisis in credibility, a paralysis in inner renewal, a default of leadership, a schism in the soul.

As Finlator continued to express his opposition to our involvement in Vietnam, feelings within the congregation ran higher and higher. A letter, written on December 11, 1967, by another long-time church member and leader, and addressed to the minister, the Chairman of the Board of Deacons, the Chairman of the Business Board, and the Church, expressed what many—but not all—of the church members were thinking and feeling.

> For some time I have found myself in sharp disagreement with our minister's viewpoint, and related activities concerning the war in Vietnam. There was a mild reaction on my part upon seeing my minister stand in front of the Post Office for an hour on Wednesdays in silent protest against the war in Vietnam. I disagreed with this, and felt that the general effect was harmful to our country and damaging to the possibilities of ending the war, since it must encourage Ho Chi Minh to continue the war.

> I reacted strongly to a sermon preached last summer on the war in Vietnam, copies of which were distributed to the press. I was shocked by this, and felt as if I were listening to Hanoi, and not the pulpit of Pullen Baptist Church.

> The march on the Pentagon subsequently, like the silent vigil, disturbed me somewhat. The resolution at the State Baptist Convention disturbed me somewhat. Each reference, directly or obliquely, in Sunday services disturbed me, and there have been many of them. The Council of Churches resolution, described by Bishop Frazier as naive (and whose description is wholeheartedly concurred by me) added some fuel to the fire.

> In last week's paper, even after clarification, is the story of counselling the students who picketed the induction center and the Selective Services office in Raleigh, and acting as spokesman for them. In Sunday's service there was a further defense of these "clean-smelling" weird looking protestants. As a related matter in Sunday's sermons, I would protest against labelling the President of the United States as an inveterate liar. I fear that Mr. Finlator is so wrapped up in the cause that he does not distinguish hearsay and accusation from that which he knows of personal knowledge, and repeating such statements from the pulpit runs far afield from my understanding of Christianity.

> I have repeatedly instructed my children that when in a group in which mischief is afoot, they should disassociate, and get away. They are

legally aiders and abetters if they remain. The burning of draft cards, attempts to interfere with induction centers, etc. are in clear violation of the law, as well as being a divisive and undermining factor in the strength of this country against communism. I do not state that Mr. Finlator is violating the law, but I do state that his actions and his words aid and abet such violators by easily-led young people.

Mr. Finlator has a right to protest, and I have felt for some time, that when it goes to the extreme which I feel it is now going, I should exercise my right of protest and that I will be doing less than my duty not to register a counter-protest.

The author of this letter concluded my resigning from all the offices he held in the church and announcing his intention to leave Pullen. He was persuaded to withdraw his resignations, however, and he continued as an active member of the church until he retired from his profession and moved away from Raleigh.

Two days after the above letter was written, on December 13, 1967, Finlator addressed a letter to the congregation in which he responded to the rapidly-growing dissatisfaction among the membership. He wrote:

To the Members of Pullen Memorial Baptist Church:

I write this personal message voluntarily to express deepest regret for the distress and anguish I have brought you during the past two years with regard to the involvement of our nation in Vietnam. Most of you have not shared my views and all of you have been patient and long-suffering. I feel that in the warmth and depth of my convictions I have taken advantage of your kindness, and your silence, in sermons and articles and direct action. I am aware that I may have gone too far and presumed too long upon your forebearance and I want so much to find the right word and do the right thing to make what amends I can.

For this reason I am this week severing my relationship with the Raleigh Peace Vigil and shall no more on Wednesdays stand with the group in silent protest against the war in front of the Post Office. I realize that my decision to participate in the vigil was made completely on my own. I also realize that, however I might wish it otherwise, I can never, as long as I am pastor, fully dissociate my actions from Pullen Memorial Baptist Church and that they, in a measure, always involve you.

Furthermore as I review my preaching I must acknowledge that all too frequently, perhaps repetitiously, the matter of Vietnam has been in my sermons. I would be the first to find fault with a fellow minister who preached on such a subject as drinking or gambling Sunday after Sunday. And now I stand self-accused of the same judgment. Again, I have felt deeply and you have listened patiently, but obviously this must not go on and on. Because I am convinced that Vietnam presents the foremost issue facing our nation, and humanity, it will be difficult to me, yet nonetheless, I am hereby subjecting myself to the rigorous discipline of proportion, perspective and self restraint and shall in future sermons temper my speech with a more hearty request for your own honestly arrived at and strongly held convictions.

Of course I am embarrassed for all of us, and offer apologies, over the unfortunate publicity in connection with the recent picketing by students here in Raleigh. Please believe me when I say the students came to me and not I to them. While it may not have been necessary for me to make the original statement concerning their views, I was, in a measure, responding to their overtures to a minister and doing what I could publicly to avoid the violence in our community that was actually taking place in other areas in the country.

Thus it is my pledged intention that future statements within, and activities beyond, our church and community, without compromising the witness one feels he has to make, indicate a deference to your feeling and honor our relationship with one another here at Pullen Memorial.

I am sorry that it is at the Christmas season I write you these words. Another time might have been much more appropriate. But this is not only the time of peace on earth but also of reconciliation and understanding and my heart goes out to you in love and in thanksgiving and in prayer.

Sincerely,
W. W. Finlator

It proved to be impossible, however, for Finlator to remain completely silent on this explosive issue or on other matters of social concern. Although he did not speak quite as often on the controversial issues, he did speak on them from time to time. While he was preaching on other topics he often made passing references that kept the matters before the congregation. For example, in a sermon entitled "Speaking of Priorities," delivered on February 8, 1970, Finlator asked "What shall be the new order of priorities in the United States?" In summarizing his response to that question he said:

> I have my own very firm convictions here and you will find yourself in varying degrees of agreement and disagreement with them. I think our first priority is total military disengagement from the Vietnam tragedy, if not precipitately, at least on a time schedule of not more than one year. Along with this, as a second priority, is the radical demilitarizing of our national life and economy. Some of our most respected leaders speak of us as a military state or as a garrison state and one look at the national budget gives an awesome confirmation of this description.

After these two priorities, he spoke of the ending of poverty in our country, the extending of full citizenship to every American, and protecting our ecology.

In late 1969 President Nixon announced his plan for "Vietnamization"—the replacing of American ground forces with South Vietnamese troops. But in April, 1970, he announced an extension of the war into Cambodia! Troop withdrawal was begun, however, and in 1971 the number of Americans in Vietnam dropped to 159,000. As the troops were gradually being withdrawn, a great deal of concern was expressed in this country about the prisoners of war. A number of groups and individuals began to try to find ways of persuading Hanoi to release those prisoners. In a "Point of View" article in the *News and Observer* for Sunday, April 18, 1971, Finlator said:

> The Hanoi government both at home and through its representatives at the peace conference in Paris has indicated to our government its willingness and desire to begin releasing prisoners when the United States announces a specific time by which all American troops will have been withdrawn. Hanoi will not even wait for the withdrawal to be completed before the exchange begins. In the light of all this let us continue to work for and pray for the safety and the security and the early return of our service men and for the peace of mind and strength of soul of their families here at home. And let us keep on writing those letters by the thousands upon thousands.
>
> But in the future, if we really want the men home, address the letters, not to Hanoi, but to Washington.

Many members of the congregation were solidly behind Finlator. Some of them agreed with his stand on Vietnam, and others did not. But there was a strong commitment to the ideal of a free pulpit and a genuine appreciation of a minister who would speak his mind on controversial topics. Some wrote letters of appreciation and encouragement to him, many assuring him of their support even when they disagreed with his views. One example of official support for his position came from the Community Concerns Committee. On May 10, 1972, that group issued to the congregation the following statement:

> We, the members of the Pullen Memorial Baptist Church Community Concerns Committee, strongly oppose the escalation of the bombing in Indo-China and the mining of the harbors of North Vietnam. We feel that such actions are inconsistent with our Christian concern for peace and the wellbeing of the human community, and we urge the President to reconsider his decisions for increased bombing and harbor mining. We also urge Congress to reconsider its funding of the Indo-China conflict in light of these actions.
>
> The Community Concerns Committee urges the congregation to express its concern over the escalated Indo-China War in one of the following ways:
> (1) Search for an appropriate time to talk with your family about American policy, Christian perspective, and war as "a way of life."
> (2) Share your concern with your congressional representatives in person or by letter or telegram.

(3) Share your concern with your friends at every possible opportunity.

(4) Take symbolic action or make statements available to the news media.

Pullen Memorial Baptist Church was, therefore, in a crucial situation when T. Melvin Williams began his work there. It was divided on the question of what to do about the "Long Range Plan" for the educational facility, and it was in turmoil because of the controversial activities and public pronouncements of its minister. Williams did not involve himself in the decision-making process about the building. Neither did he speak to the issues to which Finlator spoke. Rather in that tumultuous situation he began to work on those matters which he understood to be his ministry at Pullen.

Williams' greatest strength lay in working with groups and with individuals. He attended the meetings of the deacons with some regularity, and reported to them on his activities, particularly his work with young people. Often Finlator took note of that work and commended Williams for what he was doing. According to the minutes for November 2, 1969, "Finlator invited attention of board to Mel Williams and work he is doing. Youth group, impression on total congregation, pastor's heart in visitation, committee work, Pullen discussion group, personal study." The next month, December 7, 1969, Williams "chatted informally" and spoke of what he saw to be his work:

1. Campus ministry and youth—chaplain ministry at N.C. State, university residence hall work, counseling, chaperoning, etc.
2. Educational ministry at Pullen (though more inclined toward pastoral)—on-the-job training.
3. Involvement with Senior Highs—understanding and friendship.
4. Sharing pulpit—encourages study and reflection.
5. Function as resource person for classes and worship.
6. Sees church as shared responsibility.
   Problems: communication among groups and members—may be met by "encounter" groups extending deeper than Sunday morning contacts.
7. Work with Poteat choir.
8. Suggestions for retreats—possibly a deacon's retreat.
9. Contacts with older members—encompassing wide range of folks.

From this report it is easy to observe that Williams was more interested in group work and in "pastoral" activities than in organizational administration.

Two of Williams' reports to the deacons reflect this kind of interest. The minutes for March 1, 1970, state:

Mr. Williams then mentioned the April Arts Festival plans and introduced the idea for a Youth Coffee House for the four Friday nights in April. The Coffee House would be for teenagers and would be held in the Fellowship Hall. Mr. Williams introduced three members of the Youth Council who described their plans.

191

The minutes for June 11, 1972, state:

> Mel Williams made the following reports: (1) Day camp enrollment is full; program begins tomorrow. Union service on June 18 will conclude the week. (2) Sam Hill's visits last week were attended by about 75 each night and were well received. (3) Dance class on Monday and writing class on Tuesdays for the next 6 weeks. (4) Early services are off to a good start.

One of Williams' first programs was the creation of Encounter Groups, using the commercially-produced *Encountertapes*. Working in cooperation with the Baptist Student Union, he invited participation by students from N.C. State and Meredith. The literature sent to prospective group members to describe the program stated:

> The ENCOUNTERTAPE Personal Growth Program is a serious educational instrument. For many people the exercises are deeply involving emotional experiences. Those who decide to participate might become deeply involved or they might not, but they should know that there is this possibility when they join the group.

A total of twenty-six people were involved in the first three groups.

In the spring of 1971 the Worship Committee, working with Williams, invited Carlyle Marney to preach for three days at Pullen. Marney was former pastor of the Myers Park Baptist Church in Charlotte and currently was operating "Interpreter's House," an ecumenical center of study and work at Lake Junaluska, N.C. In a letter to Pullen members announcing Marney's visit Williams said:

> Those of us who have been blessed by Southern Baptist backgrounds have long considered Carlyle Marney to be the preacher *par excellence*, whose reputation has risen far beyond Southern Baptist circles. . . .
> Pullenfolk are not accustomed to springtime "revivals." Therefore, we have carefully titled Marney's visit "a series of sermons." Despite the semantics, we who have invited Marney feel that he is a man who may help "revival" to happen for some of us. The renewal of faith and the rededication to the living of the Christian life ought to be a goal for all of us.

Although most of Williams' work in the years 1970-1972 was with young people, in 1971 he suggested something for the deacons' which was ultimately to become a regular activity. On October 3, in a discussion in the Board of Deacons on ways of strengthening the spiritual life, he suggested a retreat. "As to the type of meeting and the purpose, he said it would probably center upon getting to know one another better and enabling the group to work together better." A committee to plan the retreat was appointed, and at the next meeting a date was announced and a program "centering on some theological reflection with a guest leader and a goal of interaction was suggested."

After Williams had been at Pullen for a number of years he produced a leaflet, entitled "For You at Pullen," in which he included a statement on "Christian Education at Pullen" which puts quite succinctly the philosophy which undergirded his career at the church:

> The goal of education is to draw forth the growth and potential of each person; we therefore see each person not as an empty vessel to be filled, but as one who already has resources to be discovered. In the context of the Church and at Pullen in particular, our goal is to help each person develop a lively awareness of the personal-spiritual resources within. It is a pilgrim's progress of on-going movement toward wholeness in the company of fellow travelers—sharing with each other our insights and strengths. In the total learning life of the church, we are involved in bearing witness to the truth that God is at the center, living in us, drawing out and freeing our power to love and serve. As sons of God we are in continual process of claiming and reclaiming this power, always striving toward wholeness, waking up inside, discovering newness, finding our depths and through this process seeking to give ourselves with passion to the needs of the total community. We invite all who share our hope and witness to join us in this pilgrimage.

A new issue was beginning to emerge within the Baptist denomination which was to affect Pullen for the next several years. When Pullen adopted its first Constitution on April 20, 1958, it abandoned the category of "associate membership" and began to accept into full membership people who came from "another church in the evangelical tradition." In the 1971 revision of the Constitution the policy was changed again, and Pullen began to accept transfers from "another Christian communion." Outside Pullen little attention had been paid that membership policy. In 1967, St. John's Baptist Church in Charlotte adopted a policy of receiving into its membership anyone who had been baptized as a believer, regardless of the mode of baptism. That action received a great deal of publicity throughout the state. In October the Mecklenburg Association, of which St. John's was a member, excluded St. John's by adopting a policy limiting membership to churches which required their members to be baptized by immersion. In other associations efforts were made to have the same policy adopted, but those efforts were not successful. There was also a move to have the North Carolina Baptist State Convention adopt that policy. The issue was arising also in other states, notably in Arkansas and in California. Throughout the rest of the 1960's and on into the 1970's the matter was debated in North Carolina, and hardly a month went by without the *Biblical Recorder* having at least some reference to it. Pullen members of course followed the discussions with interest and concern. Not for some time, however, did they have to deal with the matter because neither the Raleigh Association nor the State Convention took action during this period. The only reference to the issue in the church's official documents was a note that a question came up in the deacons' meeting on October 3, 1971, "about the possibility of the Southern Baptist Convention purging certain churches. Dr. Finlator doesn't think this will happen, but he admitted that activities are afoot in the State Convention to expel certain churches which have been denied the fellowship of their local associations." It was not to be long, however, before Pullen would have to face the issue.

Chapter 8
A Caring Church
In An Era of Disintegration
(1973-1984)

Richard Nixon was re-elected President in 1972 with a near-record 520 electoral votes out of a total of 538. As recently as 1970 the possibility of his winning a second term was very much in doubt. He had not fulfilled his promise made in his first campaign that he would get the United States out of Vietnam without losing the war. His heralded "Vietnamization" policy had failed. The peace movement had revived and there had been tragic confrontation between students and the National Guard on the campus of Kent State University. In New York City marching students were attacked by construction workers, and at Jackson State University in Mississippi two black students were killed by state police. The disclosure of the massacre at My Lai touched off waves of criticism of the Administration. The publication of the Pentagon Papers added fuel to the fire. Nixon was at loggerheads with Congress and with the Supreme Court, particularly on matters having to do with desegregation. A Gallup Poll conducted in mid-1971 revealed that less than half of the people supported the President. Yet successes in foreign affairs coupled with bitter divisions in the Democratic Party handed Nixon a landslide victory.

From the outset of his second term Nixon had to deal with increasing public indignation over the Watergate incident. The arrest of the four burglars at the Democratic National Committee headquarters, on June 17, 1972, proved to have been the beginning of the end for him.

In the midst of the Watergate investigations his Vice-President was forced to resign because of charges of tax evasion. Finally, to avoid impeachment, on August 9, 1974, Nixon resigned.

Gerald R. Ford completed Nixon's unexpired term. He faced the problem of trying to restore confidence in the integrity of the administration, all the while dealing with a suspicious and philosophically hostile Congress. In his twenty-six months, he exercised the veto sixty-six times. He barely won his party's nomination to run for re-election in 1976, almost losing his bid to Ronald Reagan.

In what has been characterized as a "lackluster" contest for the presidency Jimmy Carter defeated Ford. Throughout his term Carter had to deal with a critical energy problem. His support of a treaty which surrendered control of the Panama canal subjected him to criticism for giving away something that "rightfully belonged to the United States." He fought for the ill-fated Equal Rights Amendment. The SALT II treaty which he negotiated was not approved by Congress. His most notable achievement was to bring together for peace talks Israeli Prime Minister Begin and Egyptian President Sadat. His most agonizing problem was the seizure of the American Embassy in Iran and the holding of the American hostages.

Ronald Reagan easily defeated Carter in 1980, campaigning with promises to cut taxes, balance the budget, and reduce unemployment. He got a tax cut through Congress, although its effects were unevenly distributed. Unemployment, which had reached the double-digit level in 1979, continued to rise. The deficit in the national budget continued to increase. The Equal Rights Amendment was finally defeated. The peace initiative was renewed with a rising tide of support for negotiations for an end to the build-up of nuclear weaponry. Campaigning for re-election in 1984, he had to deal with terrorist activities in Lebanon. Yet he won 59% of the popular vote, losing only in Minnesota and the District of Columbia.

Since 1972 there has been no peace in the Middle East. Although Egypt and Israel came to terms, no other Arab nation accepted that fact. Israel continued her struggle for existence in the midst of a hostile Arab world. Lebanon, torn by internal strife since gaining independence in 1943, had to deal with the presence of the PLO and with Israeli activities against that organization, with the peacekeeping troops sent into the country by the United Nations, with Syrian interference, and with continuing terrorists activities directed mainly against the United States. The Shah of Iran was overthrown in 1979, and the Ayatollah Khomeini returned to his country in complete control of the government.

Revolutions broke out in Zimbabwe, Chile, Cyprus, Portugal, Uganda, Equatorial Guinea. Guerrilla warfare ravaged Zambia, Mozambique, Central Africa. The Russians invaded Afghanistan; the British fought the Argentineans in the Falklands; and the United States engaged in swift military activity in Granada. In Central America the United States actively supported the government in El Salvador and the rebels in Nicaragua.

In the world of religion there was significant change. Pope Paul VI died in August, 1978, bringing to an end an administration of fifteen years in which some of the policies of John XXIII and Vatican II had been fully implemented, but in which others of those policies had been attenuated. Paul VI was clearly more conservative than his predecessor. John Paul I, successor to Paul VI, lived for only one month after his election to the Papacy. John Paul II assumed the papal throne in October, 1978, the first non-Italian Pope since 1523. He proved to be even more conservative than had Paul VI, and there has been little effort to carry the spirit of Vatican II any further.

The churches in the United States struggled with the question of the status of women. Some people in the Catholic Church advocated the ordination of women as priests, but there was little prospect that that would be done. The Episcopal Church finally approved the ordination of women. The Presbyterians ordained a number of women, though they were slow to place them in positions other than Ministers of Christian Education or Associate Ministers. The American Baptists, who for years had had a handful of women pastors, became more open to women serving in that position. Southern Baptists began to ordain women, though only a handful of women have served as pastors of churches. In nearly all denominations women have been members of local church boards. The Southern Baptist Convention, however, in June, 1984, passed a resolution disapproving of women serving as deacons or as ministers. After the passing of that resolution there was a wave of protest both against the attitude expressed toward women and against the Convention's attempted invasion of the rights of the local congregations.

The most dramatic development in religion was the rise of the Moral Majority. There had been a shift to the right in the political arena, and this group represented such a shift in religion. An alliance between the Moral Majority and the political New Right played a major role in the national elections in 1980 and 1984. The shift is seen also in the organizational life of most major denominations. It was particularly noticeable among Southern Baptists, where throughout the period there was a well-organized and carefully-directed strategy for getting control of denominational institutions and agencies by placing people on the boards of trustees.

One characteristic of the extreme right is an unwillingness to tolerate differences. This characteristic became evident in the movement among Southern Baptists to exclude churches which had membership

197

policies that differed from those of the majority. The movement began to take shape in the last half of the decade of the 1960's, and it focused on North Carolina.

For North Carolina Baptists the controversy began in the Mecklenburg Association. St. John's Baptist Church, in Charlotte, adopted in the spring of 1967 a policy of accepting into membership persons who had been baptized as believers in churches of other denominations, regardless of *how* they had been baptized. The essence of their policy statement was:

> In keeping with earliest Baptist tradition, we . . . will accept a candidate's baptism as valid, without regard to mode, if it was for him an act of obedience which followed conversion and symbolized his identification with the Christian faith and the whole Church as the Body of Christ. (BR, 4/8/67)

The announcement of that policy evoked immediate debate among Baptists. A number of pastors in the Mecklenburg Association announced their plan to propose an amendment to the Association's constitution which would restrict membership to churches that require all members to be immersed. On October 20, 1967, the Association adopted the following constitutional amendment:

> All churches affiliated with this association shall be churches who use the New Testament as the statement of their faith and church policy and require that all candidates, who are physically able, to be immersed in water, on the basis of belief in Jesus Christ as Savior and Lord, to qualify for membership.

By that action not only St. John's but also Myers Park, which had had an open membership policy since 1949, were disqualified for membership in the Association.

The action of the Mecklenburg Association raised the possibility of similar action being taken by the North Carolina Baptist State Convention. The Arkansas Baptist State Convention had set a precedent in 1965 by refusing to seat messengers from a church which practiced open membership, and in 1968 by withdrawing fellowship from four churches for the same reason. The *Biblical Recorder* published a number of letters which dealt with the possibility of an amendment to the constitution of the State Convention, and it became apparent that the issue would have to be faced.

M. O. Owens, pastor of Parkwood Baptist Church, Gastonia, proposed the following amendment for consideration at the annual convention held in 1971:

> Article IV. Composition, shall be amended as follows: the lines—"a cooperating church shall be one that supports any object of the Convention and which is in friendly cooperation with this Convention and sympathetic with its purposes and work" shall be amended by the addition, after "purpose and work," of the following: "and which is Baptist,

following the New Testament teaching of salvation by grace, and practicing believer's baptism by immersion only, thus consisting of immersed professed believers in Jesus Christ (excepting where a professed believer's immersion is prevented by physical disability)." (BR, 11/20/71)

Although a slight majority of the messengers to the Convention voted in favor of the amendment, it fell far short of the two-thirds vote necessary for adoption. Owens tried again the next year with the same proposed amendment. When it became apparent that his proposal would fail, he joined President Tom Freeman, pastor of the First Baptist Church of Dunn, in support of a "compromise motion" that was overwhelmingly passed:

> That we reaffirm our faith in the Bible as our sufficient guide in matters of faith and practice and that we reaffirm our faith in the autonomy of the local church. That we reaffirm and declare our conviction that believer's baptism by immersion in water is the teaching of the New Testament and should be a requirement for members in any church that calls itself Baptist;
>
> 2. That we hereby, in spirit of Christian love, earnestly plead with the churches differing at this point to recognize that though freedom allows such practice, Christian love and the welfare of our denomination override such freedom and ask that they choose the course and follow the practice followed by the other 99 percent of N.C. Baptists in insisting on believer's baptism by immersion in water as a prerequisite to church membership.
>
> 3. That we earnestly request any other churches considering this course to refrain from following the pattern set by these 20 or so churches.
>
> 4. That we authorize the President of this Convention to appoint a committee of 11 of which he shall be a member and chairman, and one which shall be strong, and representative of both conservative and liberal view points, to take this resolution and this plea to any and all churches in our fellowship now receiving people into membership without requiring of them baptism by immersion; that they urge these churches in love and for the sake of harmony and our labors together to comply with this request; that this Committee make a full report to North Carolina Baptists in the pages of the BIBLICAL RECORDER at least 60 days before our annual Convention in 1973; and that this report be without any recommendations.

The original draft of section 2 of the motion referred to the churches as "erring" rather than "differing" and "demanded" rather than "asked" that the churches give up their freedom to differ.

Freeman appointed the committee in February, 1973. In its organizational meeting the committee tried to underscore its intent to be a reconciling agency. Initially they had difficulty in determining how to go to the churches, for they did not wish to appear to violate the autonomy of the local congregation. After three meeetings they decided to ask the *Biblical Recorder* to publish the following "Open Letter to Differing Churches":

> Any Baptist Church in our fellowship that is following a policy of receiving members into full membership in the Church without requiring baptism by immersion, is respectfully requested to write to the Chairman of the Committee of 11, and if possible, to send a copy of the church membership policy as a matter of shared information, to be kept confidential, if required.
>
> In addition, the Committee would like to know whether such churches would be willing to meet with the Committee. In fact, several churches have already written to express a willingness to meet with the Committee. If your church is one of those affected by the resolution, the Committee of 11 would like to know whether (1) You wish to meet with us, and (2) Whether you would prefer us to come to your church or would prefer to join two to four other churches in sending representatives to meet with us at a mutually-chosen site. (BR, 3/24/73)

There was not complete harmony on the committee because there were significant differences of attitude. Their work was complicated by rumblings in the Convention that no matter what the committee found, another amendment would be proposed at the next session of the Convention.

At the meeting of the deacons of Pullen Memorial Baptist Church on April 1, 1973, W. W. Finlator presented the content of the "Open letter." He also read a letter "from Warren Carr of Wake Forest Baptist Church proposing a meeting with one minister and three laymen representing each church. The Board of Deacons agreed to consider this matter and come together at a special meeting Sunday, April 8th at 2 p.m."

At the April 8 meeting, W. W. Finlator reviewed the background of the controversy and reported on the meeting at Wake Forest. At that meeting Warren Carr had proposed that the eleven churches make a joint response to the committee's overtures. Finlator outlined what he saw to be Pullen's alternatives:

1. To sit tight, do nothing, and let the committee make the overtures, to which Pullen would respond accordingly.
2. To follow through on the procedure proposed by Warren Carr and others (i.e. join with the other churches and deal with the committee as a group).
3. To send our own statement to the committee and ask them to come to speak to us at our church.

Finlator favored the third alternative, and said that he thought that some of the other churches would take the same position. After lengthy discussion, in which wide variety in opinion became apparent, the deacons directed the pastor and the chairman of the Board of Deacons to draft a letter to the committee expressing the concensus which the Board had reached. That letter, dated April 17, 1973, stated:

> We have read the indirect communication from you and the Committee of Eleven in the pages of the Biblical Recorder. While we are sensitive to and sympathetic with the anomalous position of your committee in carrying out the mandate of the 1972 Convention, an unprecedented act which we think presents serious challenges and has disturbing implications and overtones for our Baptist people, we should have nevertheless preferred a direct communication from you rather than the open letter in the Recorder with the request for information from our church and the listing in the same issue of the names of the "differing churches."

> Our concern for the ambiguity of your situation, however, does not turn us from our firm obligation in our own local church to be faithful to time honored basic principles to which all of us as Baptists adhere. We are convinced that an affirmative and unexamined response to your communication, despite our desire to be cooperative and our wish to make your difficult assignment as easy as possible, would still be violating the principle of local autonomy in the individual churches.

> Nevertheless, because of our strong and rewarding association with our fellow churches in the Baptist State Convention over the many years we make a counter proposal: Should the Committee of Eleven wish to come to Pullen Memorial Baptist Church to share with us the position and concern of the Baptist State Convention of North Carolina on the matter of baptism, and should the committee wish to explore with our people the theological, biblical and doctrinal considerations of this ordinance, and should the committee by direct communication request permission to visit our church for this purpose, we do hereby assure you that our Board of Deacons will promptly and courteously grant such permission and that the Committee of Eleven would be accorded every kindness and consideration. The Committee would come as guests of our Board of Deacons and a meeting would be held to which all members of our congregation would be invited.

On May 5, 1973, in an article in the *Biblical Recorder*, Toby Druin, reporting on the work of the Committee of Eleven, stated:

> Freeman last Friday read responses he had received from 10 of the 12 churches previously named. No additional "differing churches identified themselves.

> All except one indicated their willingness to meet with the committee along with representatives of other churches. Only Pullen Memorial Church, Raleigh, failed to indicate that it would send representatives to a joint meeting with other churches and the committee. Chairman of deacons Mrs. Roger Crook said, however, that they would be glad to meet with the committee and discuss the matter.

In response to that statement Pullen's pastor and the chairman of the Board of Deacons addressed a letter to the Committee, to the other "Differing" churches, to the *Biblical Recorder*, and to the Baptists of North Carolina. Dated May 24, 1973, the letter stated that Pullen had notified the Committee that they had chosen one of the options which the Committee had offered in its "Open Letter." It observed, "The only response we received to this letter was a form, exactly the same as that received by other churches, acknowledging our letter, but making no reference to our invitation to the Committee to request a meeting time." Another paragraph added:

> At the meeting of the Committee with area churches in Raleigh, May 27, Pullen Memorial will not be represented, not because this church wishes in any way to appear uncooperative, but because it wishes to entertain the Committee in its own way, according to the Committee's first request. Rather than let it seem that Pullen is unresponsive, we would hope to draw from the Committee a response that is at once personal, within Baptist tradition, and Christian as it deals with us as persons, as an autonomous congregation, and as a part of the Body of Christ.

The proposed May 27 meeting in Raleigh did not take place. The chairman of the Committee of Eleven responded to Pullen's request with the information that the Committee was to meet on July 2 with Watts Street Church and Binkley Memorial Church. The Committee, according to the minutes of the deacons' meeting of June 3, "would like to have us to attend that meeting. If we are unwilling to do so, they will set up a meeting with us alone." The deacons reiterated their insistence on Pullen's meeting with the Committee alone.

Plans were made for the Committee to visit Pullen on Monday evening, July 30, 1973. Roger Crook, Professor of Religion at Meredith College and a Pullen member, was asked to prepare a statement of the church's position. His statement was distributed to the church membership for its study and suggestion. After reviewing the process by which Pullen had reached its position, the document declared:

> Baptism, as we understand it, is the symbol of a person's Christian experience of salvation, of his movement from unfaith to faith. It signifies repentance, a dying to sin and rising to new life in Christ. The time for this symbolic action is the beginning of the new life in Christ. We believe it inappropriate to employ this meaningful symbol as a mere initiation ceremony, the means by which one who has already been a Christian for many years now becomes a Baptist. Baptism, in our judgment, is far too important for that.

The document then placed the Pullen position within the context of Baptist history. It concluded with a reaffirmation of the nature of the Convention as a cooperative agency intended for the support of missionary causes, not one which exercises any right to draw up a creed for its member churches.

Some seventy-five members of Pullen Memorial Church attended the session on July 30. After the chairman of the Committee of Eleven reviewed the responsibility of the Committee, the church's statement was read. Representatives of the church presented individual statements. A lengthy discussion followed, with some elements of "debate" involved. The Committee gave a good deal of attention to the question of biblical support for the church's position. When some members of the church asked about the possible exclusion of Pullen from the Convention, a member of the Committee reminded them that the Committee was to make no recommendations. The moderator of the meeting expressed appreciation for the clarification, but added, "I hope you will understand, however, that the thought of exclusion is very uppermost in our minds, not by the committee, but by the convention." (Notes on the meeting taken by Suzanne Newton)

On Sunday, November 11, 1973, just prior to the meeting of the Convention, Finlator preached a sermon entitled "One Lord, One Faith, One Baptism." After reviewing the work of the Committee, including its meeting with Pullen Church, he examined and evaluated the proposed constitutional amendment. He concluded:

> For ourselves at Pullen Memorial we are honored to be a part of the Baptist State Convention and treasure and cherish our involvement in its fellowship, its program, and its history. While there are other sources and vitalities available to us as a congregation we would respond to exclusion from our Baptist State Convention of North Carolina with the anguish of a son driven from his family. We would survive and continue our witness but the expulsion would be nothing less than spiritual trauma. We shall hope and pray that this will not happen, that North Carolina Baptists will not let it happen. At the same time it must be said again that we have reached together as a responsible and autonomous Baptist body the position we hold on baptism, and are convinced of its rightness for us both biblically and doctrinally. We have, as our Baptist Convention requested, reconsidered our practice and have emerged from the study only more deeply convinced of the validity of what we have done. We must therefore in all love and integrity say that not even the threat of exclusion from our Convention can make us forsake a principle nor deny a conviction.

As instructed, the Committee on Eleven published its report in advance of the meeting of the Convention. Seven Baptist pastors, including M. O. Owens, Jr., who had introduced the amendment at earlier conventions, and who had been a member of the Committee of Eleven, announced their intention to propose the amendment again at the 1973 Convention. During that Convention, however, when it became apparent that the proposal would fail again, one of the seven signers withdrew it "in a spirit of unity."

The issue was not finally disposed of until the next year. James M. Bulman, Convention parliamentarian, proposed the amendment at the 1974 session, with ony a slight change in wording. The debate on his proposal lasted 45 minutes, and the debaters were for the most part the same people who had spoken in previous Conventions. When the vote was taken, the amendment was defeated "by as much as 3 to 1." After that vote, the Convention was to be troubled by the issue no more, and neither was Pullen.

Throughout the history of Pullen Memorial Baptist Church, the deacons have been concerned with understanding their role as deacons and with their involvement in the spiritual development of the church. Beginning in 1971, for help in their own spiritual growth and to get a better sense of direction for the church, they began to hold annual retreats. In those retreats they usually gave attention to biblical and theological considerations. At almost all of them at least one session was devoted to a consideration of the role of the deacon. Sometimes members of the Pullen congregation were leaders of the sessions, and sometimes outside resource persons were asked to lead.

Another development in the life of the church in the early 1970's was the formation of a close association with the Method Day Care Center. For several years prior to 1973 the Center had been in operation in the Method community, located on the edge of Raleigh between Hillsborough Street and Western Boulevard. For several years there had been some interest at Pullen in the operation of a day care center. In 1973, when the Center needed to find new facilities, it entered into an agreement with Pullen Church that served the interests of both groups. By that agreement Pullen provided space and facilities; the Center maintained its own operation, was governed by its own Board of Directors, and was responsible for all expenses associated with the operation. Pullen was to have a liaison person to maintain official contact with the Center. The Center began operation at Pullen on February 1, 1974.

In the spring of 1981 an arrangement for expanded services was worked out. The Method board and staff wished to provide infant care and brought to the Board of Deacons a request that Pullen "extend the stewardship of the building to serve this need." The deacons engaged in a lengthy discussion, not on the merits or demerits of the request, but on the complicated queston of "which boards and committees had the authority/responsibility to act or to be consulted on this issue." The secretary observed that the Method board representative "was bewildered with the response and confused as to the procedure he would have to follow to finally get an official response from the church on the proposal." At last, according to the minutes:

> Allen Page moved and Jim Greene seconded that the Board of Deacons approve, in principle, the recommendation made by Method Day Care Center with regard to enhancing the Pullen facilities to include infant care, subject to the support and approbation of the Business Board, the Board of Education, the Building and Grounds Committee, the Minister of Education, and the Sunday School Superintendent. The motion passed unanimously. (5/1/81)

In the fall of 1983 the deacons asked for a special study of "Method Day Care Center and its relation to Pullen." A special committee was appointed for this purpose. The committee worked quickly and circulated to the deacons a report dated October 26, 1983, which stated that the relationship should be "reaffirmed and deepened." It contained four recommendations, the most important of which were the placing of five Pullen members on the Method Board of Directors and significantly increasing Pullen's contribution for scholarships for children of low income parents. The deacons approved the recommendations.

Although the Method Day Care Center is not an agency of Pullen Memorial Baptist Church, the relationship between the two is such that many people consider Method an extension of Pullen's ministry. A number of Pullen people have served on the Method Board of Directors and a number of others have worked as volunteers in the Center. Pullen's Community Concerns Committee, which worked out the plans for Method's location at Pullen, provides scholarship funds for children from economically deprived families. The arrangement has clearly been a happy one both for Method and for Pullen.

Of all the developments at Pullen in the decade of the 1970's, one of the most unusual was the establishment of a relationship with Coventry Cathedral in Coventry, England. An industrial center famous for the manufacture of automobiles, in World War II Coventry was converted into a center for the production of airplane engines. It was targeted for total destruction by the Germans, and on the night of November 14, 1940, bombs virtually leveled the city. The great 11th century cathedral was left an empty shell. After the war a new building was constructed, with the theme of reconciliation permeating both the architecture of the building and the life of the congregation. One expression of that theme was the creation of "The Community of the Cross of Nails," with centers in churches around the world dedicated to the effort of reconciliation.

Pullen's first official relationship with Coventry was the sending of a group of young people to spend a month studying, working, and worshipping there in the summer of 1974. Mary Ruth Crook proposed the idea after she had visited the cathedral in the summer of 1972. It was she who won the approval of the deacons, recruited the leadership, and planned a program of study., Mel Williams led the group of twenty young people and five adult leaders on the pilgrimage. From the point of view of both Pullen Memorial Church and Coventry Cathedral the project was an outstanding success. Two years later, in 1976, a second group of twenty young people and five adult leaders went to Coventry. They too had a specifically tailored program which involved them in the life and work of the cathedral. Other groups went in 1979 and in 1982.

The visit of those student groups to Coventry led Pullen to another connection with the cathedral. In 1977 Pullen became a center of Coventry Cathedral's Community of the Cross of Nails. Shortly after the 1976 group returned home Alan Eakes, who had been the leader of the group, received a letter from Father John McGuire, dated September 14, 1976, which included the following paragraphs:

> I have spoken to the Provost about how much you and your young people have meant to us and also their great affection for the Cathedral and also the important part they played in our Ministry this Summer.

> He is very keen to deepen our association with them and, indeed, the entire Pullen Community. So impressed is he by your Church's dedication to Coventry and its vision that he feels very inclined to make your Church a Cross of Nails Centre.

> Would you please discuss this with your Pastor and see how he would feel about this coming to be. I am sure that all it would take at this point would be his requesting Provost Williams to make Pullen one of our Coventry Centres of Reconciliation. The fact that two large groups have come here in the past two years, and have been so exceptional, means a great deal to us, and I do hope this deeper affiliation can come about.

The deacons reponded favorably even though they were unsure about what that association might entail. W. W. Finlator wrote to McGuire expressing appreciation for what Coventry had done for the Pullen young people and responding to the invitation to ask for membership in the Community of the Cross of Nails. He said:

> In response to the overture in your letter we brought the matter to our Board of Deacons on Sunday evening, October 3. The Board of Deacons promptly directed me to write you conveying our gratitude and our desire to take affirmative action. The Board requests that you give us suggestions for procedure to become officially a part of the Coventry fellowship and that the matter be brought before the Board for further action.

On December 15 Father McGuire replied, "The Provost welcomes your request, and would like to suggest to your Board of Deacons that he come to present your Church with a cross of nails in the evening of Sunday October 30th, next year, accompanied by Mrs. Eloise Lester, Director of the Community of the Cross of Nails, and myself."

For some months after that, communication was limited, and there was some uncertainty at Pullen about what the status was and what the relationship meant. On August 15, 1977, Finlator wrote Provost Williams:

> Through our Board of Deacons our church has taken official action requesting status as a Cross of Nails Center. Will you do what is necessary to carry through on this for us at the Cathedral? Will you also direct me to tell the congregation what is further expected of us to achieve full status?

Williams responded on August 23: "I am most grateful to you for your letter. The Cross of Nails, properly engraved for the Pullen Memorial Baptist Church, is already in Washington for me to bring to you on Sunday, October 30th."

The Cross of Nails, which hangs on the rear wall of the sanctuary, was presented in the service on Sunday evening, October 30, 1977. Participants in the service were H.C.N. Williams, Provost of Coventry; Eloise Lester, Director of the Community of the Cross of Nails; Kenyon Wright, of Coventry Cathedral; Roger Crook, Chairman of Pullen's Board of Deacons; Alan Eakes, Chairman of Pullen's Coventry Committee; Mary Ruth Crook, Founder of the Pullen-Coventry Pilgrimage; T. Melvin Williams, Jr., Associate Minister at Pullen; and W. W. Finlator, Minister of Pullen. The theme of the service as "Father Forgive." A brief statement on the back of the bulletin explains the significance of the service:

> The Community of the Cross of Nails is a world-wide community of individuals and groups, who share a commitment to a practical vision of reconciliation and genuine intention to live a disciplined Christian life. It springs directly from the united efforts of the community of Coventry Cathedral, exercised, since the loss of the old Cathedral under attack from the air in 1940, throughout the period of destruction and the incitement to bitterness which followed.
>
> The symbol is a cross made by a priest from three fourteenth century iron nails which fell from the blazing timber of the roof. The symbol was an immediate expression of hope, and of a resolve that there should be a resurrection from the rubble. This resurrection was accomplished in physical terms with the building of the new Cathedral, which was completed and consecrated in 1962.
>
> But far more important than the reconstruction of the building was the establishment of a dynamic experimental twentieth century ministry among people, with reconciliation at its heart. The Community of the Cross of Nails is the worldwide expression of this vision.

The months following the presentation of the Cross of Nails were again a period of somewhat limited communication, and that failure to communicate created some feeling of concern. In the summer of 1978 Mary Ruth and Roger Crook, with a group of students from Meredith College, spent two weeks at Kennedy House, an international hostel at the Coventry Cathedral. On July 4 Mary Ruth Crook wrote to the Pullen Church staff:

> The provost also spoke to our group. He ended on a disturbing note which is the object of this letter. Because he has not had regular communication with Pullen, he is of the opinion that we have not fulfilled our commitment as a Cross of Nails Center. He spoke rather sharply about this, and I immediately made an appointment to discuss the matter. Roger and I went, but the Provost had been called away, so we had

207

two subsequent conversations with Connie Downes. Eloise Lester was away on holiday, or we would have talked with her as well. I had taken the book of photographs, leaflets, pages from the yearbook and especially significant bulletins of Sunday worship all laid out in a way that described Pullen's year (or so) since October 30. We explained our understanding of our purpose, and she explained the Cathedral's (i.e., the Provost's) expectations. It seems that he and Eloise and John Maguire *should have* had a session with our ministers or Coventry committee explaining about the beginning of a *Chapter* which is a group of volunteers who pledge themselves to the "Discipline" (as outlined in the leaflet) and indicate such to the Cathedral through the "Application" and payment of $4.00 *each* to cover costs of mailing materials regularly from the Cathedral. We need a designated correspondent to inform the Provost regularly of the activities of this Chapter which should meet at least quarterly to share ideas. Roger and I identified points of the Discipline with Pullen's program of Bible Study and corporate worship and community involvement. So all that is lacking is the formal designation of a Chapter and a correspondent. Connie suggested that upon our return we form this Chapter from any who have been to Coventry and any others interested, then choose a correspondent, send in our money for the regular mailings, and *keep the Provost* informed! She was very sorry that we did not know all this (maybe I was the only ignorant one) but said that communication from our end was essential. She felt that Pullen is fulfilling its purpose (and has *always* been a center of reconciliation) and will explain to the Provost what we explained to her. Eloise Lester is to be based in the U.S. next year for the purpose of keeping in touch with and helping American churches, and will come on our invitation to talk and work with our chapter.

Eloise Lester did establish her headquarters in the United States, at St. Anne's Episcopal Church in Atlanta. In due season, on March 17 and 18, 1979, she spent a week-end with Pullen. Among other matters, she shared information about an additional feature of the Community, the system of Foyers. According to the literature, "This is the formation within the church membership of small groups of about eight which meet monthly in the homes of members for a simple meal and relaxed conversation. The Foyer groups are changed every six months." Pullen proceeded immediately to set up this system, and that has proved to be one of the most helpful features of the church's involvement in the Community.

Whatever dissatisfaction Provost Williams may have felt initially, the situation was resolved. In February, 1980, he was again a guest of the church. Following that visit he wrote to W. W. Finlator:

At long last I am back at the desk after concluding the travel and fighting off a flu bug. I wanted to thank you and all of the wonderful people at Pullen for your most gracious hospitality and the opportunity of being with you several weeks ago. This is my third visit with all of you, and each time I come away with a real sense of having been with a very committed and Christian community . . . a group of Christians who have all of the characteristics of those marvelous people of the early church . . . loving, sharing and knowing their ministry in God's world. Much of this is certainly due to your very fine leadership. Bless you!

Pullen's involvement in the Community of the Cross of Nails has continued primarily through the operation of the Foyer system, through individuals maintaining their membership through annual dues and contributions, and through continuing support of the pilgrimages of the young people to Coventry.

A year and a half after he had led the first group of young people on the Coventry pilgrimage, Mel Williams was granted a six-months sabbatical. Although he had come to Pullen as Minister of Education in 1969, his work had been more inclusive than that. His title was changed to "Associate Minister" when the 1971 Constitutional revision provided for that position. His early interest in group work grew throughout his ministry. Although the records are incomplete, there is enough information to understand how he worked. In August, 1973, he conducted a "Leadership Training Retreat" for church school workers, and in September he held a "follow-up session." In October, 1973, he began two "Enabling Groups" which met over a ten-week period on Sunday evenings. For the participants he described the nature of the groups:

> As you know, each group is self-determining. Your own personal agendas will very much influence the direction your group will take. I have provided some basic guidelines, which have already been enumerated. I see the goal of the group as personal grwoth through the development of group trust. It's an attempt to get to know each other in a substantial way, through personal sharing. Hopefully, you will enable each other to be more fully the kind of person you want to be. A support group.

Such Enabling Groups were to be a continuing part of Williams' work at Pullen.

From time to time Williams preached at the Sunday morning service. His sermon titles give a clue to the dominant concerns in his ministry: "Afraid to be (Me) (Free)"; "The Way to Radical Amazement"; Beyond Obedience"; "The Fellowship of the Weak"; "The Alarming Possibility of Being Able": "Giving Up, for God's Sake"; "What Do You Want Me to Do for You?"; and "Healing with Loneliness."

Williams' sermon on "The Alarming Possibilities of Being Able" summarizes his objectives for himself and for the people with whom he worked. He began by saying, "Beneath all the issues of life which clamor for our attention, there is one basic issue: What does it mean to be a person—an able person?" After describing his own pilgrimage, he summarized his conclusions:

Here are the elements in my vision of possibilities for being a person:
1. This person has a solid sense of his or her own *specialness* as a person. Uniqueness. . . .
2. He or she has a sense of worth and competence as a Person—a sense of Self, so that my bubble bumps into your bubble. You emerge as a distinctive being. . . .
3. There is a naturalness and spontaneity, with a minimum of self-consciousness or self-preoccupation.
4. You have the will to be fully yourself—living from within, from inner resources, rather than from the expectations of others. . . .
5. He has an absence of fear—and I'm convinced that fear is the Great Obstacle that blocks and prevents us from seeing the wild possibilities for our lives.
6. The person I want to be lives with the sure faith that his needs will be met as he can *give* himself to others. . . .
7. He takes the "givens" of his life—his circumstances, abilities, history, parents, etc.—and weaves them into the fabric and fullness of his person. In other words, he has a courageous self-acceptance, and a sense of satisfaction with who he is, limitations included . . . .
8. I am in charge of me. I am responsible for my feelings, my judgments, my failures. I am a victim only if I *allow* it. . . .
9. This person in my vision knows what his or her strengths are. So that you can live out of those strengths rather than from your weaknesses.
10. This person assumes that his inner resources and strengths are great. Your creative potential is high. . . .
11. This process of self-discovery means that every day is exciting. . . .
12. This commitment to personal growth and discovery means that I am an *adventurer*. I am constantly interested in my journey taking me to some new ground, some new trail where I've never been. Like moving up a mountain, gaining new standpoints as you go. When you see your life as an *adventure*, you will see also that you are committed to *risk*, to *courage*, and to a *radical trust in yourself*. In other words, you are a free person. You know the grace of freedom.

Williams' understanding of Christian education was thoroughly consistent with the ideas which he expressed in that sermon. On January 23, 1973, he released a document entitled "A Point of View for Christian Education at Pullen, in which he stated:

I have ceased to view education in terms of the inculcation of a body of knowledge. I do not think we are here to "teach religion," though I recognize that some biblical and theological facts are essential. I think of education, especially Christian education, not as a pouring of facts into empty heads, but as a leading forth, a leading out (*educere*) of what is within each person. The teaching I see is definitely informed by biblical foundations (so that means we will study the Bible). But I'm most interested in the learning here that is not academic but existential; that is, related to where you are in your life. Real learning takes place when the subject matter touches the learner's personal life. In theological terms, How and Where does the life of God touch my life?

In the context of Pullen Church this kind of learning is vital, even crucial. I don't think you can *teach* a person to be a Christian, for the process of becoming a Christian is a process of self-discovery. I want to help people discover for themselves that the Christian life is a worthy life to lead—that it's important to ground your life in a "spiritual" base. That is to say, your relationship to God is crucial as a base for your relationship to people around you. Who then is God for you? What is *your* Christian faith like? What do you want to understand with regard to your faith? What do you want your children to get from this church school?

This is what I want from Christian education here: First, I want a sense of community—where I feel a good level of acceptance and belonging. In order for existential learning to happen in any educational setting, I think the accepting community is vital. . . . Rather than imparting a body of knowledge as we are teaching each other *how to live.* We are enabling each other to discover values by which to live. And how are values taught except by self-discovery? So—if I want to teach a person how to live. . . . No, if I want to ENABLE someone to live—i.e., help him to discover his own resources and strengths—I need to have some notion of what a real person (a Christian) is.

Here Jesus is my model, for he shows me most clearly who God is and what God desires for my life. Ah now, a camera gets a clearer focus. For I look at Jesus and see a man-human-me. I identify with this man, and I say, "Now educate me to be like this man." Educate me to accept his kind of life. After all, I have some of Jesus' same capacities in me.

In addition to his work with groups and with the church school, Williams spent an increasing amount of his time in counseling, particularly with married couples who were experiencing some difficulty and with divorced people. In this way he ministered both to members of the congregation and to people not associated with the church. Because his theological preparation had not included training in that area he wished to have help in developing his skills. He presented his request to the Board of Education and they in turn made a recommendation to the Board of Deacons. Mary Cochran had chaired a committee "to explore questions about granting pay and allowances during the leave and plans for covering Mel's responsibilities during the leave." At the meeting of the deacons on July 12, 1975, Mrs. Cochran presented the report which recommended a six-months leave with full salary and allowances. The committee also recommended that "approval of the leave and pay and allowances be placed before the full congregation in Church Conference." The deacons approved the recommendation for the leave. The minutes do not report the discussion that took place, but for some reason they decided against the recommendation that the matter be taken before the church in conference. Instead they passed a motion "that the issue not be taken to the

Congregation for a vote, but that a full and detailed report be mailed to the church membership." In a letter dated July 30, 1975, the congregation was notified of the action.

In another major action the deacons began in 1976 a study of the church's organizational structure. From time to time various deacons had commented on the need for such a study. Finally, on November 7, 1976, they appointed a task force "to study in depth the organization of the church" and asked for a final report no later than March 6, 1977. That report, which was not presented until April 3, found that "The Board and committee structure does not coincide with the budget structure, and some committees and boards have lack of continuity and absence of memory of past events. Some committees are confused about their mission." It offered specific suggestions about how the organization should be revised. The proposals were circulated in writing to the congregation, written responses were invited, and a church conference for discussion of the proposals was held on December 11, 1977. After that discussion the deacons further considered the ideas that came out in the meeting and made some revisions in the plan.

After more than a year of discussion and of committee work the deacons presented their proposals to the church. In a conference held after the worship service on Sunday morning, April 30, 1978, the motion was made:

> That the proposed amendments to the church constitution and by laws be adopted, effective October 1, 1978; and that the Nominating Committee and Service Board, in establishing new committees and in adding to the membership of existing boards and committees, divide the nominees for such new posts into equal classes of one, two or three year terms.

Most of the proposed amendments dealt with the problems of inconsistency between community structure and budget structure and with clarification of responsibilities. One changed the church calendar so that the church year would begin on July 1 rather than on October 1. The most significant change was the creation of a Church Council composed of certain committe chairmen and church officers which would help coordinate the activities of the church. In addition, the Council would be responsible for making the nominations which thus far has been made by the Service Board. After full discussion, the motion was passed as presented.

The revision of the organizational structure did not affect the responsibilities of the Minister or of the Associate Minister. It did not, therefore, deal with a problem that was in the offing. After his return from his sabbatical, in July, 1976, Mel Williams had resumed and expanded the work that he had been doing earlier. He began to feel, however, that the responsibilities assigned him within the church structure were unduly limiting for him. He had hinted at that feeling even before he had taken his sabbatical. On September 12, 1976, he had concluded his remarks in the deacons' meeting "with the observation that he felt a need to re-examine the organizational structure of the church." That statement was a part of the discussion which had led to the creation of the task force on the church organization. His growing concern, however, seems not to have been so much a matter of constitutional statements as it was one of personal relationships. Increasingly he came to feel that he was not being given the opportunity to exercise his ministry at Pullen to the best of his abilities.

At last Williams concluded that he needed to get official reaction to his concern for his status at Pullen and for his future there. The minutes of a called meeting of the deacons on August 27, 1978, state:

> Board of deacons met in a called session at the request of our associate minister, Mel Williams. In an opening statement, he asked for support while he shared with us his process of deciding to continue to minister at Pullen. The terms under which he would remain are as follows: to be able to preach on a regularly planned basis, to be able to participate in the design of the 11 a.m. worship service on a regular basis, and to increase his leadership of lay ministry in our church.

The minutes are brief, but the session was long, lasting from 7:30 until 10:40. Williams' request was understood by everyone to deal with matters which Finlator saw to be under his jurisdiction. Williams desired a pastoral relationship that might be described as one of "collegiality," while Finlator preferred the maintenance of the "Associate Minister" status in which Williams had come to Pullen. After the lengthy and sometimes heated discussion, the board drew up the following resolution, which it addressed to both Williams and Finlator:

> The Board wishes to convey to both ministers a rededication of itself to its part in this church's expanding ministry.
>
> The Board of Deacons resolves its support for an expanding role for Mel Williams with such responsibilities to be more clearly identified.
>
> At the same time we appreciate and support Bill Finlator's continued dedication to his calling and his expressed dedication to reach mutual agreement on their respective roles.
>
> We recognize that precise delineation of duties is not easily achieved and that frequent review is needed.
>
> Therefore, the Board of Deacons, mindful of their mutual efforts, respectfully requests the ministers to share their progress with the Chairman of the Board prior to the next meeting of the Board, toward a plan for sharing the ministerial duties of the church including the pulpit ministry.
>
> The Pullen Board feels that this church is most fortunate and thankful to have two men of such caliber ministering to its needs. We appeal

213

to their understanding of our support and express our confident expectation of their contribution in a fruitful ministry together in Pullen Memorial Baptist Church.

The ministers did attempt to work out an agreement. On August 31, Williams addressed a note to the Board of Deacons in which he said:

> Since the meeting last Sunday I have sensed an openness from Bill concerning my desire for larger responsibilities. Our conversations have been honest, and I am grateful to the Deacons for helping to facilitate this development.
>
> Specifically, I am grateful for Bill's willingness to include me in the process of designing worship, and I appreciate his granting me advance notice of the times I am to preach.

Finlator's response, dated September 1, included the statement:

> Mel and I have been in several conferences since last Sunday and, as I assured the Board, we have worked through the considerations and recommendations he brought to the Board. He knows that he is welcome to share in the preparation of the worship service, that he will bring unique enrichment in his contributions to such preparation. I have invited him to name such Sundays and occasions as will be most significant and meaningful to him for preaching assignments and these dates have been calendared. He runs a crowded schedule in our church and wishes to confine his preaching appointments to some 12 or 14 times during the year.

In *Pullenews* for October 4, 1978, however, the following statement from both ministers appeared:

> While the church constitution holds the senior minister ultimately responsible as administrative head and names him ex officio member of all committees and Boards, we wish to advise the congregation of a current division of special assignments during the new church year beginning October 1 to the end that each of us may make'the best use of time and involvement.
>
> Mel will work more closely with the Board of Education (which includes the church school and youth groups) and with the Committee on Community Concerns, the Family Life Committee, the Nursery Committee and, in addition, he will supervise the work with seminary interns.
>
> Bill will work more closely with the Business Board, the Board of Trustees, the Area Ministry Committee, the Building and Grounds Committee, the Funeral, Music, the Esthetics, the Library and the Ushers Committee.
>
> Both ministers will continue their responsibilities in pastoral care and counseling, in worship services and with the Board of Deacons.

Another matter which some members of the congregation perceived as a need had not been addressed by the revisions in the constitution.

There was a personnel committee which dealt with personnel and administrative policies in the day-to-day operation of the church. At the deacons' retreat held on November 11, 1978, the chairman reported that he had appointed a special committee whose duties would be to:

1) Write job descriptions for all staff except the ministers
2) Formulate policy for sick leave, vacations, maternity leave, and the retirement for each staff member
3) Recommend to the Board of Deacons a general range of benefits appropriate to each staff member.

After considerable discussion it was moved that "we establish a Personnel Committee as a standing advisory committee to the Board of Deacons." The duties of that committee were to be identical with those stated by the chairman except that in item 1) the phrase "except the ministers" was omitted. The minutes note that "After further discussion, it was decided that the description of the standing committee needed further development and Bob Savage agreed to do this before the next meeting." The following statement was approved at the meting of December 3, 1978:

The duties of the Personnel Committee shall be consistent with the church constitution and involve the following matters:

1. Write and periodically revise a description of responsiblity of all staff members.

2. Formulate a policy for sick leave, vacations, retirement, and maternity leave for each staff position.

3. Recommend to the Board of Deacons a general range of benefits appropriate to each staff position.

4. Recommend to the Board of Deacons a starting salary for any prospective staff member being considered for employment by the church.

5. Periodically the committee shall review items 1 through 4 above and make recommendations for changes as needed.

6. Be available to the ministers for counsel and keep them advised concerning conditions within the congregation as they affect relations between ministers and people.

7. Be available to help resolve personnel problems which may arise.

This committee was to function as an advisory committee to the Board of Deacons, not as a committee of the church.

Before the committee could get well-started on its task another controversy arose over an action taken by the minister in his capacity as chairman of the Advisory Committee on Civil Rights. By the time the last United States ground troops had left Vietnam in 1972, criticism of Finlator for his stand had ceased. Meanwhile, Finlator was making the news on other controversial issues. In an April 8, 1973, "Point of View" article in the *News and Observer* he observed that "Sen. (Sam) Ervin's amiable purpose prose is often more picturesque than accurate." He was one of several ministers interviewed for an article on the integration in the Raleigh churches, published in the *News and Observer* on May 27, 1973. The week after Billy Graham's "Central Carolina Crusade" in Raleigh, he was quoted as saying that the crusade "was not really a live matter" of concern. On November 10, 1974, in another "Point of View" article, he said that President Ford's stand on amnesty for the Vietnam war resisters and evaders "perpetuates the Vietnam trauma." On October 26, 1975, in another "Point of View" article he talked of North Carolina's anti-union stance. He wrote on the Christian academies, on Christian economics, on the Far Right, on the use of "code words." He frequently made the news for his activities with the American Civil Liberties Union and for his work with the United States Commission on Civil Rights. Whenever he spoke as a representative of either of these latter groups he tried to make it clear that it was in that capacity that he was acting. Yet almost invariably the news articles identified him as pastor of Pullen Memorial Baptist Church.

Against this background of constantly speaking to controversial issues, and of close involvement in the work of the American Civil Liberties Union and the President's Commission on Civil Rights, Finlator's telegram to President Carter urging the cut-off of funds for the University of North Carolina should have come as a surprise to no one. Since 1970 the Department of Health, Education, and Welfare had been in constant communication with the officials of the University, pressuring them to eliminate all traces of segregation from the system. The case had been brought before HEW by the NAACP Legal Defense and Education Fund. The chief areas of concern were the proportion of blacks and whites in the student bodies and in the faculties of the various institutions, the limited programs and course offerings in the traditionally black institutions, and the relatively inadequate facilities of the traditionally black institutions. Several times it appeared that HEW and the University were about to come to terms. Always, however, something interfered with a settlement. Early in 1979 HEW was under a court order either to approve the University desegregation plan by March 14 or to cut off federal money to the University. HEW officials visited the campuses of the University system in February and were not satisfied with the steps that had been taken. HEW officials proposed additional actions for the University, and the University made counter-proposals. HEW rejected the University offer, but did not announce a decision about the cut-off of funds.

Nine days after the deadline had passed without any HEW action, on March 23, 1979, in his capacity as Chairman of the North Carolina Advisory Committee to the U.S. Commission on Civil Rights, Finlator sent the following telegram to President Jimmy Carter:

In the spirit of your State of the Union statement that you "take no obligation . . . more seriously than that of striving to secure full civil rights and equal opportunities for all Americans," you are urgently requested to take administrative action to end illegal separation in higher education. The North Carolina Advisory Committee is deeply concerned that high regard for and strict compliance with Federal law shall prevail in our state.

North Carolina officials have failed to meet the latest deadline (March 14) for submitting to the Department of Health, Education and Welfare an acceptable plan to desegregate the State's institutions of higher education and to increase resources available to North Carolina's historically black colleges.

As Chairman of the Advisory Committee, I therefore request that you direct Secretary Califano to comply with outstanding Federal court orders requiring effective enforcement of Title VI of the Civil Rights Act of 1964 by the Department, and that you specifically direct Secretary Califano to initiate immediately administrative proceedings that will, absent compliance, terminate Federal funds for distribution to continue in North Carolina, and all the states, segregation and racial discrimination against minorities in the higher education system.

On March 26, 1979, Califano took steps to cut off federal funds. The University then went into the courts to block the cutoff. The issue was not finally settled until an agreement was signed on July 2, 1981.

Although the press paid little attention to Finlator's telegram to the President, merely reporting it on March 24 and saying little else about it, the matter created a furor within the church. A number of members of the congregation were associated with North Carolina State University; nearly all of them were committed to the objectives of desegregation; and some of them had indeed been hard at work to rectify such problems as existed at State. Some of the congregation were distressed by the telegram; some approved of it; and some simply regarded it as another expression of Finlator's commitment to the work of the Advisory Committee. Many people wrote to Finlator and to the Board of Deacons about the matter. Many writers were either distressed or indignant, and many others were supportive of Finlator. One person notified the Chairman of the Business Board that he was withdrawing financial support from the church, and another resigned from the Board of Deacons.

At their meeting on April 1, 1979, the deacons discussed the matter at length and at times with considerable heat. One motion which had a great deal of support, but which was defeated, proposed a letter to the *News and Observer* disavowing Finlator's views but supporting his effort "to invoke Christian principles into the policies and practices of our society." Finally the deacons passed a motion made by Finlator "that he and Bob Savage will sign a brief statment in the Pullen News, inviting church members who are concerned to come to

217

the church parlor on a Sunday afternoon to talk." That statement was published in *Pullenews* for April 4, 1979, inviting concerned persons to a session to be held at 2:30 on Sunday afternoon, April 22. Some forty to fifty people attended the meeting.

At the next deacons' meeting the chairman reported on the discussion. The board then authorized a committee to draw up a statement to be presented to the church. The following statement was prepared, approved by the deacons on May 13, and on May 14 sent to the members of the congregation:

> The Board of Deacons has engaged our minister in three prolonged, sometimes heated, discussions relative to the relationships between the minister and members of the church. Members of the Board have expressed their views to him about the effects of such public statements as his recent telegram to the President and have attempted to convey to him the views that you have shared with us. We assure you that to our knowledge, all matters of concern to you, to us, and to Bill Finlator, which have grown out of this issue, were fully and openly discussed and considered by the Board.
>
> Our minister, Bill Finlator, is acutely aware of the deep concern and feelings of hurt and frustration that some of you, and us, are experiencing. He has expressed to the Board of Deacons a sincere desire to effect reconciliation. He proposes to do this by seeking conversations with those individuals who are troubled and apprehensive. He pledges to listen to you and to respond to you as part of the effort to deal with your concerns.
>
> Even though there remain strong differences of opinion among the Board members themselves, we recognize that the future ministry of Pullen depends upon a reconciled church—a church with heart and spirit to work out its differences in Christian charity. Let us join together with Bill Finlator in his endeavors to reach this reconciliation. The Board of Deacons pledge their continued concentration on these areas of concern. We therefore call upon our members to join us in this *constructive first step* in a mission of growing together in Christ. We must do this so that we might minister to one another and the community at large.

Both Finlator and the deacons were distressed at the alienation between the pastor and some members of the congregation, and both were deeply concerned that the problem be resolved. At no point did the deacons suggest any attempt to restrict the freedom of the minister to speak, either from the pulpit or as a private individual or even in his capacity as an official of the Advisory Committee. At no point did Finlator indicate that he thought that the church or the deacons were infringing on his right to speak. Yet feelings had run high and at times intemperate expressions had deepend the division. The minister and the deacons made the conciliatory efforts indicated in the statement of May 14, and those efforts were met with some success. A complete reconciliation between all parties, however, was not to be.

The work of the church went on, however. Finlator preached the same kind of sermons, with their social emphasis, that he had been preaching in the past several years. The worship services, with some decline in attendance, continued to be meaningful to the participants. The Boards and Committees functioned as usual. The educational program followed its normal procedure. And the church took steps to enhance its work and worship and to function more effectively as a congregation.

One major step was the installation of a new organ in the sanctuary. In the late 1970's it became apparent that the old organ was going to have to be replaced. Maintenance became expensive, and there was some suggestion that an effort to secure a new one should be made even before the debt on the building had been paid off. By 1979 the situation had become critical. At their meeting on April 1, 1979, the deacons heard a report from the music committee which indicated that the repair of the old organ would be prohibitively expensive and that the committee was getting information on the cost of a new one.

On July 1 Bob Petters, chairman of the Music Committee, was back with a request that the board approve a drive to obtain funds for a new organ. "The committee reported that the business board had approved its plan to approach the church for a commitment not to exceed $100,000 to purchase and install a new organ." The deacons approved the recommendations and appointed a committee to plan the presentation to the church. In a letter to the congregation dated August 20, 1979, the Chairman of the Board of Deacons announced a church conference to be held on September 9, at which time the church would be asked to approve a recommendation for the purchase of the new organ. The recommendation from the Organ Committee, endorsed by the Board of Deacons, stated:

> The Organ Committee recommends the purchase of a new pipe organ from the Austin Organ Company at a cost of between $95,000 and 100,000. Included are installation costs and the removal of the present organ. If pledges received exceed $100,000, it will be possible to add more ranks (sets) of pipes to the new organ.

The old organ, which has been installed in 1951, had had "an experimental electric action (which has proven to be mechanically defective)" and had "deteriorated through the years." The cost of rebuilding the old organ would exceed $60,000 and if it were rebuilt the "inherent mechanical and musical problems would still exist."

According to *Pullenews* for September 13, 1979,

> By strong affirmative vote the church in conference this past Sunday voted to purchase a new organ from the Austin Organ Company for $100,000. On Sunday, 61% of this amount was reported as "Intended pledges" by Leroy Martin, co-chairman of the Organ Campaign. A contract will be signed when at least 70% of the cost of the instrument has been pledged.

Geraldine Cate
Minister of Music 1944-

Pullenews for October 3 announced that 70% of the cost had been received in cash and pledges, and that the contract had been signed. On October 7 the deacons approved a recommendation, brought from the music committee, that the organ be named in honor of Geraldine Cate "as a symbol of our love and respect, in appreciation for her long and distinguished service to Pullen Memorial Baptist Church and its music program."

Construction of "The Geraldine Spink Cate Organ" was completed in May, 1981, and a service of dedication was held on May 31. During the summer two other dedication programs were presented by James Good of Southeastern Baptist Theological Seminary, and David Lynch of Meredith College.

The price of the organ was $97,815. Necessary repairs and alterations to the building to accommodate the organ ran the total cost to $122,678. While the organ was being installed the church was completing payment on its note for $115,000 which it had signed on

November 29, 1976, to finance the completion of the building program. It was no small achievement for the church, therefore, to complete payment for the organ on September 1, 1981.

Meanwhile the Personnel Committee which had been appointed as an advisory committee to the deacons had been working at its assigned responsibilities. Its task was complicated by the controversy over Finlator's telegram. It was further complicated by speculation as to when Finlator might retire and by efforts to persuade him to announce his retirement plans. In a progress report dated April 30, 1979, the chairman of the Personnel Committee stated, "the committee unanimously recommends to the Board of Deacons retirement at age sixty-five for full-time employees subject to annual negotiation and approval for extension until age seventy, at which time retirement will be mandatory."

On May 6, 1979, the deacons discussed "the church's retirement policy, or lack of retirement policy." The chairman indicated that the Personnel Committee was considering the issue and would be submitting a statement for discussion. On November 4, 1979, however, the deacons received notice that the committee had not been able to agree on a proposal. The board requested the committee to continue its work and to make at least a status report in December.

In November, 1979, the committee mailed a copy of its status report to each deacon, and the board held a called meeting on December 16 to discuss it. Staff members had also received copies and had been invited to respond. At the meeting the deacons heard responses from W. W. Finlator and Geraldine Cate, both of whom were nearing retirement age. At the next meeting a response from Betsy Wooden, who was also approaching retirement age, was read. After further discussion it was agreed that the deacons would be divided into "task forces" to work on each section of the report. Two "Pullen Town Meetings" had been called for discussion of the future of the church, and the report of the Personnel Committee became involved in those discussions. The Personnel Committee, with one change in membership, continued to work in cooperation with the deacons' task forces. At last the committee submitted its final report and the deacons spent a long session on May 4, 1980, working on a draft of personnel policies to be recommended to the church. Copies were mailed to the church members for their study in advance of a congregational meeting on June 8, at which action was to be taken.

Action on the proposed policies required two congregational meetings rather than one. Meeting on June 8 and June 22, 1980, the church approved a long document on "Personnel Policies." One part of the document authorized the establishment of a Personnel Board which shall concern itself with the overall administration of the personnel policies, which apply to all employees. The Personnel Board shall be responsible for recommending to the Board of Deacons changes and/or revisions in policy, and the Board of Deacons will in turn recommend changes to the congregation. The Personnel Board shall also be responsible for facilitating good relationships between employees and the church.

The document also spelled out in quite general terms a "Work schedule for ministers," and in more specific terms a work schedule for other staff members. It specified holidays, vacations and leave, sick leave, retirement and disability plan, and salary administration and reimbursements. Two sections of the document evoked a great deal of discussion. The one was the requirement that the Personnel Board

> review with each staff member at least once a year, the employee's performance in relation to the duties and specific goals as set forth in his/her contract and up-dated by mutual consent between the church and the employee. The Personnel Board shall make a written report to the Board of Deacons.

The other was the statement:

> Normal retirement for full-time staff will be at the end of the church program year in which the employee's 65th birthday occurs. However, by mutual consent of employee and church, employment after 65 is permissible. Mandatory retirement will be at the end of the church program year (June 30) in which the employee's 70th birthday occurs.

Although Finlator was already past 65, and although a significant number of people were trying to get him to make his retirement plans known, setting a policy on retirement was not an effort to force him out. The deacons had made that clear in their action on May 4 in which they passed a motion "that employees over 65 be exempted from these policies." They were trying to deal with the matter of a permanent policy as a separate issue from Finlator's retirement.

In the aftermath of the controversy over Finlator's telegram to the President, and in the midst of the efforts to establish a personnel policy, three things happened in rapid succession that affected the church. They were not the result of the controversy, but they added to the total picture. First, Mel Williams resigned to take a position as pastor of the Oakhurst Baptist Church in Decatur, Georgia. His letter of resignation, dated December 2, 1979, was addressed to the Board of Deacons and to the congregation of Pullen Memorial Church. At their meeting on December 2 the deacons approved the following statement which was then published in *Pullenews* for December 12, 1979:

> Without prior knowledge or preparation for responding officially to Mel Williams' resignation, it is difficult to articulate coherently all the emotional and logical factors appropriate to moving acceptance. We do so, however, with the heartiest support for his future work. We do so

sadly in the prospect of losing him but gladly in thanksgiving for a decade of service to this church as a musician, preacher, educator, and counselor.

He has been a minister and close personal friend to many of us. He has introduced a new love and warmth to Pullen which had not been exhibited previously. He now makes a courageous decision to launch into a new phase of life. It is not only our duty to support him but to send him forth with our prayers and greatest foundation strength this church can provide.

We therefore recommend that the congregation accept the resignation of Mel Williams, effective January 2, 1980, and send him to Oakhurst Baptist Church, Atlanta, Georgia, with our warmest support and prayers for God's greatest blessings on his future efforts. He has been one of us and will always remain so.

With the following letter, dated December 5, 1979, the chairman of the Board of Deacons notified the congregation of Williams' resignation:

At the monthly meeting of the Board of Deacons last Sunday evening the Rev. T. Melvin Williams submitted his resignation as our Associate Minister. Enclosed is a copy of his letter of resignation, which has been accepted on behalf of the church by the Board of Deacons. We are saddened by Mel's impending departure, but we send him forth with the assurance of the abundant love of Pullen people and with our prayers that the peace of God may be upon him,

That same issue of *Pullenews* carried also the motion which the church adopted on December 9:

I would like to move that the congregation accept Mel Williams' resignation with the greatest regret and with even greater love and understanding. I would also like to move that this church pledge Mel its continued support, as his wonderful and inspired ministry reaches out to touch new lives and eagerly greets a new set of challenges.

Following his last morning worship service at Pullen, Williams was honored at a farewell dinner given by the church. The deacons, noting his "ceaseless activity" at Pullen, invited him to sit in a large, comfortable leather chair being given him, while he listened to words of appreciation from many members of the church. He was presented with a book of photographs representative of his work, and a number of people presented individual gifts.

The second event was an article about W. W. Finlator which appeared in the *Christian Century* for January 30, 1980. Written by Bill Finger, the article chronicled Finlator's social activism and focused on the controversy arising frm the UNC-HEW matter. Finger said:

Combining southern graciousness with an outspoken social conscience requires an unusual talent. And retaining the good graces of a congregation in the conservative Southern Baptist tradition demands an instinct for survival. For 42 years now, W. W. Finlator has combined such talents and instincts.

After giving a brief account of Finlator's religious and educational background and a summary of his career before he came to Pullen, Finger summarized some of Finlator's controversial activities:

Finlator has needed all the resources he could muster for this Raleigh ministry. During the civil rights protests, he spoke out for equal rights. He preached against the Vietnam war, when opposing it was an unpopular stance even in secular circles. He became an early supporter of the North Carolina Civil Liberties Union, serving as a lobbyist in the state's General Assembly and a watchdog for First Amendment rights. He's stood side by side with Angela Davis calling for a pardon for Ben Chavis and the Wilmington Ten.

In explaining Finlator's relationship to the congregation, Finger quoted Mel Williams:

"Pullen is a diverse congregation," notes Mel Williams, the associate pastor. "Most of the longtime members have supported Bill's right to say what he wants, even if they disagree. Over the years, they have had their grievances, and this was the last straw. It's the toughest battle he's had."

Finger concluded his article with a paragraph that prompted a response from the deacons. He said, near the end of the article:

For the first time in his 42-year ministry, Finlator may in fact have gotten "too involved." Prompted by the telegram to President Carter and a congregational airing of grievances that followed, the church has formed a personnel committee to look at the current situation.

At their meeting on March 9, 1980, one of the deacons called attention to errors in the *Christian Century* article. At the request of the deacons, the chairman addressed the following letter, dated March 10, 1980, to the editor:

In the cover story of the January 30, 1980, issue, "W. W. Finlator: "Risk-Taker," by Bill Finger, there is an error which needs to be corrected. Regarding Mr. Finlator's relationship with his congregation Mr. Finger wrote: "Prompted by the telegram to President Carter and a congregational airing of grievances that followed, the church has formed a personnel committee to look at the present staff situation."

On December 3, 1978, the Board of Deacons of the Pullen Memorial Baptist Church appointed a personnel committee to study such matters as employment policies, retirement and job descriptions for all staff positions. Eventually recommendatons growing out of this study will be presented to the congregation.

It was several months later in 1979 when the controversy arose over Mr. Finlator's telegram to President Carter. Consequently, Mr. Finger erred in stating that the personnel committee was appointed as the result of the controversy; it had been assigned specific duties growing out of wholly different circumstances. (*Christian Century*, 4/9/80)

The third event was the retirement of Betsy Wooden from her position as church secretary. Her letter is not found in the records, but the minutes of the deacons, dated April 27, 1980, state:

Bill Finlator read the resignation, effective June 1, of Betsy Wooden who has served the church for 32 years. Bill stated that he wanted to go on record as saying that he "honors this wonderful woman and does not look forward to the future here without her." Bill urged the Board to see that the church show its appreciation to Betsy Wooden.

The deacons adopted the following resolution:

Whereas she has served faithfully as secretary at Pullen Memorial Baptist Church for thirty-two years, and has, in addition to discharging her regular duties, gone far beyond what was required of her to be friend, advisor, confidante, resource person, and counselor to countless numbers of people, and whereas her daily presence has for years exemplifed the heart of this church.

Be it hereby resolved that the Board of Deacons, on behalf of Pullen Memorial Baptist Church, offer this expression of love, gratitude, support, and affection to Betsy Wooden as she begins a new phase of her pilgrimage.

Betsy Wooden
Church Secretary 1948-1980

Betsy Wooden had grown up in Pullen Church. Her parents had joined the church while it was still located on Fayetteville Street, and she had attended Sunday school and worship services there. She had known both Jack Ellis and Lee Sheppard as pastor. She had begun her work as secretary at Pullen late in 1948, at just about the same time that McNeill Poteat returned for his second pastorate. Over the years her responsibilities had expanded and in addition to the usual secretarial duties she did a great deal of the administrative work of the church. Because she was a long-time member of the congregation, and because she knew the membership well, she could do many things for the church which do not normally fall into the job description of a church secretary. Her long years of service to the church were celebrated by a reception following the morning worship service at which she was honored with tributes, songs, and a significant gift.

In light of their uncertainty as to how long Finlator might remain as pastor, the Board of Education and the Board of Deacons decided that the church should not seek a permanent Minister of Education but rather should employ someone on an interim basis. Sue McDaniel accepted that responsibility and began her work in May, 1980. She was a graduate of Meredith College and of Southeastern Baptist Theological Seminary. She had worked as a nursery school teacher and as an assistant to the Baptist chaplain at North Carolina State. She had been a member of Pullen since 1972, when she moved to Raleigh with her husband who was joining the faculty at N.C. State.

McDaniel had not been ordained when she began her work at Pullen, and after six months on the job she requested ordination. After the appropriate steps had been taken and the church had approved, her ordination service was set for September 13, 1981. The minutes of the deacons' meeting on July 12, 1981, state:

> Sept. 13 has been selected for the ordination of Sue McDaniel, Minister of Education. The ordination sermon will be preached by Dr. Dale Moody, father of Sue McDaniel and faculty member at Southern Seminary in Louisville, Kentucky. Sue McDaniel requested that the new deacons who need ordination—Phil Letsinger, Pat Levi, Betty Moore, and Paige Robinson—be ordained in the same service on September 13. Her purpose is to illustrate the idea that the church consists of many members who are all equal though called to different tasks.

Although the minutes give no reasons, the deacons were not entirely sure that McDaniel's request was appropriate. After much discussion they finally enunciated three possibilities: (1) Follow McDaniel's request. (2) Have two separate services on the same day. (3) Have two separate services on different days. They left it to the pastor to decide! At the next meeting Finlator announced that he had opted to follow McDaniel's request and that she and the new deacons would be ordained in the same service.

Sue McDaniel
Minister of Education 1980-1982

The minutes for the deacons' meetings throughout McDaniel's ministry reveal her regular involvement in the meetings, with reports both on the educational work and on pastoral concerns. On October 3, 1982, after a total of a little more than two years on the job, and some three months after Finlator's retirement, she announced to the Board of Education and to the Personnel Board "her intention to resign, because of health and family reasons, effective October 21, 1982." She agreed to continue on a part-time basis for several weeks if she were needed, and served until mid-December.

Meanwhile, Bill Finlator had come under pressure from some members of the congregation to announce his plans for retirement. Bill Finger was correct when he stated in his *Christian Century* article that "For the first time in his 42-year ministry, Finlator may in fact have gotten 'too involved.'" Although there had been no effort to fire him during the furor over the UNC-HEW situation, many people had begun to speculate about his retirement date. In spite of the fact that current staff personnel who were already 65 were exempted from the retirement policy adopted by the church in June, 1980, some people thought that the action might influence him to decide to retire shortly. Finlator, on the other hand, insisted that the decision about when he would retire should be his to make. He refused to discuss the matter either with those who were pressuring him to retire or with those who wanted him to stay as long as he chose to do so.

The issue of Finlator's retirement was formally raised in the meeting of the deacons on April 13, 1980. The deacons were presented with a proposed course of action designed to help the church achieve certain goals. Three items in the six-point proposal stated:

2. Ask the present minister to step down as Senior Minister no later than June, 1981, in order to make way for a new full-time staff person.
3. Begin the search for a person for the position of minister whose responsibilites would include those now being performed by the Senior Minister—worship planning, visitation, preaching. In addition this person would also help the laity plan and carry out an effective total program of outreach and nurture.
4. Offer the present minister the option to remain connected to Pullen Memorial Church if he so desires, not in an administrative or decision-making capacity, but as minister-at-large or Emeritus, with certain specified responsibilities and with an agreed-upon stipend to supplement other income he may have.

Although there was considerable discussion, the proposal was not voted upon. Instead, the deacons authorized the chairman to appoint a small committee "to meet with the minister to talk with him concerning his retirement and all issues of retirement." At the next meeting, on April 27, the chairman reported that he and two other deacons had discussed the matter with Finlator.

They quoted Bill Finlator's statements that he had thought of retiring before the age of 70, which would be June, 1983; that more recently he had thought of retiring after 25 years at Pullen (August or September, 1981); that he desires no emeritus status; that he will be willing to step down at any time that he felt it would be in the best interest of the church; and that a long-range retirement policy probably would be a good thing.

Bill Finlator was asked to comment, and he thanked the committee for the sensitive way they conducted the meeting and carried out their difficult assignment. He stated that he will retire when he believes the time to be right, and that could be in six months or three years or anytime in between. He asked that he be allowed to make the decision on when to retire.

There was some sentiment on the board to elect a committee to discuss the matter further with the minister, but a motion to that effect was not carried.

The issue, however, would not die. At their meeting on June 1, by a divided vote the deacons passed a motion

that the committee that was appointed to discuss retirement with the minister meet with him again to set a definite date for this retirement, to be on or before August 31, 1981, and that the committee attempt to receive a voluntary statement of retirement in writing, but if this is not possible that the date of August 31, 1981 be the retirement date recommended to the congregation by the Board, and that the committee present its report to a called meeting of the Board of Deacons on June 15 at 7:30 pm.

With a recorder present a three-member committee met with Finlator on June 25, 1981. Finlator remained unwilling to do the one thing that the committee had been asked to try to get him to do—set a date for his retirement. At a called meeting of the deacons on June 29 the committee reported on the session and their failure. The deacons then adopted the following statement:

WHEREAS, after more than a year of rigorous scrutiny of the needs, priorities, goals and possibilities of Pullen Memorial Baptist Church, the Board of Deacons perceives the church to be at a critical point requiring knowledgeable, long-term planning, and

WHEREAS, said planning must take into account the personnel requirements of the church in relationship to its membership and goals, and

WHEREAS, the minister of the church is currently serving in a pre-retirement position of indeterminate length, and

WHEREAS, the Board of Deacons perceives that the declaration of a definite date of retirement would provide a tangible timeframe in which the church could work to effect the orderly transfer of the ministry of Pullen Memorial from one Senior Minister to another, and

WHEREAS, having such a date would greatly facilitate the general understanding of church members and clear the air of seeming indecision and lack of direction, and

WHEREAS, the Board of Deacons deems it very appropriate that the church be able to demonstrate its belief in and capacity for a democratic resolution of such matters, and

WHEREAS, the Board recognizes the profound and significant ministry of W. W. Finlator at Pullen Memorial Baptist Church, and

WHEREAS, the Board desires that this ministry continue strongly, viably, and without abatement until an appropriate climactic point, and

WHEREAS, the 25th anniversary date of August, 1981, previously alluded to by the minister as a possible retirement target seems to be a propitious moment in which to celebrate the past twenty five years and to make a commitment to a new beginning,

THEREFORE: The Board of Deacons directed that the Committee that was appointed to discuss retirement with the minister meet with him again to set a definite date for his retirement, to be on or before August 31, 1981, and that the Committee attempt to receive a voluntary statement of retirement in writing, but if this is not possible the date of August 31, 1981, be the retirement date recommended to the Congregation by the Board and that the Committee present its report to a called meeting of the Board of Deacons on June 15, 1980.

Again, the deacons were not unanimous in their approval of the action.

On July 6 the deacons again struggled with the question of taking their recommendation to the church. The division on the board was still apparent, though the majority favored calling for congregational action. They voted "that a date in September, to be set by the staff and deacons by mutual consent, for consideration of the single issue of the minister's retirement and that it be held after the morning service."

Pullenews for July 9, 1980, carried an "Update of Major Actions Taken by the Board of Deacons" which rehearsed the steps taken by the deacons and announced their intention to ask for congregational action in September. On August 5 a letter was sent to the congregation announcing a "Town Meeting" for September 4 at which the board's resolution would be discussed, and a congregational meeting for September 28 at which action would be taken. After the appearance of *Pullenews* many members of the congregation wrote to the board, and more spoke to individual deacons. Within the congregation there was strong opposition to the proposal as well as strong support for it. A petition calling upon the deacons to rescind their action was circulated among the congregation and was signed by more than 250 members of the church. The explanatory statement prefacing the petition rehearsed the steps which the deacons had taken, listed a number of points which the petitioners found troublesome, and affirmed:

> Although the issue is now to be put before that large number of people by means of a church conference scheduled for September, the following people wish to assure the minister beforehand that we do not believe that the motion of June 1 and the resolution of June 29 deal with him fairly and honorably. We are deeply concerned about the feeling of our minister and his family. We are also concerned that Pullen Memorial Baptist Church continue to be known in the Christian community and in the world at large as a champion of fair play and of religious liberty. We believe that recent events concerning the closing of Mr. Finlator's ministry are contrary to the spirit of this church.

Citing reasons for their action, concluding with the statement that "we believe that the Board of Deacons has proceeded without understanding the will of the majority of the congregation," the petition stated:

> WE, THEREFORE, repudiate the resolution adopted by the Board of Deacons and strongly recommend a reconsideration of that action, and
>
> WE, HEREBY, express our gratitude and loving support for the minister whose integrity and courage shine as brightly today as in years gone by and whose service has brought lustrous distinction to this congregation.

The matter became public, with many people outside the congregation discussing it. Former members of the church wrote to the board, and some people who had no connection with the church wrote. The deacons were assured by many that they were doing the best thing, but found themselves having to defend their position to many other people. A real polarization was developing, with people choosing up sides in a way that they had never done before. A number of people wrote to the deacons to urge them to find a way of avoiding an open conflict. One such letter contained a sentence which stated what many people felt: "In the spirit of reconciliation, I urge you to take whatever action and use whatever resources necessary to prevent further confrontation because the church will be the loser."

The resolution of the difficulty came on Sunday, August 24, 1980. On that date, well before the congregational meeting planned for September 28, Finlator announced his plans for retirement. He set the date as June 30, 1982, nearly a year later than the date set by the deacons and one year before he reached his 70th birthday. In announcing his retirement date Finlator said, "In making this decision, I call upon the congregation, its leadership, committees and boards to join me in pledging our full mutual commitment in working together more abundantly toward achieving what St. Paul called the unity of the spirit in the bond of peace." After that announcement, the planned Town Meeting and Church conference were canceled. The matter of Finlator's retirement was settled.

The idea for holding "town meetings" had first come up in the deacons' retreat which was held at Meredith on September 29, 1979. There had been some discussion of the need for better communication between the Board of Deacons and the congregation, and someone suggested the holding of "open forums or 'town hall' meetings on key topics of continuing concern." (Minutes, 10/7/79) At the meeting on November 4, 1979, the deacons passed a motion that

> the board of deacons sponsor a series of three town meetings in 1980. The meetings will provide a forum to discuss some of the issues raised at the deacons' retreat, among them, "What is the distinctive mission of Pullen Memorial Church?"; "Do our activities and actions demonstrate our commitment to what we say is our mission?"; and "In order to carry out our distinctive mission, what will be our goals for the next three, five, ten years?"

The first town meeting was held on January 22, 1980, and was planned to allow discussion on any topic that the congregation wished. Approximately 100 people attended and a wide variety of subjects came under discussion. Most had to do with the unique nature of Pullen and the direction which Pullen should take in the future. Feelings were still running high about Finlator's telegram to the President, and the report of the deacons' Personnel Committee was only two months old. While neither of those matters dominated the discussion, as indeed no one topic did, they were clearly in the thinking of many persons who spoke. The second town hall meeting was held on March 6, with comments and observations focusing on "the church as a nurturing, worshiping, serving, and educational community." The third town meting was announced for September 4, 1980, to discuss the deacons' proposal having to do with setting a retirement date for Finlator. As has been noted, that meeting was canceled after Finlator announced his retirement date. The next call for a town meeting came in the deacons' meeting on November 1, 1981, for the purpose of giving some direction to the Ministerial Search Committee. By that time the idea of occasional town meetings called for the purpose of discussing, without taking action, matters important to the life of the church seems to have become an accepted and expected practice at Pullen.

The church celebrated Finlator's twenty-fifth anniversary at Pullen on Sunday, August 30, 1981. The deacons planned only a "mini-celebration" so as not to detract from "subsequent events to honor W. W. Finlator upon his retirement." The celebration consisted of a worship service in which Bill and Mary Lib Finlator sat with the congregation. They heard a sermon by Stewart A. Newman, emeritus professor of philosophy at Meredith College, in which Newman set Finlator within the context of a long history of prophetic preaching at Pullen. A reception after the service gave the opportunity for both congregation and visitors to speak personally to the Finlators.

One reason for Finlator's reluctance to make an early announcement of his retirement plans was his fear that the time after his announcement would be a "lame duck" period. That in fact was what happened. He continued to conduct the worship services and to preach as he had been doing. For all practical purposes, however, after his announcement the church began to look beyond the time of his last Sunday. He did not actively participate in the discussions of the future of Pullen. He attended the meetings of the deacons and made the appropriate announcements and spoke of the work that was being done in the various organizations, but attempted to exercise no influence over decisions about long-range plans. Apparently he felt that it would be inappropiate for him to do so. For their part, the deacons did not feel the necessity of seeking his advice. The situation was at best awkward.

Just prior to the effective date of his retirement, Finlator was honored at a service held at 3:00 P.M. on Sunday, May 23, 1982. The program included music by both the choir and the congregation. Statements of appreciation were delivered by former N.C.S.U. Chancellor John T. Caldwell; U.N.C. President William Friday; Bishop Joseph Gossman of the Catholic Diocese of Raleigh; Professor Daniel Pollitt, of the U.N.C. School of Law; Rev. O. L. Sherrill, Executive Secretary Emeritus of the General Baptist State Convention; Mr. Claude Sitton, Editor of the *News and Observer*; and President Ralph Scales of Wake Forest University. A portrait of Finlator was unveiled and placed in the recently re-named "Finlator Fellowship

Hall. Finlator was presented with a book of letters of appreciation written by church members and by other friends throughout the country. In describing the event, the *News and Observer* (5/24/82) said:

The Rev. W. W. Finlator's last hurrah was laced with irony. The outspoken liberal Baptist often has sparked controversy, but Sunday his friends agreed that his voice would be missed.

Before a packed congregation at Raleigh's Pullen Memorial Baptist Church, about 800 people gathered to pay tribute to Finlator, the church's 69-year-old minister who will step down next month after 26 years at the church.

Finlator, a civil rights and anti-war activist and civil libertarian, listened Sunday to ministers, educators, journalists and congregation members pay tribute to work he had done inside the church and out for more than two decades. . . .

While his stands provoked criticism, Roman Catholic Bishop F. Joseph Gossman of Raleigh praised Finlator's career of bringing the church actively into social issues. . . .

The Rev. O. L. Sherrill, executive secretary emeritus of the General Baptist State Convention, said Finlator had made life richer for everyone because of his stand for civil rights. . . .

William C. Friday, president of the University of North Carolina System, also paid tribute to Finlator. Two years ago, Finlator set his own retirement to end an internal church split that was caused by a letter he had written to the U.S. Department of Health, Education and Welfare saying funds should be cut off to the university system because it had failed to meet federal desegregation requirements.

The letter upset some of the church's 700-member congregation, and Finlator announced plans to retire in two years to ease the friction.

But Friday, a longtime friend of Finlator's, had nothing but praise for the retiring minister. Friday recalled that Finlator had given the invocation when he was sworn in as UNC president 25 years ago.

"Bill Finlator sent me on my way as a new administrator," Friday said. "All these years he has remained a faithful friend.

"His wide-ranging views caused others to enjoin he should stick to his religion. To his everlasting credit, that is exactly what he has done."

Similar words of praise came from Daniel Pollitt, UNC law professor; Dr. John T. Caldwell, former chancellor of N.C. State University; Dr. James R. Scales, president of Wake Forest University; and Claude Sitton, editorial director of the News and Observer and the Raleigh Times. . . . .

Amid the accolades, Finlator kept his sense of humor. Looking at the portrait, he said a member of the deacon's board had asked him if he wanted a photograph or a portrait.

"I told him, 'How about a stained glass window?' " he said with a smile.

Because Finlator was so much in the news, and because his public stands on issues were so often controversial, other aspects of his ministry have generally been overlooked. Yet he was thoroughly conscientious and genuine in his exercise of what might be called "pastoral duties." He made no effort to visit in the homes of all the members of the congregation, as do few modern ministers. But he regularly visited church members—and others—who were in the hospital, and he conscientiously made himself available to people who were having crises of other sorts. Not trained as a counselor, and having no real interest in doing that kind of work, he nevertheless saw himself as a pastor and he genuinely cared for his people. He was at his best in funeral services, delivering messages that were appreciative of the person who had died and helpful to the family and friends. One member of the congregation who wrote a response to Finger's *Christian Century* article on Finltor, while voicing criticism of certain aspects of Finlator's ministry, nevertheless said, "The many of us who have received notes or visits from him would emphasize, in addition, the supportive role he plays in times of stress or crisis." (*Christian Century*, 4/2/80)

Finlator was well known for the letters to which that church member referred. He wrote not only in times of crisis but also in times of achievement. He wrote to people about their bereavements, their sicknesses, their economic reverses, their family problems. He wrote to them about their marriages, about their becoming parents or grandparents, about their publications, about their job promotions, about their public recognition for service, about their activities in the political arena. He wrote in appreciation of their participation in church activities and about their involvement in the causes of social and economic and political justice.

Finlator's sermons were always timely, speaking to current issues and bringing the gospel to bear upon them. His involvement in controversial issues, and his speaking about them, has already been made abundantly clear. At the same time, many of his sermons were quite personal, and many of his stances were surprisingly traditional.

As a text for his final sermon at Pullen, preached on June 20, 1982, Finlator used 2 Timothy 4:6-8: "For I am now ready to be offered, and the time of my departure is at hand. I have fought a good fight, I have finished my course, I have kept the faith; Henceforth there is laid up for me a crown of righteousness, which the Lord, the righteous judge, shall give me at that day; and not to me only, but unto all them also that love his appearing." He called it an inappropriate passage for him to use, but based his reminiscences about his ministry at Pullen upon it. Mindful of the turbulence of the times, and of the fact that the church had never been placid and serene during his ministry, he spoke of the spirit of the church and of his own spirit:

But I have not fought the good fight. True, I have often been in the fray, not often enough for my conscience, too often perhaps for some of you, and while I think there is no Sir Modred in me, I also know that there is too little of Sir Galahad. Many of you cheered me on and joined ranks with me. Some of you will say I have spoken when I might have been silent, silent when I should have spoken, some that I have often gone too far, and others have not quite forgiven me for backing down and moderating. And perhaps all of you might agree that at times I have reminded you of the knight errant who mounted his horse and rode off in all directions! All of this does not average up to fighting a good fight!

But you, my Pullen people, have made it possible for me to enter into the lists and given me the strength to "say not the struggle nought availeth". Never once did you, as a church, tell me what to preach and what not to preach, what to engage and encounter, and what not to engage and encounter, and though many of you might have privately dissented, never once, as a church, have you penalized me or imposed economic sanctions. On the contrary, my salaries came every month and always without the freeze! I pay tribute to you for this!

So, while it may not have been the good fight, it certainly has been an exhilirating one, and I would hate to have missed one moment of it. There is zest and a throb in trying really to hear the word of God, and translating it in the language of the day to well-intentioned friends who often really do not want to hear, are discomforted and threatened by hearing, and then taking the message beyond the sanctuary to the market places to confront the legalized securities that are at enmity with it. This can be painful and devastating to both the hearer and the bearer of the word. But then again, the zest and the throb! What a sadness to have missed this.

John Carlton, professor of preaching at Southeastern Baptist Theological Seminary, was chosen to serve as interim pastor following Finlator's retirement. Carlton was a graduate of Baylor University, attended Southern Baptist Theological Seminary and received his M.Div. and Ph.D. from Duke University. He taught preaching at Duke Divinity School and at Southern Baptist Theological Seminary before joining the faculty at Southeastern. He had served as interim pastor in a number of churches both in Kentucky and in North Carolina. Early in his career in North Carolina he had been interim minister at Pullen following McNeill Poteat's death.

Carlton began his ministry at Pullen on the first Sunday in July, 1982, and continued through the last Sunday in July, 1983. His preaching at Pullen was for the most part focused on traditional biblical and theological themes. Typical sermon titles were "The Cost of a Word," "Who Do You Think You Are?" "On Examining Ourselves," "When Virtue becomes Vice," "Standing By the Best," "Holy Waste," "The Fellowship of His Suffering," and "Seekers and Possessions." The sermons were basically expository, with practical applications. His illustrations were more from great literature than from the daily newspaper. His words were well-chosen, his diction polished. He represented classical, traditional preaching at its best.

Although Carlton, during his year at Pullen, had primarily a responsibility for the morning worship service, he also involved himself as much as possible in the pastoral ministry. He was particularly concerned with hospital visitation, and he was called upon for some other pastoral visitation as well. Upon a few occasions he was called upon for weddings and for funerals, and in both kinds of service he ministered effectively to the congregation.

Pullenews for August 1, 1983, carried a comment on Carlton's last Sunday with Pullen:

> John Carlton Day, July 31st, was a great success. The congregation turned out in full force, the choir was in great voice, Martha Buchanan outdid herself and the sermon was one of John's best. Carter Williams was the liturgist and also presided very ably over the short ceremony at which John Carlton was made an Honorary Member of Pullen with all its rights and privileges. . . . Then "Nic" Nahikian presented John with a "Love Gift" from a number of his Pullen friends amounting to a little over $2,000.

While Carlton was serving as interim minister H. M. "Nic" Nahikian was serving as interim administrator. The church had found it advisable to employ an interim administrator because Carlton could not take on that side of the work in addition to his full load at Southeastern, and neither the Minister of Education nor the church secretary could add those responsibilities to their already full load. Nahikian was a long-time member of the church who had served several terms on the Board of Deacons. He had also served the church for many years as Treasurer and was already familiar with much of the details of the daily operations. He was recently retired from his position in the department of mathematics at North Carolina State.

Beginning some six months before Finlator's retirement, the Ministerial Search Committee was hard at work on its assigned task of finding the person whom they would recommend to the church. The Committee had been organized in November, 1981, when the Chairman of the Board of Deacons culminated nearly six months of work on his part in selecting a large committee that would be representative of the congregation at large. He presided over the first meeting, held on November 29, at which all ten members and all ten alternates were present, and in which John Steely was chosen chairman.

The Ministerial Search Committee had two valuable pieces of material to help it determine what kind of person to look for. The first was a summary of a survey done by the Board of Deacons and the Church Council from May through September, 1981. Those two groups set out to talk to as many members of the church as possible. The focus

for the interviews was five goals for the church which had been identified by the Board of Deacons. The questions were open-ended and the
responses were not of the sort that could be easily tabulated. They did,
however, give a feel for the judgment of the congregation about the
strengths and weaknesses of the church and about the direction which
the church should take. The areas under consideration were worship,
education, fellowship, service/witness, and support. This material
was to help the Committee interpret the church to the persons being
considered for the position of pastor. The interviews did not deal
directly with the kind of minister which the congregation might
want, but in most of the interviews that matter came up. The report,
therefore, included a statement "Concerning the Pastoral Leadership":

> The strongest signal from respondents concerning future pastoral prior-
> ities calls for attention to the program of the church—coordination of
> activities and providing leadership and boards through warmth, en-
> couragement, listening and negotiation. There also is evidence of
> strong support for a prophetic role for the minister, continuing the
> church's tradition as an advocate of human rights. Members also value
> the ability of a minister to be helpful in times of personal and family
> need. Respondents asked for a strong minister/preacher who will call
> forth professions of faith from both adults and children.

The second item which the Search Committee could use was the
"Personnel Policies" documents as finally approved by the church in
conference on June 22, 1980. That document had to do with the entire
church staff, not with the minister only. Its statements about the work
of the minister were of necessity rather general. It was quite precise,
however, in specifying the responsibilities of the other staff persons
who would be working under the supervision of the minister. It was
also quite precise in spelling out benefits, in planning for performance assessment, and in procedure for job termination.

The Ministerial Search Committee spent some time making their
plans. They advertized the position nationally and prepared a ques-
tionnaire to be sent to interested persons. They asked Mahan Siler,
Director of the School of Pastoral Care at the Baptist Hospital in
Winston-Salem, to meet with them as a consultant. More than a
hundred persons either applied or were recommended for the position, and the committee gave careful consideration to each one. The
chairman reported to the committee on June 6, 1982, that at that time
he had corresponded with all but six of the candidates, providing each
with a copy of the history of the church, a data sheet, three reference
sheets, a copy of the job description, and a recent worship bulletin.

At almost every meeting of the Board of Deacons there was some
report from the committee. On April 10, 1983, according to the minutes of the deacons:

E. Johnson reported that the committee had decided on an individual and was negotiating with that person. He said the individual could not be identified as it would be damaging to his present situation. He hoped that an announcement could be made within a matter of weeks. The Search Committee had discussed a sequence of events and would provide written information to the congregation. About the same time there would be an opportunity for the deacons to meet with the Search Committee to receive information and to discuss the candidate. There would be an event on a Saturday at which time the congregation would meet the person and his family. The deacons would be invited to meet him the evening before. The next day the man would preach. There would be a called meeting of the congregation that night to vote on calling him. The election would be held and then the person would need to work out notice before leaving his present position.

On May 1, 1983, a member of the committee reported to the deacons that "there would be a business meeting of the church on May 22 to vote on the new minister, but the person wants to remain in his present position through June, take vacation in July, and be ready to begin at Pullen on August 15."

On May 15, 1983, the chairman of the Search Committee mailed a letter to the congregation notifying them of the plans for a visit by the prospective minister and his family on the week-end of May 20-22 and calling for a church conference on Sunday evening, May 22, to vote on calling the new minister. The following official recommendation from the committee was enclosed:

M. Mahan Siler is a native of Knoxville, Tennessee, who was educated in public schools, Baylor School, Vanderbilt University, University of Edinburgh, and the Southern Baptist Theological Seminary. He grew up in the First Baptist Church, Knoxville. Mahan is married to Janice Edwards of Wilmington, and they have four children: Jeannine, Marshall, Julia, and Mark.

Since 1977 Mahan has been Director, School of Pastoral Care, North Carolina Baptist Hospital, Winston-Salem, and for 3 1/2 years prior to that was a member of the staff of the department with responsibilities for the educational needs of the department. His pastoral experiences include two years at Coffee Creek Baptist Church, a 250 member congregation of the American Baptist Churches; three years as pastor of an 80 member mission church in a lower income section of Louisville, Kentucky; three years as assistant pastor of the 2000+ member Crescent Hill Baptist Church, Louisville; and five years as pastor of the 700 member Ravensworth Baptist Church, Annandale, Virginia. In North Carolina Mahan has been active developing pastoral counseling centers, providing special counselors for ministers and their families. He was chairman of the commission on the ministry which made its report to the Baptist State Convention of North Carolina in 1981.

Janice met Mahan when they were both students at Southern Seminary, Louisville. They have walked together for twenty-five years, yet they have also learned the benefits of walking as individuals. Currently Janice is working on a master's degree as an external student of Goddard College. She plans to continue to work as a marriage and family counselor. She has shared leadership roles with Mahan in many counseling and marriage enrichment seminars. On two occasions they have been sent to Japan by the Foreign Mission Board, Southern Baptist Convention, to provide resources for missionaries there. Together they will publish (Broadman, 1984) a book on teaching values to children.

Jeannine, who graduated from Chapel Hill last week, is one of ten North Carolinians appointed to the Journeyman program of the Foreign Mission Board. After training this summer she will go to Japan for two years. Marshall is a junior business and economics student at North Carolina State University. Mark and Julia are rising juniors in high school.

Mahan Siler's sense of his most important contributions to his present position points to the skills he will bring to Pullen:
1. a climate of trust and high participation
2. pastoral care
3. leadership through goal setting, envisioning the future, communication and conflict resolution

The members of the Ministerial Search Committee unanimously recommend to Pullen Memorial Baptist Church that M. Mahan Siler be called to become the senior minister of Pullen Memorial Baptist Church with his duties to begin August 15, 1983, at an annual compensation rate of $40,729 including benefits. A copy of the proposed covenant to be signed by elected representatives of the church and the minister upon extension and acceptance of the call can be examined in the church office.

During the week-end a large percentage of the congregation had some contact with the Silers. On Friday evening Siler and his family met for supper with the Search Committee, the Board of Deacons, the Busines Board, the Board of Education, the Board of Trustees, the Church Council, the Personnel Board, and their spouses. On Saturday morning there was a coffee in the church parlor to which all members of the church were invited to meet the Silers. There was a cookout for the young people on Saturday evening and an ice cream social on Saturday night for all church members. Siler preached at the morning worship service on Sunday, and there was a reception following the service. At the Sunday evening conference the vote to call Siler was unanimous.

For the next issue of *Pullenews* Siler wrote:

I accept your invitation to be your pastor with excitement and anticipation. Janice, Jeannine, Marshall, Julia and Mark join me in these feelings.

It has been said that a wise person is one who knows what time it is in his or her life. "What time it is in the life of Pullen?" has been a question you have been raising over these past years. It's a question concerning my own life I have been addressing as well. I have been assessing how my particular set of gifts and experience might best be utilized during the coming years. Gradually it began to feel "timely", by the Search Committee and us, that we join you in your ongoing life together and ministry. Last weekend seemed to confirm, on your part and ours, the "rightness" of the decision. We appreciate all who made possible the experience of the weekend.

I'm not one to use glibly the phrase "God's will". Most of us have experienced the abuse of those words. More is laid at the feet of God than is usually deserved. Yet, I pray that our mutual decision is God's will—in the sense that our common humanity, our partnership in ministry will lead to vibrant expressions of our Lord's spirit of love and justice. I do sense among you and in myself a readiness, a "timeliness" for beginning a new era. I come with deep respect for who you are and who you have been. I look forward to coming alongside, anticipating what we can become together in the understanding and service.

In the interim between Finlator's departure and Siler's arrival the church had the services not only of an interim pastor and an interim administrator but also of an interim worker with young people. Following Sue McDaniel's resignation, only a few months after Finlator's retirement, the church employed Janice Patty to work with the youth. A native of Greensboro, Patty was a graduate of Meredith College and at the time of her employment was a student at Southeastern Baptist Theological Seminary. Pullen ordained Patty on Sunday, June 26, 1983.

Janice Patty
Minister of Education 1983-

While Patty was working with the young people, the church recognized the need for someone to minister to college students. Nancy Howell, a student at Southeastern Seminary, was employed part-time for that responsibility. A graduate of the College of William and Mary and of Southeastern Baptist Theological Seminary, she was currently working on a graduate degree at Southeastern.

With Patty and Howell working together, the young people's program was functioning well. At the end of the academic year Howell left to do graduate work elsewhere. Patty, who had completed her work at Southeastern, accepted an extended contract with an expanded responsibility. She was given the title, "Associate Minister in Christian Education," and was to be responsible for both student ministry and youth ministry. She was to work thirty hours per week and it was understood that she could continue her theological education by taking "Clinical Pastoral Education" and by taking additional courses at Duke Divinity School. The proposal stated as the advantage for Pullen in this arrangement:

> The availability of the continuation of Janice's ministry and at the same time incorporating the momentum begun under the leadership of Nancy Howell in serving students. This also gives Pullen the opportunity during the spring of '85 to look at staff needs in regard to overall church ministry.

As scheduled, Mahan Siler began his work as Senior Minister at Pullen Memorial Baptist Church on August 15, 1983. He preached his first sermon as pastor on Sunday, August 21. Using Mark 14:1-9 as his text, he spoke on the subject, "An Act of Gratitude." In that sermon he said:

> I'm wondering with you this morning—what's the essential fire around which we huddle for survival, for life as a church? How would we describe that motivational flame that must not go out? What best fuels our ministry of Christ together?
>
> My answer? *Our sense of being graced.* The essential awareness, it seems to me, is that we are a gifted people. I don't mean talented, though we are certainly full of talent. We are gifted. We regularly confess here that we are not self made persons. We are the product of the gifts of many others and the Other. We love because were were first loved. We live because life is given. It's a gift, not our creation. The fire of life and love is not stolen from the gods as Greek mythology would present it; the creative fire of life and love is given by God the Creator, freely given, given through mother, father, sister, brother, teacher, friend, son, and daughter and the many others through whom the gift of caring affirmation touches us.

Siler considered this sermon a pace-setter, outlining the kind of ministry he envisioned. Writing about it in *Pullenews* for August 23 he stated:

Also, we are making available copies of the sermon I delivered last Sunday. I'm doing this in the interest of dialogue. During these next number of Sundays I plan to preach on themes related to the ministry of our church. I want them to stimulate your own perceptions and convictions, leading, I hope, to discussions among us.

Titles of the sermons preached during the next two months give further clue to what Pullen might expect as pulpit emphases: "The Church: A Place of Summons and Support," "Not by Bread Alone," "The Church's Ministry: Promise and Partners of Liberation," "The Audacity of Ministry," "A Story to Be," "Reframing Your Past," "Church's Ministry: A Place for Children Only," "Church's Ministry: A Place to Worship," and "Living Reminders."

Siler attended his first meeting with the deacons on September 4 and heard a discussion of plans for his formal installation, to be held on Sunday, September 18. He heard a report on the up-coming deacons' retreat, a report from the church council, a report from the church treasurer, and a report from the communion committee. He had the opportunity to talk with the deacons about how he was beginning his work. Although there was an air of excitement about the future, there was also an air of "business as usual."

The installation service was held at 3:00 P.M. on Sunday, September 18, 1983. The address was delivered by Dr. Wayne Oates, of Louisville, Kentucky. Oates, a teacher and long-time friend of Siler's, was a pioneer in the field of education for pastoral care. Special music included an organ and trumpet prelude with Michael Arrowood and Tom Funk, followed by the processional, Ralph Vaughan Williams' arrangement of "All People That on Earth Do Dwell." The choir sang both "Jubilate Deo," composed for that service by Pat Elliott, and Warren Martin's "Anthem of Dedication." James Rochelle sang the prayer of St. Francis, "Lord, Make Us Instruments of Thy Peace." Other participants in the service were Carter Williams, John Steely, Donna Forester, Libby Gourley, and Mary Ruth Crook.

Once he had been settled into his new situation Siler began to try to get to know the congregation and to understand better the direction which the congregation wished to take. Working through the Area Ministry network, he met with the members of the congregation in small groups to get their "views and feelings" about Pullen. In preparation for those discussions he asked the congregation to think about two questions: "What do you appreciate about Pullen's ministry? What needs would you like to see more effectively addressed?" In the sessions Siler encouraged all those present to express themselves, and in the process he discovered how varied are Pullen people and how broad are their concerns.

In *Pullenews* for October 2, 1983, Siler announced his plans for his daily and weekly schedule:

First, I want you to know of my basic schedule. Generally, I study and prepare for worship leadership in the mornings. Between 11:00 and 12:00 I try to be in the office to receive and return telephone calls. The afternoons and often evenings are spent in meetings, pastoral conversations and visitation. Mondays are my Sabbath. Nancy Littlefield, our able administrative secretary, generally knows where I am and how I can be reached for emergencies.

Siler was not long in beginning some new projects which were characteristic of his own ministerial emphasis. *Pullenews* for October 4, 1983, announced a marriage "Information Night." The announcement stated, "We invite any married couples who would like to make their marriage stronger and more meaningful to an 'Information Night' for Baptist Expression of Marriage Encounter." The same issue of *Pullenews* carried an announcement about the worship service:

One of the challenges of worship leadership is to design a service of worship that has in mind all ages. In the near future we want to plan ways through which the younger people can become more involved— both in leadership and participation. During next Sunday's service the children in grades 1-6 will be invited forward for a time of sharing specifically designed for them. Would you who are parents of these children help us by alerting them of this special time for them? I appreciate your cooperation.

The October 17 issue of *Pullenews* carried a note addressed to "Seminarians and students" inviting them "to the Silers' home . . . for a light lunch and conversation" immediately following the morning worship on October 23. In the October 31 issue Siler announced:

For close to ten years now I have directed a journal writing experience during Advent season called *Journey into Advent*. I invite any of you to join me on Thursdays, December 1, 8, 15, 22, from 12:00-1:15 at the church. If there is sufficient interest another group can meet with me from 5:45-7:00 on the same days.

This weekly series will offer the opportunity to interact autobiographically with the coming of Jesus. The meaning of his birth will serve to stimulate the further meaning of our own lives. Participants will be encouraged to make use of journals for private reflections upon selected scripture. The event is designed to be a reflective, devotional experience that will further personalize the deeper meaning of Christmas.

When Mahan Siler came to Pullen he found a church with a distinctive worship service. Since the days of McNeill Poteat the service had demanded that the congregation be involved both intellectually and emotionally in what was done. The congregation voiced as their own the prayers and the affirmations that have been used by the church through the centuries, and they did the same with the words of great spirits of the twentieth century. They sang the great hymns and they heard great music from the choir. They became accustomed to the eleven o'clock hour not just as "preaching" but as a worship service.

Yet the church also stressed the importance of preaching. Siler followed in the footsteps of John Pullen and Jack Ellis and Lee Sheppard and McNeill Poteat and Bill Finlator. He stood in a pulpit which had a tradition of thoughtful and forthright proclamation. He faced a congregation which expected to be challenged by what they heard from the pulpit.

Siler found a church staff working efficiently and with dedication to the kind of church Pullen was trying to be. Gerry Cate, who had been Minister of Music since 1944, had helped McNeill Poteat develop Pullen's pattern of worship. She saw music as an integral part of worship and insisted that a choir and a congregation should offer to God only the best. The Pullen choir, therefore, was well-known for the high quality of its music. Miss Cate enriched that quality by bringing into the choir some of her students, both from the white community and from the black. In that way she had integrated the church racially long before the congregation took official action to open its membership. Janice Patty, who had been employed in January to work with the young people, had been well-received and had established a program that was attractive and challenging. Nancy Littlefield, who became church secretary in September, 1982, was efficiently operating an office that was vital to almost all the organized activities of the church.

Siler found a church structured with Boards and Committees whose members took their responsibilities seriously. Some dealt with regular, and therefore, central activities of the church: matters having to do with the worship service, with fellowship activities, with business, with physical facilities. Others dealt with less common, and therefore more innovative, activities: new forms of outreach, of concern for social issues, of response to crises. Siler found a readiness to create new committees when the need became apparent, and to allow committees to die when they had outlived their usefulness. He found a church using its organization rather than maintaining it.

When Siler came to Pullen he found a congregation that was very much alive. He found a wide variety of people—business people, doctors, lawyers, writers, educators, social workers, secretaries, government employees, nurses, retired people, students, ministers, administrators—expressing their faith in a variety of ways through the church. He found people of all ages and people in varying circumstances in family life—all a part of the community of faith. He found them in Sunday school classes and in circles of the Women of the Church and in committees and on boards. He found them ministering to one another and reaching out into the community. He found them

M. Mahan Siler
Minister 1983-

concerned with the inner life and with social reform. He found them worshipping and he found them questioning. He found them committed to the cause of Christ and he found them uncertain about much that they were doing. He found a congregation of people like the man who said to Jesus, "I believe; help my unbelief" (Jn. 9:24). He found a congregation ready to move ahead with its mission.

To help determine the direction which the church should take, Siler involved the deacons in careful consideration of matters basic to the church. He led them in their first retreat after his arrival, held on October 21-22, 1983. The stated agenda was:

— deeper interpersonal relationships between deacons and between deacons and pastor
— clarify expectations and functions of deacon/pastor and their working relationship
— utilizing both data from "town meetings" and more current observations, assess present and future directions for Pullen's ministry
— enjoy one another and the setting

At the next meeting of the deacons he asked the chairman to appoint a committee "to spend some time with him thinking about this mission." The committee was appointed, met regularly over a period of months, and by May had prepared a report which was to be the basis for further discussion. Some salient observations in that report offer at least a part of Pullen's agenda for the future:

We noted that our reputation for involvement in ministry in the community has not been matched by performance in many instances. Most of our involvement is through individual efforts with minimal group and church support. Our organizational structure is weighted towards our own needs as a congregation. . . .

We next took a look at the nature of our own congregation. From this internal look we felt the need to have a study made of our internal organization. . . .

Another concern within the organization was to strengthen the involvement and focus upon the children. . . .

Again, looking internally, we noted the importance of new member assimilation during this time of transition. We also lifted the concern for the alienated member who is either on the periphery or has lost interest in the life of the congregation.

Next we, as a committee, began to focus on the environment of Pullen. We raised the question—What are the current needs/changes of our community (local, national, international) and how would these affect our priorities of mission?. . .

Next as a committee we wrestled with some of the theological/biblical concepts that should guide our selection of priorities.

Although this report was prepared by a committee of the deacons, and was intended for the deacons, it had significant implications and possibilities for the church as a whole. The committee asked that "the deacons consider a way of involving the larger church in some refining of our future priorities during the Winter/Spring of 1985."

Pullen Memorial Baptist Church celebrated a "Homecoming" on Sunday, September 23, 1984. In his sermon on that day Mahan Siler, preaching on the subject of tradition, issued a challenge for Pullen's future that was faithful to Pullen's past. He said:

> What a great time to be a Baptist congregation in the Free Church tradition. One contemporary Baptist congregation has spawned a network for peacemaking that now extends throughout the nation. Another Baptist congregation has initiated a similar network around the concern for world hunger. Is there a freer institution than Pullen? There are no binding ecclesiastical restrictions upon us. The freedom to be creative and courageous is awesome. And so are the responsibilities.

PROLOGUE

"What's past is prologue."
—Shakespeare

Because a prologue is an anticipatory statement, the Prologue to the history of Pullen Memorial Baptist Church belongs at the end of the book. Pullen's one-hundred year history is an anticipation of things to come. The enduring ideals, the fixed commitments, and the confident hope which have characterized the church demand a continuing embodiment in a believing, worshipping, and working fellowship. That is the Pullen of the future because it has been the Pullen of the past.

The ministers of Pullen Memorial Baptist Church will not have to demand a free pulpit; rather the church will demand of its ministers a courageous and forthright application of the gospel to the needs of the world—both personal and social. The ministers will not be the church's professional holy persons; rather they will be a part of "a kingdom of priests." The ministers will not be "hired" by the church; they will be "liberated" for the ministry of the Word. They will not be expected to minister only to the members of this congregation; they will be supported by this congregation in their ministry in the world. They will not be expected to fit a mold or play a role; they will be expected to be men and women exercising their gifts in their own way.

Pullen Memorial Baptist Church will not be a club for religious people but a community of faith. The congregation will not be held together by their friendship with another but by the love of God. They will not be a people who come to enjoy the Sunday morning service but a people who present themselves in worship before God. They will not be a people who measure success by numbers but a people dedicated to making a difference in the world. They will not be a people concerned with the survival of the church but a people committed to the ministry of the church. They will not be a people bound by the past but a people who draw strength from the past. They will not be a people who despair of the future but a people whose heritage offers hope.

"Beloved, we are God's children now; it does not yet appear what we shall be."

—1 John 3:2

Appendix: Statistical Table

Year	Pastor	Church Clerk	Baptisms	Other Affiliations	Resident Members	Non-resident Members	Total Members	Grand Total – All Funds For All Purposes	Sunday School Superintendent	Enrollment	WMU President	Missionary Organizations	Enrollment	Total Mission Gifts*
1884														
1885														
1886	C.A.G. Thomas	Geo. L. Tonnofski	56	8	69			$ 374	John T. Pullen	211				
1887	Alvin Betts	Geo. L. Tonnofski	5	6	75			250	John T. Pullen	171				
1888	S.H. Thompson	Geo. L. Tonnofski	5	1	78			532						
1889		J. A. Baker	27	2	78			601						
1890	O.L. Stringfield	J. A. Baker	2	2	72			552						
1891	Jonathan Wood	J. A. Baker	6	3	86			343						
1892		J. A. Baker	29	8	115			196						
1893		John T. Pullen	23	17	147			$ 2,708						
1894	O.L. Stringfellow	John T. Pullen	41	14	182			2,079						
1895		John T. Pullen	13	8	180			680						
1896		John T. Pullen	28	18	210			1,090						
1897	W. C. Barrett	John T. Pullen	12	12	221			2,232						
1898	W. C. Barrett	J. D. Briggs	6	4	214			1,744						
1899	W. C. Barrett	J. D. Briggs	19	18	232			1,189						
1900	A. A. Butler	John T. Pullen	3	9	162			1,347						
1901	A. A. Butler	John T. Pullen	10	7	173			1,164						
1902		John T. Pullen	43	25	201			1,164						
1903	R. J. Bateman	John T. Pullen	6	10	197			1,653						
1904		John T. Pullen	20	3	170			1,112						
1905	R. J. Bateman	John T. Pullen	3	36	159			1,826	John T. Pullen	150	Miss Ella Ford			$ 146
1906	E. Y. Pool	John T. Pullen	59	12	208			2,186	John T. Pullen	149	Miss Addie Waite			168
1907	P. G. Elsom	John T. Pullen	25	7	278			3,046	John T. Pullen	234	Miss Addie Waite			200
1908	P. G. Elsom	John T. Pullen	6	34	197			2,661	John T. Pullen	213	Miss Jennie Bonner			301
1909	J. E. Cooke	John T. Pullen	1	27	180			1,847	John T. Pullen	185	Miss Maggie House		15	317
1910	L.E.M. Freeman	L. R. Norris	34	28	262			4,022	John T. Pullen	239				243
1911	F. D. King	L. R. Norris	26	21	310			3,194	John T. Pullen	215				293
1912	A. V. Joyner	L. R. Norris	9	4	333			6,488	John T. Pullen	291				201
1913	A. V. Joyner	L. R. Norris	15	14	341			4,008	T. W. Blake	236				146
1914		L. R. Norris	14	14	335			2,965	S. A. Sutton	210	Mrs. Fred Senter		15	277
1915	W. H. Dodd	L. R. Norris	14	14	285			2,562	W. P. Baker	210	Mrs. W. H. Dodd		40	263
1916	Lyman K. Dilts	L. R. Norris	0	0	196			2,890	W. P. Baker	200	Mrs. S. M. Lane		15	122
1917	R. D. Stephenson	J. E. Moore						1,805	W. P. Baker		Mrs. R. D. Stephenson		15	181

*Including the Cooperative Program and all organizations; excludes local expenses

Table of annual church statistics (1918–1951).

Year	Pastor	Church Clerk	Baptisms	Other Affiliations	Resident Members	Non-resident Members	Total Members	Grand Total - All Funds For All Purposes	Sunday School Superintendent	Enrollment	WMU President	Missionary Organizations	Enrollment	Total Mission Gifts
1918	J. G. Davis	E. G. Green	0	0	196			$ 1,805	W. P. Baker	200	Mrs. R. D. Stephenson	4	15	$ 181
1919	J. A. Ellis	L. R. Gilbert	9	23	191			1,758	J. J. Bernard	168	Mrs. J. E. Blair	4	15	227
1920	J. A. Ellis	L. R. Gilbert	9	25	220			6,628	R. L. McMillan	318	Mrs. J. A. Blair		22	1,350
1921	J. A. Ellis	L. R. Gilbert	2	55	260			7,319	R. L. McMillan	405	Mrs. J. A. Ellis			748
1922	J. A. Ellis	L. R. Gilbert	26	37	245			8,701	R. L. McMillan	262	Mrs. G. H. Ferguson	3	94	7,143
1923	J. A. Ellis	L. R. Gilbert	18	86	265			12,827	R. L. McMillan	447	Mrs. R. L. McMillan, Sr.	3	93	1,263
1924	J. A. Ellis	L. R. Gilbert	12	53	304			12,395	R. L. McMillan	515	Mrs. Z. M. Caviness	4		2,546
1925	J. A. Ellis	L. R. Gilbert	7	80	380			22,922	R. L. McMillan	648	Mrs. Z. M. Caviness	3	67	1,219
1926	J. A. Ellis	M. B. Maynard	15	57	408			14,815	R. L. McMillan	595	Mrs. Z. M. Caviness	2	98	2,275
1927	J. A. Ellis	M. B. Maynard	4	47	396			19,902	R. L. McMillan	611	Mrs. J. S. Mitchener	1	136	2,291
1928	J. A. Ellis	Thos. J. Martin, Jr.	6	42	417			11,257	R. L. McMillan	659	Mrs. J. S. Mitchener		109	2,045
1929	E. McNeill Poteat, Jr.	Thos. J. Martin, Jr.	4	6	366			10,034	Geo. W. Coggin	580	Mrs. Guy Allen		105	2,671
1930	E. McNeill Poteat, Jr.	C. G. Mumford	13	65	409			10,219	W. E. Jordan	635	Mrs. Guy Allen		98	2,198
1931	E. McNeill Poteat, Jr.	C. G. Mumford	11	32	420			8,712	W. E. Jordan	766		5	75	1,360
1932	E. McNeill Poteat, Jr.	C. G. Mumford	12	18	437			8,394	R. Ray Carter	600	Mrs. W. L. Mayer	5	75	1,561
1933	E. McNeill Poteat, Jr.	C. G. Mumford	10	24	447			7,244	R. Ray Carter	460	Mrs. L.E.M. Freeman	4	171	1,166
1934	E. McNeill Poteat, Jr.	C. G. Mumford	7	10	437			7,403	D. E. Stewart	522	Mrs. Z. M. Caviness	2	173	1,142
1935	E. McNeill Poteat, Jr.	C. G. Mumford	13	13	449			7,879	D. E. Stewart	564	Mrs. Z. M. Caviness	2	160	1,640
1936	E. McNeill Poteat, Jr.	C. G. Mumford	17	64	434			9,689	Stirling Abell	502	Mrs. E. A. Branch	3	120	1,956
1937	E. McNeill Poteat, Jr.	C. G. Mumford	8	14	385			10,076	Mrs. G.H. Ferguson	478	Mrs. E. A. Branch	3	130	1,642
1938	Lee C. Sheppard	C. G. Mumford	19	5	343			8,297	P. H. Wilson	496	Mrs. E. H. Rolston	5	155	2,229
1939	Lee C. Sheppard	C. G. Mumford	7	31	414			8,898	P. H. Wilson	479	Mrs. E. H. Rolston	5	131	2,130
1940	Lee C. Sheppard	C. G. Mumford	10	31	388			10,199	P. H. Wilson	407	Mrs. E. H. Rolston	4	129	1,482
1941	Lee C. Sheppard	C. G. Mumford	7	38	398			11,464	P. H. Wilson	516	Mrs. E. H. Rolston	5	163	2,672
1942	Lee C. Sheppard	C. G. Mumford	17	37	404			13,431	C. G. Mumford	448		4	158	1,785
1943	Lee C. Sheppard	C. G. Mumford	30	30	405	40*	405*	22,266	C. G. Mumford	493		6	157	2,935
1944	Lee C. Sheppard	C. G. Mumford	8	23	365	65	427	11,202	C. G. Mumford	424	Mrs. Lee C. Sheppard	5	142	2,301
1945	Lee C. Sheppard	C. G. Mumford	12	40	362	65	459	15,093	C. G. Mumford	401	Mrs. E. H. Rolston	5	132	2,530
1946	Lee C. Sheppard	C. G. Mumford	23	59	399	60	482	17,764	C. G. Mumford	446	Dr. Mary Yarbrough	4	180	4,449
1947	Lee C. Sheppard	C. G. Mumford	31	29	422	60	490	19,966	C. G. Mumford	552	Dr. Mary Yarbrough		168	4,672
1948	Hugh A. Ellis	C. G. Mumford	4	35	409	75	469	17,731	C. G. Mumford	429	Miss Carolyn Mercer		169	3,606
1949	Ed. McNeill Potest, Jr.	C. G. Mumford	12	75	415	75	490	46,708	C. G. Mumford**	437	Mrs. Roy N. Anderson		217	5,358
1950	E. McNeill Poteat, Jr.	C. G. Mumford	2	72	455	85	540	220,437**	C. G. Mumford		Mrs. Roy N. Anderson		195	2,862
1951	E. McNeill Poteat, Jr.	C. G. Mumford	18	116	542	82	624	64,745	C. G. Mumford	569			222	1,466

*First year setting our resident members as a separate category on report to Association **$200,000 was for new building and equipment

Year	Pastor	Church Clerk	Baptisms	Other Affiliations	Resident Members	Non-resident Members	Total Members	Grand Total – All Funds For All Purposes	Sunday School Superintendent	Enrollment	WMU President	Missionary Organizations	Enrollment	Total Mission Gifts
1952	E. McNeill Poteat, Jr.	C. G. Mumford	10	106	604	80	684	$ 42,313	J. A. Rigney	706	Mrs. Roy L. Yelverton	4	250	$5,584
1953	E. McNeill Poteat, Jr.	C. G. Mumford	13	76	635	75	710	39,684	J. A. Rigney	534	Mrs. Roy L. Yelverton	4	249	4,397
1954	E. McNeill Poteat, Jr.	C. G. Mumford	13	87	666	50	716	43,660	J. A. Rigney	566	Mrs. W.E. Bolton, Jr.	3	215	3,813
1955	E. McNeill Poteat, Jr.	C. G. Mumford	17	41	650	40	690	86,178	J. A. Rigney	535	Mrs. W.E. Bolton, Jr.	3	203	4,831
1956	William W. Finlator	C. G. Mumford	23	41	663	40	703	46,181	Charles E. Bishop	506	Miss Grace Yow	3	207	6,382
1957	William W. Finlator	C. G. Mumford	21	74	640	106	746	51,883	Charles E. Bishop	570	Miss Grace Yow	3	238	4,865
1958	William W. Finlator	C. G. Mumford	15	42	575	179	754	45,283	James W. Reid	600	Mrs. W.W. Finlator	3	251	5,095
1959	William W. Finlator	C. G. Mumford	24	64	602	169	771	55,843	James W. Reid	584	Mrs. W.W. Finlator	3	257	8,625
1960	William W. Finlator	C. G. Mumford	15	62	607	69	676	65,073	T. C. Blalock	620	Mrs. B. F. Bullard	15	245	8,503
1961	William W. Finlator	C. G. Mumford	13	56	506	56	562	64,312	T. C. Blalock	542	Mrs. B. F. Bullard	17	211	8,172
1962	William W. Finlator	C. G. Mumford	8	49	550	42	592	68,632	H. Ed Beam	495	Mrs. Leroy P. Richardson	17	228	8,923
1963	William W. Finlator	C. G. Mumford	12	53	538	74	612	67,355	H. Ed Beam	488	Mrs. Leroy P. Richardson		255	6,233
1964	William W. Finlator	C. G. Mumford	24	44	635	95	730	72,021	R. J. Volk	495	Mrs. W. W. Wooden	8	244	7,430
1965	William W. Finlator	C. G. Mumford	8		641	89	730	75,069	R. J. Volk	461	Mrs. W. W. Wooden	9	205	8,234
1966	William W. Finlator	C. G. Mumford	10	48	623	118	741	74,624	R. J. Volk	443	Mrs. C. T. Smith	6	179	8,540
1967	William W. Finlator	C. G. Mumford	10	37	629	115	744	75,122	R. J. Volk	435	Mrs. C. T. Smith	5	195	8,495
1968	William W. Finlator	C. G. Mumford	8	39	621	136	757	71,248	R. J. Volk	436	Mrs. Roy L. Yelverton	5	214	9,168
1969	William W. Finlator	Wm. P. Ingram, Jr.	9	45	633	140	773	75,668	Phillip G. Little	369	Mrs. Roy L. Yelverton	4	163	9,372
1970	William W. Finlator	Wm. P. Ingram, Jr.	13	36	612	152	764	76,279	Phillip G. Little	371	Mrs. Carter Mackie	2	125	15,869
1971	William W. Finlator	Wm. P. Ingram, Jr.	9	35	617	154	771	82,255	Phillip G. Little	352	Mrs. Carter Mackie	6	150	10,242
1972	William W. Finlator	Wm. P. Ingram, Jr.	9	30	515	128	643	138,057	Phillip G. Little	346	Mrs. Carter Mackie	4	170	9,242
1973	William W. Finlator	Wm. P. Ingram, Jr.	9	53	541	135	676	85,888	Phillip G. Little	337	Mrs. R.A. Prichard	4	177	13,484
1974	William W. Finlator	Wm. P. Ingram, Jr.	5	60	577	145	722	89,850	Frank A. Gourley, Jr	276	Mrs. R.A. Prichard	3	166	12,190
1975	William W. Finlator	Wm. P. Ingram, Jr.	9	37	592	125	717	97,861	Frank A. Gourley, Jr	323	Mrs. T. W. Mitchell	2	144	11,860
1976	William W. Finlator	A. C. Barefoot	13	37	607	138	745	126,536	Elmer Johnson	343	Mrs. W. P. Ingram	3	124	8,056
1977	William W. Finlator	A. C. Barefoot	9	45	655	125	760	130,811	Elmer Johnson	387	Mrs. W. P. Ingram	3	157	7,962
1978	William W. Finlator	A. C. Barefoot	12	47	682	102	784	167,890	William Correll	383	Mrs. W. P. Ingram	5	120	8,956
1979	William W. Finlator	Jesse Doolittle	9	42	638	172	810	173,371	William Correll	204	Mrs. Norman Watson	5	110	15,613
1980	William W. Finlator	Jesse Doolittle	9	37	665	163	828	212,025	William Correll	195	Mrs. Barbara Volk	5	125	13,723
1981	William W. Finlator	Larry Matthews	5	8	628	163	791	212,689	Robert Savage	195	Mrs. Barbara Volk	1	118	34,124
1982	William W. Finlator	Larry Matthews	11	19	628	164	792	221,805	Robert Savage	147	Mrs. Barbara Volk		106	16,804
1983	M. Mahan Siler, Jr.	Larry Matthews	3	29	635	163	798	203,852	Frank A. Farmer	199	Mrs. Barbara Volk	1	105	33,005
1984	M. Mahan Siler, Jr.	Thornton Mitchell	5	55	763	65	828	218,743	Frank A. Farmer	237	Mrs. Mary Ruth Crook	1	95	36,680